ADMINISTRATOR'S GUIDE TO STUDENT ACHIEVEMENT & HIGHER TEST SCORES

MARCIA KALB KNOLL, Ed. D.

JOSSEY-BASS
A Wiley Imprint
www.josseybass.com

Published by Jossey-Bass
A Wiley Imprint
989 Market Street, San Francisco, CA 94103-1741   www.josseybass.com

Jossey-Bass books and products are available through most bookstores. To contact Jossey-Bass directly call our Customer Care Department within the U.S. at (800) 956-7739, outside the U.S. at (317) 572-3986 or fax (317) 572-4002.

Jossey-Bass also publishes its books in a variety of electronic formats. Some content that appears in print may not be available in electronic books.

Acquisitions Editor: *Win Huppuch*
Productions Editor: *Jacqueline Roulette*
Page Design/Layout: *Robyn Beckerman*

Library of Congress Cataloging-in-Publication Data

Knoll, Marcia Kalb.
    Administrator's guide to student achievement and higher test scores / Marcia Kalb Knoll.
        p.   cm.
    Includes bibliographical references (p.) and index.
    ISBN 0-13-092337-0
    1. School improvement programs.   2. Academic achievement.   3. Educational tests and measurements.   I. Title.

LB2822.8 .K66 2002
371.26—dc21   2001036195

About the Author

Marcia Kalb Knoll, Ed.D. (St. John's University) is a career educator who has served in all the educational seats. She began her career in education as a teacher and then administrator in the New York City Public Schools, serving as assistant principal and then principal of P.S. 220 and Director of Curriculum and Instruction for District 28 schools in Queens, New York. In 1988 she became Assistant Superintendent for Educational Services in the Valley Stream Central High School district on Long Island, New York. Dr. Knoll is currently a Professor of Educational Administration and Supervision at Hunter College of the City University of New York.

She has had a variety of opportunities to serve, guide, and influence the educational community in New York State, across the nation, and around the world as a member of many prestigious committees, such as the Professional Standards Board, a member of the board of examiners for NCATE (National Council for Accreditation of Teacher Education), an invited speaker for groups, such as the United States Department of Education, and as a consultant for professional development for Regional Labs, State Education Departments, counties, and school districts.

Dr. Knoll has been recognized and honored by the educational community having received numerous awards and citations, including a tribute read into the Congressional Record of the 99th Congress of the United States of America. She has had many leadership opportunities in elected positions for ASCD (Association for Supervision and Curriculum Development) and PDK (Phi Delta Kappa). Dr. Knoll is a past president of ASCD.

She is the author of *Elementary Principal's Survival Guide* (Prentice Hall, 1984), *Supervision for Better Instruction* (Prentice Hall, 1987), the curriculum bulletin *Personalized Instruction* (New York City Board of Education), graded levels for main idea and critical thinking in the "Developing Reading Comprehension Skills" and "Developing Problem-Solving Skills" series (Oceana Educational Publications), as well as over fifteen articles.

How This Book Will Guide You to Student Achievement and Higher Test Scores

Student success is what schools are all about. Meeting standards measured by standardized tests are high stakes for our students. Passing mandated tests mean promotion and even graduation in many states. It is to these ends of student achievement that this book is directed—successful students who achieve high test scores.

The *Administrator's Guide to Student Achievement and Higher Test Scores* is intended for all of you who guide, facilitate, direct, support, and assist teachers to reach the highest levels of effectiveness with their students. This book addresses the work of principals, assistant principals, department chairs, directors, coordinators, staff developers, coaches, and mentors. It is a guide to making classroom instruction work for students in several ways:

- It deals with the range of real topics that influence effective instruction for students' achievement in a practical and easy-to-use format.

- It is filled with charts and forms that clarify the strategies presented and make applications to your situations easy.

- It presents samples, examples, and case studies of actual activities.

You can use the *Administrator's Guide to Student Achievement and Higher Test Scores* as a complete guide to all aspects of teaching and learning that influence student success. Or, use it as a guide to those particular aspects of the teaching and learning process that most concern your work. The book is presented in six parts that comprise the elements required for student success:

1. How to Establish Teaching Standards that Make Students Successful
2. How to Determine What Teachers Need to Make Students Achieve
3. How to Match Growth Plans to What Teachers Need to Make Students Achieve
4. How to Communicate for Student Success
5. Professional Development that Impacts Student Achievement
6. Enhancements for Student Success

A closer look at each part will help you determine how you can use this book to make students successful.

PART I: HOW TO ESTABLISH TEACHING STANDARDS THAT MAKE STUDENTS SUCCESSFUL

The first section begins with focusing teachers on student achievement and building a collegial effort. The critical element of gaining trust by demonstrating the behaviors that characterize it are fully explored. Ways to maintain the trust you have built by replacing evaluation with documented teacher growth, reflected in student achievement, are presented.

Next, the section concerned with the establishment of standards for teaching presents six specific criteria that influence learning and target students' achievement:

- Classroom environments that enhance learning

- Management of the learning environment that maximizes learning

- Preparation for effective instruction

- Instruction that fosters learning and achievement

- Professionalism and student success

- Parent/community interaction

Each of the six aspects and its significance for student achievement are fully presented. The composite summary can be used by you to guide your work with teachers and as an outline for teachers to use as they reflect about their practices that foster student learning.

PART II: HOW TO DETERMINE WHAT TEACHERS NEED TO MAKE STUDENTS ACHIEVE

Here you'll find a full range of data that can be collected about teaching and used to determine what teachers need to help students achieve. How to place teachers in charge of their own data collection, through the construction of portfolios, is clearly presented with specific criteria. Next, six different data-collection tools are presented in detail, with a rationale for their selection, specifically designed forms, and step-by-step directions for their use.

The types of data-collection tools presented include:

- Holding overview conferences about student achievement

- Making informal visits to view students achieving

- Observing classroom environments to support learning

- Conducting time-on-task reviews to observe learning in progress

- Reviewing artifacts to document learning

- Conducting observations that target student achievement

Each data-collection tool is accompanied by strategies for analyzing and using the collected data to diagnose the needs of teachers and communicate with the teacher. A specific conference plan and suggestions for sample language are presented.

PART III: HOW TO MATCH GROWTH PLANS TO WHAT TEACHERS NEED TO MAKE STUDENTS ACHIEVE

The first section describes in detail how to match growth plans to diagnosed teachers' needs. First, the "why" and "how" growth plans for teachers result in increased student achievement is discussed. Both how to select and who selects the growth objective and the growth plan that matches determined teachers' needs are detailed as well as how the growth plan is communicated to the teacher.

Next, three different growth plans are presented, each with a complete process for its use including the preparation, monitoring, and review, and an actual case study model. The three growth plans are: directed growth plan, collaborative growth plan, and teacher-directed growth plan which includes teachers working either together or independently on a self-directed growth plan.

The next section of Part III discusses how building a learning community is a vehicle for teacher growth and student achievement. Steps for building a learning community and supporting and monitoring its growth and effectiveness are detailed.

This part concludes with details of your specific role in the growth process and presents a procedure for having the staff rate you, with step-by-step directions for analyzing, interpreting, and using the results.

PART IV: HOW TO COMMUNICATE FOR STUDENT SUCCESS

The essential topic of communication is presented, beginning with the importance of providing a secure climate in which teacher growth can flourish, and then discussing the two elements of this climate that must be present: an understanding of basic needs and the power of listening.

Conferencing as a vital communication tool that results in student achievement is detailed, including guidelines for effectively transmitting feedback. The powerful communication skills of active listening (with the actions for its delivery and the messages it sends) and reflection (which is essential to teacher growth) are fully developed.

The next section of Part IV describes various forms of written communications and gives techniques and strategies for making them achieve their purposes. The last element, communicating with yourself, completes Part IV. Detailed forms and strategies are presented to help you keep track of what you are doing to focus on student achievement by effective informal and formal recordkeeping and efficient use of time.

PART V: PROFESSIONAL DEVELOPMENT THAT IMPACTS STUDENT ACHIEVEMENT

Part V begins with a discussion of the characteristics of adult learners and how to use these characteristics to support professional-development efforts. A guide to professional development that leads to student achievement is then presented. The strategies to use for selecting the topics, as well as the time, place, and frequency for professional development, are discussed. The components of effective workshops are presented with a description of how to plan to include all of them.

Next, the link between the workshop and student achievement is detailed. Making professional-development efforts work in the classroom by guiding and promoting the process, providing time for teachers to visit each other, and making time for discussion and interaction are presented. Using peer coaches and study teams to effectively transfer professional-development strategies to classroom practice that impact student achievement is discussed. Each is presented with details and guidelines for making them work effectively and efficiently, often with minimal funding.

The last section of Part V presents two ways to ensure that professional development impacts student achievement: by incorporating the professional-development objectives into teachers' growth plans, and with strategies for monitoring the progress of the study teams.

PART VI: ENHANCEMENTS FOR STUDENT ACHIEVEMENT

This final part is concerned with five ways to enhance student success. First, standards and their relationship to student success and teachers' control of their delivery are presented. A discussion of motivation explores how self confidence, praise, and rewards impact student achievement. Organization of classrooms presents tracking and detracking as ways to inhibit or foster student achievement. Social–emotional learning and its contributions to student success in school and in life are explored. Last, technology and how to maximize its use for successful twenty-first-century students are presented. Technology hallmarks for school leaders are stated.

Next, how the curriculum is interrelated with elements that lead to student achievement are presented. A framework for designing curriculum that promotes student success is presented and discussed. An outline of the framework that can be used as a guide for designing curriculum is presented and supported by curriculum samples.

The last section of Part VI discusses curriculum and instructional leadership for student achievement. The ways in which leadership can result in continuous improvement of instruction and the leadership actions that support teacher's efforts are presented.

LAST THOUGHTS

The *Administrator's Guide to Student Achievement and Higher Test Scores* presents, explains, and supports an interactive structure of six components that result in student success. The following statements form the foundation of that structure.

Student achievement and higher test scores result when:

- Teachers are active participants in their own development.
- Teachers are provided with opportunity, and then guided, facilitated, supported, and encouraged to continuously improve their effectiveness.
- Communication with teachers is honest, open, and respectful.

Marcia Kalb Knoll, Ed.D.

Contents

PART II
How to Determine What Teachers Need
to Make Students Achieve

SECTION 3
GATHERING DATA ABOUT TEACHING FOR STUDENT ACHIEVEMENT. 55

PART III
How to Match Growth Plans to What Teachers Need to Make Students Achieve

PART IV

How to Communicate for Student Success

SECTION 18
WRITING EFFECTIVE COMMUNICATIONS. 222

SECTION 19
COMMUNICATING WITH YOURSELF: KEEPING TRACK OF WHAT YOU ARE DOING
TO HELP STUDENTS ACHIEVE 233

PART V

Professional Development that
Impacts Student Achievement

SECTION 20
PROFESSIONAL DEVELOPMENT THAT LEADS TO STUDENT ACHIEVEMENT 245

PART VI
Enhancements for Student Success

SECTION 25
LEADERSHIP FOR STUDENT ACHIEVEMENT

Part I

How to Establish Teaching Standards that Make Students Successful

Focusing Teachers on Student Achievement

Student achievement is everyone's job. It is the sole purpose for which schools exist. At times the effort is exhausting and the challenges appear overwhelming. Staying focused on student achievement, believing that students can achieve, encouraging and supporting teachers' efforts, and providing the assistance that teachers need moves the work toward the goal. Teachers benefit from the strength of collaboration when they see themselves not as individuals, but as a part of a collective effort in which they work together with others to achieve student success.

Building a Collegial Effort for Student Success

Success for all students can become a reality when the collective strength of the entire school community works collegially on continuous improvement of student achievement. There are six ways in which to build the collegial effort.

1. **Support teachers' work.** The work of teachers can be supported in three ways: First, with the time to learn, experiment, observe others, and reflect on their instructional effectiveness; second, with assistance to learn the strategies and techniques that may be problematic; and third, being treated with respect and dignity, which builds self-confidence.

2. **Focus on teaching and learning.** Ongoing discussions about instructional practices and reflection about the effectiveness of those practices characterize this focus. These discussions occur whenever educators are together and are the major topics of meetings. Everything else takes a back seat to teaching and learning.

3. **Establish working together to achieve student learning as the norm.** Teachers share instructional goals with each other and then collaboratively plan the ways in which those goals may be achieved. These collaborative plans include the design of instruction and teaching materials. Teachers then analyze the student outcomes that resulted and evaluate the effectiveness of their efforts.

4. **Encourage teachers to work together in small study groups.** These study groups provide the teachers with support for ongoing learning. Teachers work together to find solutions to similar problems. The study groups also provide the teachers with a sense of belonging and a place to turn for immediate assistance.

5. **Extend professional development beyond the workshop session.** Participants in the professional-development activity are provided with time to try out the new strategies presented. Teachers are encouraged to visit each other and then talk together about what was seen as a way to learn with and from each other.

6. **Promote a spirit of continuous learning.** All members of the educational community seek new and better means to help students to be successful. Alternatives are continuously examined and considered. Ideas are shared and reflected upon. Professional journals are examined as new sources of information to be explored and discussed.

Gaining Trust

When a collegial effort is the structure for student success, trust is its foundation and interdependence is the cement that makes it strong. Since a collegial effort brings individuals together, it is dependent upon the relationships among that group of individuals who are asked to work together to make all students successful. When trust is missing, relationships among individuals can easily become problematic and result in petty differences, which divert attention from the central focus of the work. When trust is present, the members of the group hold a firm belief in the reliability, truth, and strength of the focus on student achievement.

Gaining trust is not only critical to success with collegial efforts, it is also vital to success with individual members of the educational community. Gaining the trust of all teachers is the vehicle to your effectiveness in guiding, coaching, leading, and inspiring them to grow in their abilities to help students to achieve. When a supervisor is trusted, all members of the educational community feel the supervisor is there to serve them and help them to continuously learn how to more effectively help their students to achieve.

CHARACTERISTICS OF A TRUSTED SUPERVISOR

Building that firm belief in the reliability, truth, and strength of the focus on student achievement and the supervisor's desire and ability to serve teachers' needs and help them requires much more than lip service. It is dependent on actions and behaviors. In addition, the trusted supervisor provides the model for how all of the members of the educational community conduct themselves and interact with each other. If you were to make a list of the characteristics of such a supervisor and then group them and label the groups, you will most probably identify the following three significant characteristics.

- **Being open rather than closed.** Members of an educational community must give and receive open communications. An open person models respect for the ideas, perceptions, feelings, and information that is shared. The purpose of activities planned and work that is requested is clear and agreed upon. Teachers feel comfortable about asking questions, clarifying their meanings, and explaining their point of view. They are able to present a situation from their own perspective.

- **Being supportive rather than controlling.** A supportive person encourages, reassures, and seeks to understand others, their goals, successes, and disappointments. Being supportive requires that judgment and suspicion be suspended. People are not labeled, stereotyped, categorized, or prejudged. A supportive person acts on positive intentions, believing that others truly want to be successful and try to do their best.

- **Being dependable rather than unpredictable.** Being dependable means that people can rely on you. They can depend on the constancy and confidentiality of your assistance, attention to their needs, and the collective needs of the community. Being able to predict that help is available enables teachers to be more comfortable and secure with the unpredictable nature of classrooms.

BEHAVIORS THAT ARE DEMONSTRATED

Listing characteristics is the easy part. Saying that you are open or supportive or dependable does not convince anyone that it is true, especially if your behavior demonstrates other characteristics. The hard part is consistently demonstrating the behaviors that convince others that you are open, supportive, and dependable. These behaviors are the actions and attitudes that serve as models for the entire community.

- **Behaviors that demonstrate openness.** An open person asks questions rather than makes assumptions, invites feedback from varied points of view, and makes decisions based on input. Expectations are made clear verbally and/or in writing. Being open means considering alternatives, taking calculated risks when appropriate, and acting on new ideas and initiatives. Openness requires flexibility and consensus building as a means of finding solutions to problems. An open person is both accessible and visible. He or she practices active listening, and uses positive body language such as a smile, a nod, and eye contact. Being open requires a sense of humor, revealing feelings and sharing personal anecdotes. This includes sharing areas of vulnerability, which may display some faults and mistakes, and accepting criticism for them. Teachers have stated, "I am much more likely to share something that made *me* look foolish in the classroom if you tell me something that made *you* look or feel foolish."

- **Behaviors that demonstrate supportiveness.** A supportive person listens and seeks to understand in a nonjudgmental way before responding. Demonstrating support may require that you take over someone's duties and responsibilities when your help is needed. A supportive person provides resources that are requested. Making personal contact through written notes and letters of recognition as well as verbal comments of recognition is supportive behavior. Supportive behavior includes sharing the accomplishments of others and oneself with the wider community. A supportive person avoids or prevents public embarrassment of others in the community and takes the flack when necessary. Teachers say, "A supportive supervisor won't pull the plug on you. They don't give up on you."

- **Behaviors that demonstrate dependability.** A dependable person does what he or she says. They follow up on promises and statements made. Teachers say, "They walk the talk." Dependable persons are punctual and keep commitments. They pay attention to deadlines, answer letters, and return phone calls. Dependable persons demonstrate knowledge and skill and provide the help that is needed and requested. Being dependable means being confidential in your dealings with people so what is said remains between those sharing the communication. A dependable person is consistent and predictable. Policies and practices are established and followed by everyone. Everyone in the community knows that similar situations will be handled in the same way.

Figure 1-1, "Behaviors That Build Trust," presents a summary of the behaviors that build trust for each of the three identified characteristics. Use the summary to honestly reflect on your behaviors. Look for examples to support your point of view.

DETERMINING YOUR TRUST QUOTIENT

One way to find out if the professional community with whom you interact trusts you is to ask them. You can do this by using Figure 1-2, "Survey of Behaviors that Build Trust." Introduce the survey at a faculty or department meeting and explain the purpose of gathering this information about your behaviors. Ask the members of the professional community with whom you interact to anonymously complete and return the survey. Honestly examine the responses with an open point of view. What you think about your behavior is not so important as how others, with whom you interact, see you.

Begin your examination of the responses by first totaling each returned survey to determine the number of behaviors under each characteristic that are coded as *A = Always, S = Sometimes,* and *N = Never.* Next, combine all of the responses by characteristic to determine the total number of *A = Always, S= Sometimes,* and *N = Never* you were given by the group as a whole. Review the total number of *A = Always* when compared with *S = Sometimes* for each characteristic. Identify those behaviors within each characteristic that are coded with *A = Always* and those coded *S = Sometimes.*

Pay careful attention to the number of *N = Never* that is recorded. Identify the specific behaviors that were coded *N = Never.* List those behaviors separately, by characteristic, to determine if these specific behaviors were consistently coded *N = Never* by numbers of individuals. Although every response should be considered, it is more important to pay attention to a response from large numbers of respondents than from a single individual who may be responding from personal prejudice.

Figure 1–1

For Reflection: BEHAVIORS THAT BUILD TRUST

Compare your behavior with the ones below.

BEING OPEN

Asks questions—does not assume
Invites feedback
Considers alternatives
Takes calculated risks
Makes decisions based on input
Initiates new ideas
Makes expectations clear verbally and/or in writing
Is flexible
Builds consensus to solve problems
Is accessible and visible
Follows up on ideas
Practices active listening
Exhibits a sense of humor
Shares personal anecdotes
Reveals feelings
Accepts criticism
Is vulnerable (shows faults) and admits mistakes
Uses positive body language (smiles, nods, eye contact)

BEING SUPPORTIVE

Listens and responds appropriately
Is nonjudgmental
Assumes duties/responsibilities of others (when appropriate)
Provides resources
Makes personal contact
Writes notes/letters of recognition
Makes verbal comments of recognition
Shares accomplishments of others and self with others
Prevents/avoids public embarrassment of professionals
Takes flack when necessary

BEING DEPENDABLE

Does what he or she says
Follows up on promises and statements
Is punctual
Keeps commitments
Pays attention to deadlines
Answers letters
Returns phone calls
Demonstrates knowledge and skills
Provides needed/requested help
Maintains confidentiality
Is consistent
Is predictable
Handles like situations in the same way
Establishes and implements policies and practices

NOTES AND THOUGHTS

Figure 1-2

SURVEY OF BEHAVIORS THAT BUILD TRUST

Review the behaviors listed below. Place a check for each behavior in the column that matches how it is demonstrated by the supervisor.   *A = ALWAYS,*   *S = SOMETIMES,*   *N = NEVER*

BEING OPEN	A	S	N
Asks questions—does not assume	___	___	___
Invites feedback	___	___	___
Considers alternatives	___	___	___
Takes calculated risks	___	___	___
Makes decisions based on input	___	___	___
Initiates new ideas	___	___	___
Makes expectations clear verbally and/or in writing	___	___	___
Is flexible	___	___	___
Builds consensus to solve problems	___	___	___
Is accessible and visible	___	___	___
Follows up on ideas	___	___	___
Practices active listening	___	___	___
Exhibits a sense of humor	___	___	___
Shares personal anecdotes	___	___	___
Reveals feelings	___	___	___
Accepts criticism	___	___	___
Is vulnerable (shows faults) and admits mistakes	___	___	___
Uses positive body language (smiles, nods, eye contact)	___	___	___
Total	A ___	S ___	N ___

BEING SUPPORTIVE			
Listens and responds appropriately	___	___	___
Is nonjudgmental	___	___	___
Assumes duties/responsibilities of others	___	___	___
Provides resources	___	___	___
Makes personal contact	___	___	___
Writes notes/letters of recognition	___	___	___
Makes verbal comments of recognition	___	___	___
Shares accomplishments of others and self	___	___	___
Prevents/avoids public embarrassment for all	___	___	___
Takes flack when necessary	___	___	___
Total	A ___	S ___	N ___

BEING DEPENDABLE			
Does what he or she says	___	___	___
Follows up on promises and statements	___	___	___
Is punctual	___	___	___
Keeps commitments	___	___	___
Pays attention to deadlines	___	___	___
Answers letters	___	___	___
Returns phone calls	___	___	___
Demonstrates knowledge and skills	___	___	___
Provides needed/requested help	___	___	___
Maintains confidentiality	___	___	___
Is consistent	___	___	___
Is predictable	___	___	___
Handles like situations in the same way	___	___	___
Establishes and implements policies/practices	___	___	___
Total	A ___	S ___	N ___

The analysis of the survey will provide you with information about what the professional community believes about the frequency of the trust behaviors that you demonstrate. You may be surprised, disappointed, or delighted by the results. You will be able to broaden your understanding of the feedback if you gather a representative group to review and discuss the returned surveys with you. Ask the group members to specify incidents or occasions that they recall that illustrate how you behave in particular situations. Assessing oneself is never easy, but it is always an effective way to make people believe that you are interested in their opinion. How you use this information to change your behavior is, of course, your decision.

BUILDING POSITIVE INTERACTIONS

Although we strive to make our interactions positive, at times just the opposite is achieved because of the language unintentionally used. Our words trip us up. The messages sent might be interpreted with an implied negative assumption that speaks directly to the emotions of the listener, builds resistance, and diminishes trust. Examine the questions below that contain an implied negative assumption and compare them with the ones that are positive.

NEGATIVE ASSUMPTIONS	POSITIVE ASSUMPTIONS
What mistakes do you find with your lesson planning?	Did your lesson plan achieve what you thought it would?
Since these students usually give you a hard time, how have you planned to keep them involved?	How have you planned to maintain the students' active involvement in the lesson?
Why do you think so many students were lost after your instructions?	How did your instructions assist the students in understanding what to do?
What could you have done to make the lesson more interesting?	How can you measure student interest in the lesson?
Before you teach a lesson, wouldn't you want to assess students' readiness for learning?	How do you determine students' readiness for learning?
How could you call on more students?	How do you determine which students to call on?
Do you believe the materials were distributed fairly?	How do you determine the way in which materials will be distributed?
How could you prevent students from abusing materials?	What instructions do you give students about the use of materials?

Section 17 in Part IV provides a full discussion of nonverbal communication that will also prove helpful in gaining trust.

Teacher Growth Is Reflected in Student Achievement

There is a direct relationship between teachers' growth in effective instruction and students' growth in achievement. Obviously, skillful teachers positively impact student achievement. The job is therefore to focus on helping teachers to grow and develop increasingly more effective means of instructing students. This focus can be maintained with good results when criticism, judgments, and ratings are replaced by ongoing assistance that considers the individual teacher's abilities and needs.

Teacher growth for student achievement is directly related to the following set of beliefs:

- Students can achieve when instruction is effective.

- Teachers are capable of growing, learning, and becoming increasingly more skillful in delivering instruction that positively impacts student achievement.

- Teachers have individual levels of abilities with a wide range of knowledge and skills that impact instructional effectiveness.

- The administrator's supervisory purpose is to help each teacher to learn and grow through an individualized process of ongoing support.

SUPERVISING FOR TEACHER GROWTH

The first step in helping teachers to grow in instructional effectiveness is to find out what they know and do not know. To determine these growth needs, data about the teaching and learning process must be gathered. Part II discusses a full range of tools that can be used to gather these data.

The next step in the growth process is to develop an individualized growth plan with the teacher that focuses on one specific area of growth at a time. This specific focus makes the growth plan realistic and manageable. It builds the teacher's confidence in being successful. Part III discusses how to develop individualized growth plans.

The growth plan is then implemented using the materials and human resources specified to support the teacher in the learning process. The teacher and the administrator on an ongoing basis review progress being made on the identified skills. The review involves the teacher in a reflection about the activities that have been implemented and their resulting outcomes. The teacher is encouraged to express ideas, suggestions, and possible reasons for the results demonstrated thus far as well as how the results will be used to guide future work on the growth objectives. Judgmental, evaluative, and critical language lead to defensiveness, combativeness, or resentment and stifles discussion. Part IV discusses how to communicate for student success.

The teacher's growth in reaching the objectives specified in the growth plan is documented by gathering data showing student achievement. The types of data to be gathered are specified in the growth plan. These data are reviewed collaboratively by the teacher and the administrator and become a part of the teacher's record of growth for the school year. See Figure 1-3 for a sample growth plan for Ms. Moore, a first-year teacher.

RESULTING OUTCOMES

Designing, supporting, monitoring, and assessing teacher growth by implementing a well-developed growth plan results in documented success and student achievement. The attention to individual teacher needs and the ongoing support that is provided have two outcomes:

1. Teacher confidence is built leading to the accomplishment of the growth objectives. Success is motivating and acts as an incentive for the teacher to continue to strive for higher goals.
2. The supportive nature in which work on the growth plan is conducted results in a climate of mutual respect and reinforces the trust that has been built.

How to Replace Evaluation with Documented Growth

Evaluation at the end of the school year is necessary for several reasons. It provides closure to the teacher's work during the year on one or more growth plans. In addition, yearly teacher evaluation is usually a requirement of the school district and the state.

GROWTH PLAN SUMMARY

Rather than evaluate the teachers with ratings and labels, or the value judgment language of satisfactory, outstanding, or unsatisfactory, provide a summary of the growth plan(s) that were undertaken and the results achieved. The growth plans that were undertaken with documentation of student achievement used as criteria for evaluation should be attached to your summary. Figure 1-4 presents a sample growth plan summary for Ms. Moore for the year.

This summary serves four purposes:

1. To record the knowledge and skill areas that were targeted for this teacher's growth over the course of the year.
2. To specify the time frames during which a growth plan was conducted.
3. To present the resulting outcomes specifying student growth and/or achievement.
4. To identify future areas of growth to be targeted.

The growth plan summary should be prepared in consultation with the teacher. There should be agreement on all aspects of the summary. Be sure you include the teacher in reflection and discussion. You may wish to use this opportunity to get the teacher's preferences for future growth plan objectives.

Figure 1-3
SAMPLE GROWTH PLAN

Teacher: **Sarah Moore**   Date: **8/25/01**

Assignment: **Social Studies grade 7**

Objective (What behaviors, skills and abilities are to be developed?)

To establish and maintain appropriate student behavior in all class periods.

Resources (What human and material resources will be provided?)

District Student Behavior Code given to Ms. Moore and discussed in detail.

Visitation to classrooms of Mr. Jewel and Mrs. Handle is scheduled for September 1.

Discussion time following the visits with those teachers is scheduled for September 2.

Conference time provided for Ms. Moore with the grade leader.

The department chair continues to mentor the teacher as needed.

Additional visitations and/or discussions with the teachers in the department are scheduled as needed.

Specific Activities (How will the skills and abilities be developed?)

The teacher develops a useable set of class rules with the students in each class.

The teacher prepares an effective means of maintaining those rules.

A written copy of the rules is posted in the classroom.

Parents sign a copy of the rules placed in each student's looseleaf book.

The teacher learns conflict-resolution strategies, reviews them with students, and uses them to resolve all issues.

Time Frame (When will the plan begin, be monitored, be completed?)

The plan begins on September 1 and is expected to be completed by September 30.

Informal visits to all classes are conducted by the principal or the assistant principal: daily during the first week, every other day during the second week, and twice a week for the remainder of the plan.

Evaluation Criteria (How will the plan be evaluated? What student achievement data will be collected?)

Number of referrals made for student misbehavior.

A copy of the rules for class behavior is posted and referred to when required.

Parents' signature on the rules of class behavior are visible in students' looseleafs.

Students are observed: attending to task, raising their hands to respond to questions, involved with each other in activities, producing an acceptable noise level, using conflict-resolution strategies to resolve confrontational issues.

_____   _____
Administrator's Signature   Teacher's Signature

Figure 1-4
SAMPLE GROWTH PLAN SUMMARY

Teacher: **Sarah Moore**   School: _____ **8/25/01**

Assignment: **Social Studies grade 7**

Objective 1:   To establish and maintain appropriate student behavior in all classes

Time Frame: September 1 to September 30

Outcomes for the student behavior objective:

> Class rules for behavior are posted.
>
> Class rules are signed by a parent and are visible in students' notebooks.
>
> Students raise their hands to answer questions.
>
> Students attend to tasks.
>
> There is a hum of meaningful activity in all class periods.
>
> Friction and negative interactions among students are minimum.
>
> The teacher and students use conflict-resolution strategies.
>
> A minimal number of referrals for behavior are made.

Objective 2:   To increase the active participation of all students

Time Frame: October 15 to December 15

Outcomes for the active participation objective:

> Students move quickly and quietly into a think, pair, share configuration.
>
> Students actively discuss information with their peers.
>
> Students work in groups to complete assigned tasks.
>
> The work of each student is on display in some part of the classroom.
>
> At times, two of the students need a reminder to maintain attention.
>
> Referrals are attached.

Objective 3:   To design and use graphic organizers in instruction

Time Frame: February 1 to May 15

Outcomes for the graphic organizers objective:

> Students use sequence charts to demonstrate their knowledge of the events in the Civil War.*
>
> Students use cause and effect organizers to demonstrate information about immigration movements in the U.S.*
>
> Students use spider webs to explain the impact of the Industrial Revolution on life and work in the U.S.*
>
> Students use a KWL format to begin a new unit on World War I.*

*Samples attached

Future Areas for Growth Plans:

> To design higher level questions that require student reflection.
>
> To employ varied cooperative learning strategies in instruction.

DEALING WITH MANDATED EVALUATION

Despite the negative effects of evaluation, it must be completed when the school system and/or the state require it. These requirements to rate teachers and/or complete a particular checklist or form can be turned from a negative to a positive experience by involving the teachers.

- **Invite the teachers to participate.** Invite the teachers to participate in completing the form required by the district or the state. The teachers' input provides their professional opinion about the specific areas of performance that are detailed on the form. When your opinion differs from a teacher's, ask the teacher to provide specific information and data that support his or her opinion. The involvement of the teacher helps to maintain a high level of trust and communicates that you respect the teacher's opinions and care about the teacher's well being.

- **Involve the teacher in the decision.** Involve the teacher in making the decision when rating is required. This provides the teacher with the opportunity to participate in making a judgment about his or her overall effectiveness. The teacher should be encouraged to participate in an open discussion with the rater. If teacher growth is the goal, compromising over the rating as a way to more fully involve the teacher in a growth plan is a course worth considering.

Standards for Teaching that Target Students' Achievement

If you don't know where you are going, any road will get you there. On the other hand, if you know that your target is high student achievement, then using a set of standards for teaching that targets students' achievement can guide you to your goal. The discussion of standards for teaching that follows identifies the knowledge, skills, and abilities that comprise the actions of teachers whose students achieve. The standards may effectively be used as a guide to plan for teachers' growth. It may also be useful in helping teachers to understand the scope of their role, and in involving individual teachers in the identification of specific skills they wish to master.

The description of standards for teaching that target students' achievement is, however, presented with a word of caution. **It is not intended for use as an observation checklist.** Not only is it not practical to try to observe all aspects of the teacher's role during one observation, it is counterproductive to a good lesson plan. When a checklist is used in observations, teachers attempt to incorporate all aspects of the checklist, because the items are on the checklist, whether or not they should be included in the lesson.

The standards for teaching that target students' achievement are divided into six areas:

- Classroom Environments that Enhance Learning
- Management of the Learning Environment that Maximizes Learning
- Preparation for Effective Instruction
- Instruction that Fosters Learning and Achievement
- Professionalism and Student Success
- Parent/Community Interaction

Classroom Environments that Enhance Learning

In many ways, every classroom is a home for the students, a primary one for some and a second home for others. It is a place in which students and their teachers spend a great deal of time during each day, week, and year. The nature of that environment has a tremendous impact on the feelings of both the teacher and the students about their security, acceptance, and self-image. Everyone needs to feel: safe from both physical and psychological harm; accepted and wanted as a member of the group; and valued as an individual. These feelings necessarily impact on the individual's capacity to be effective, learn, and achieve.

CLASSROOM ATMOSPHERE

Teachers in classrooms that help students to learn, achieve, and perform well on tests have developed knowledge and skill in the following areas and demonstrate these in their communications and actions.

Teachers' attitudes and beliefs.   Teachers have a sense of being in charge of the classroom, the students, and instruction.

1. *They are confident and enthusiastic.* They greet students with a smile and engage in conversations with them. They express interest in the student as an individual and as a member of the class.

2. *They are problem solvers.* These teachers are faced with the same problems faced by all teachers, but they believe that problems can be resolved rather than endured. They seek solutions to problems by speaking with members of the educational community and continuously strive to find new ways to help students to achieve.

3. *They help their students.* These teachers send messages to their students that they are there to help them in whatever ways are required to make them successful. They individualize their attention to students to provide what each one needs to learn the material.

4. *They use the skills of professionals.* They are professional in their attitude, behaving as diagnosticians of needs and solvers of problems rather than controllers of behavior and parent substitutes.

5. *They have high expectations.* Most important, these teachers expect their students to learn and achieve. They believe success is possible for all their students and it is their job to find the way to make that happen.

Classroom climate.   The climate of high-achieving classrooms has two broad characteristics.

1. IT IS WORK ORIENTED.

- **Focus on expectations.** The teacher emphasizes that the business of the class is work-oriented. The teacher focuses on learning and communicates in words and actions what is expected student behavior, attitude, and work.

- **Use of rubrics.** Teachers in these classrooms develop, discuss with the students, and then post and/or distribute lists or rubrics that specify the ways in which students can demonstrate their positive behavior and the high level of work that is expected. Students use these lists or rubrics by themselves or with other students to compare their actions and work with what is expected.

2. IT IS WARM AND SUPPORTIVE.

- **Use of praise.** A warm and supportive environment is developed and sustained by the use of specific and appropriate praise, when deserved. Specific praise statements replace general statements of praise such as "good" or "great." For example, "You asked a really good question." "The examples you gave helped everyone to understand." "Using color to code the sections of your report shows your attention to details." Unearned or empty praise is replaced with acknowledgment and suggestions. For example, "You attempted to spell every word correctly, but there are some that you still need to learn." "You have completed some parts of the assignment very well, but there are parts that need to be explained."

- **Respectful treatment.** In warm and supportive environments, students and their contributions are treated with respect. Students' work is read, contains the teacher's comments, and is returned to students in a timely manner. The walls of the classroom and the halls of the school are filled with students' work. As a result, students in these classrooms model the respect and caring demonstrated by their teachers, and treat both the teacher and other students in these same ways. Students express themselves freely and ask questions. They ask for help and also listen to each other.

- **Teacher's appearance.** The teacher's physical appearance is positive. Facial expression and body language are accepting of student needs and the speaking voice is clear, easy to hear, and easy to understand. The teacher's physical vitality demonstrates involvement, energy, and interest in the teaching role.

See Section 23 for a discussion of how motivation enhances student success.

PHYSICAL ARRANGEMENT OF THE ROOM

The appearance and arrangement of the classroom contribute to achieving both a work-oriented and a warm and supportive environment.

- Teachers in work-oriented classrooms arrange the furniture to provide easy and safe movement of students. Aisles and passageways are kept clear, entrances and exits are open, and frequently used areas are accessible.

- The furniture is used to enhance instruction. Students' desks and chairs in these classrooms are grouped and regrouped for instruction. Space is used maximally to provide for students' learning needs so that areas of instruction for large groups, small groups, and individuals are available. Equipment is located in areas that make its use easy. Tables and bookcases are placed where they serve instruction.

- Teachers' and students' desks are without excess paper, and the floors are clutter-free and dust-free. Clothing, book bags, and materials not in immediate use are put away. There is a general appearance of organization.

- Classrooms that appear warm and supportive display multiple examples of the work of every or almost every student. The displays are interesting, appealing, and colorful. Students' projects that are in progress are visible, treated with respect, and carefully stored.

AVAILABILITY OF RESOURCES

Learning resources are neatly arranged, organized, and easily available to students. Resources include oral, visual, and tactile materials to provide for learning-style preferences. A variety of resources beyond textbooks—including, for example, reference books, magazines, pictures, videos, and a computer that is turned on and in use—are visible.

Section 6 provides a comprehensive discussion of effective learning environments.

Management of the Learning Environment that Maximizes Learning

For practitioners, particularly new teachers, management of the learning environment is the first priority. The focus is on the actions the teacher takes to create, implement, and maintain a classroom environment that supports learning through effective management and discipline. These systems address the day-to-day management needed to engage students in productive activities and prevent minor problems from becoming major ones. Even the most rich and appealing classrooms may turn into chaos if routines for using them have not been established. Teachers whose students demonstrate high on-task rates and academic achievement implement a systematic approach to classroom management during the first days of classes.

CLASSROOM MANAGEMENT

- **Students must learn the expectations that will govern the classroom.** These expectations and their related procedures and rules are necessary for learning to take place. How to be prepared for class, turn in homework, make up missed work, go to the rest room, signal the teacher for assistance, and participate in class, for example, must be fully understood by each student. Time devoted to teaching these expectations early in the year to establish ongoing habits of work and use of the procedures is directly related to increasing students' on-task behavior.

- **Students can learn these rules and procedures in a variety of ways.** The goal is their understanding of what the expectations are, why they are important, and how attending to them are of benefit to the students. Lessons may be taught by stating a rule or procedure and asking the students to generate why the rule or procedure is important and how they may benefit from it. Or, the rules and procedures may be taught directly through written material or a lecture. Posting the rules and procedures on the bulletin board keeps them in sight and encourages their use as a reminder. Teachers often provide the students with their own copy of the rules and procedures, which are then signed by a parent and placed in each student's notebook or looseleaf binder.

The expectations that govern the classroom with their related rules and procedures are designed so that students clearly understand them, easily use them, and feel encouraged and supported by them. They deliver the messages: *Schoolwork is important! You are capable of being successful! The teacher is a continuing resource for you.* Rules and procedures are:

- **Positive statements.** Say, "Raise your hand and wait to be called on" *instead of* "Do not shout out an answer." Say, "Be on time, all the time" *instead of* "Don't be late.

- **Short and specific.** Keep the wording a simple and clear statement that can easily be remembered and followed. For example, "Homework is due on the date stated; be prepared with books, paper, and pen/pencil."

- **Few in number.** Teachers may list those behaviors that are critical to student success and then prioritize them. Select between five and seven that are the most important. When the list gets beyond seven, students do not remember them and therefore will not consistently attend to them.

- **Related to consequences.** Students must be informed of the consequences that result from not following or meeting the rules and procedures of established expectations; for example, they might lose points on their grade, lose a privilege, lose a turn, have a parent called.

See Figure 2-1 for a summary of these rules and procedures.

Figure 2-1
CLASSROOM MANAGEMENT

Establish rules and procedures.
Use positive statements.
Give short and specific statements.
List no more than seven rules.
Relate rules to consequences.

BEHAVIOR MANAGEMENT

It is not so much what teachers do to stop misbehavior that characterizes the management of learning environments that maximizes learning, but *how* teachers prevent problems from starting. The following four factors characterize classrooms in which students are engaged in tasks, have less inappropriate behaviors, have smoother transitions, and show generally higher academic performance.

- **Establish and communicate expectations.** In both elementary and secondary classrooms, the teacher establishes and communicates expectations by teaching the rules and procedures to the students at the beginning of the school year, as discussed above. This contributes not only to good classroom management, but also to good behavior management.

- **Provide systematic monitoring.** The teacher monitors each student's academic performance by observing daily participation in class and reviewing classwork, homework, and test results. The on-task and off-task behaviors students' demonstrate are also monitored, noted, and communicated.

- **Provide feedback.** The teacher provides immediate feedback to students about both their academic progress and behavior.

- **Use time productively.** The teacher maximizes the use of instructional time and encourages student on-task behavior by planning activities that actively involve students in interesting and appropriate work with which they can be successful.

TEACHER ACTIONS THAT DE-ESCALATE A SITUATION

Of course, a carefully planned and maintained management system will not, by itself, stop all misbehavior. Teachers who effectively manage the learning environment are continuously aware of problematic students and take immediate action to de-escalate a situation. Here are the strategies they use.

- **Positive reinforcement.** The student is rewarded for positive behavior with something that is considered of value. The reward could be desired attention, a hug, or a star. A behavior that is rewarded is more likely to be repeated than a behavior that is ignored.

- **Proximity control.** The teacher moves near to the student to provide a signal that reminds the student to stay focused, remain seated, or stop unacceptable behavior.

- **Redirection.** The student is moved from an inappropriate behavior to a more appropriate behavior by changing the activity to be completed or the location of the student.

- **Reframing.** The task the student is working on is redefined, explained, or changed to make it more appropriate and appealing to the student.

- **Contingency setting.** The student is given a cause-and-effect statement or asked to predict the results of an action. This strategy may be used to prevent an undesirable action or enable the student to select a desirable action.

- **Postpone.** The teacher paraphrases the student's concern by saying, for example, "I know you are angry (hurt, upset) and we will talk about this as soon as the lesson is finished (at lunch time, in ten minutes)."

- **Timeout.** The student is given the time and space to cool off. This enables the student to gain control and save him- or herself from embarrassment.

STUDENT SELF-CONTROL STRATEGIES

Strategies that use student self-control rather than teacher control to stop misbehavior may have long-term benefits with older students. These behavior-management strategies are:

- **Self-verbalization.** Students are encouraged to talk about their anger as a means of controlling aggressive behavior and dealing with frustration. They may also be asked to control their behavior by using problem-solving strategies and suggesting alternative positive actions.

- **Self-recording.** Students are encouraged to record orally or in writing the behavior they need to control and change. They may suggest ways that they may be helped to make those changes and who could help them.

- **Goal setting.** Students are asked to create short- and long-term goals for their behavior and actions that will help them to be successful.

- **Discipline parameters.** Students are given a set of clear and consistent rules for their behavior with specific punishments and rewards that will result from their actions.

- **Student contracts.** The student and the teacher enter into a signed contract that specifies the student's rights and responsibilities. A series of logical and appropriate positive and negative consequences of the student's actions are specifically stated and implemented.

- **Guided discipline.** The student and the teacher collaborate to identify a corrective and supportive guide for the student. The teacher offers choices and encourages the student to make good decisions, and set expectations and limits—each of which has rewards and consequences.

DEALING WITH SERIOUS BEHAVIOR PROBLEMS

When behavior-management strategies do not work, teachers who manage learning environments that maximize learning know what resources the school offers to provide direct intervention. But punishment neither teaches desirable behavior nor instills a desire to behave. It is therefore best used as a planned response to repeated misbehavior of a serious nature.

See Figure 2-2 for a summary of behavior-management strategies.

GATHERING AND KEEPING DATA

Keeping accurate records about students and their work contribute to the effectiveness of learning environments that maximize learning. Most school systems require teachers to keep such records. In addition, records of student attendance are often used to determine state funding.

Formats for data collection.   Data may be kept in a variety of ways. Some teachers record student information electronically. Others prefer to keep student records in a notebook, a grade book, a looseleaf binder, or in individual student folders. The issue is not the manner in which records are keep, but rather that they are consistently kept, fair in their judgment, and both neat and accurate.

Purposes for gathering data.   Gathering data about students and their work serves two purposes.

- They may be used to identify students' emerging needs, learning gaps, and trouble spots so that appropriate intervention strategies can be conducted before too much time is lost and the student falls further behind.

- They provide a record of the students' works that become the criteria by which the students are evaluated on progress reports or report cards sent to the parents.

Criteria for gathering data.   Learning environments that maximize learning identify criteria for data gathering that have an impact on student achievement. These criteria include:

- **Class participation.** The teacher may enter a daily grade or code to record the level and quality of each student's participation in the tasks and activities that were presented. Students who are actively involved in class tasks achieve at a higher level.

- **Homework.** If homework is to be taken seriously, it should be graded for completion on time, the quality of the responses, and the care and neatness given to its appearance. Homework is a means of reviewing and reinforcing what is taught in class. It also provides an opportunity for students to reflect, construct deeper understanding and meaning, and apply new knowledge in ways that make sense to them.

- **Social interactions.** The ways in which the students behave in the classroom and work collaboratively with other students are important to the social and emotional development of students and should be recorded and noted by the teacher.

Figure 2-2

BEHAVIOR MANAGEMENT

Guidelines

- Establish and communicate expectations.
  Teach the rules and procedures at the start of the year.
- Conduct systematic monitoring.
  Observe students' participation, classwork, homework, and behavior.
- Provide feedback.
  Immediate feedback about work and behavior when required.
- Use time productively.
  Plan to actively involve students in appropriate work.

Teacher Actions that De-escalate a Situation

- Positive reinforcement
  Reward positive behavior with something considered of value.
- Proximity control
  Move to a position near the student.
- Redirection
  Move the student or change the student's activity.
- Reframing
  Redefine, explain, or change the task the student is working on.
- Contingency setting
  The student is given or asked to make a cause-and-effect statement or predict the outcome of his/her action.
- Postpone
  Paraphrase the student's concern and set a time for dealing with it.
- Timeout
  Give the student the time and space to cool off and gain control.

Student Self-Control Strategies

- Self-verbalization
  The student talks about his/her anger.
- Self-recording
  The student records the behavior that needs to be controlled and changed.
- Goal setting
  The student sets short- and long-term goals for him-/herself.
- Discipline parameters
  The student is given a set of rules and specific consequences and rewards.
- Student contract
  The student and the teacher enter into a contract of specified rights and responsibilities with logical and appropriate rewards and consequences.
- Guided discipline
  The student and the teacher collaboratively identify a guide to support the student.

- **Assessment results.** The level of achievement that each student demonstrates becomes a part of the data gathered for each student and contributes to identifying if the student is learning and growing, as well as where there are problems and gaps. The results of all assessments that are conducted and collected should be recorded, including spot quizzes, class work, oral presentations, and formal and informal testing.

- **Project work.** Work on long-term projects should be evaluated and graded using the criteria for evaluation that was established by a rubric and distributed to students at the start of the assignment. When projects are group activities, students should be informed about how they will be evaluated, either as individuals or as the group as a whole.

See Figure 2-3 for a summary of gathering and keeping data.

Preparation for Effective Instruction

Teachers whose students achieve take the time to prepare instruction that will be effective for their students. To do this, teachers must first know and understand the content material to be taught. Then the content is shaped, tailored, arranged, and manipulated into a form that can be understood by the students. This preparation involves the following factors.

ANALYSIS OF STUDENT NEEDS

The first step in preparing for effective instruction is to determine the strengths and needs of the students. Effective teachers know that what their students know and do not know about the content to be taught is critical to what and how the content is taught. The type and level of prior knowledge students bring to instruction determines at what level they begin instruction, ask questions, and design activities.

For example, it would be impossible for students to master division by a two-place number if they do not understand subtraction with exchange. Additionally, it is extremely difficult to determine the nutritional value of foods, by comparing a line graph with a bar graph, if students do not first know how to read and interpret each graph.

CULTURAL SENSITIVITY

Today's schools have many students from all parts of the world. They bring with them cultural differences in ways to behave, interact, and understand. For example, when Americans engage in conversation, they generally stand two feet apart. Hispanics, Asians, and Middle Easterners stand or sit close to others. It is considered rude to move away.

Figure 2-3
GATHERING AND KEEPING DATA

Purposes

To identify student needs and plan intervention strategies.
To provide the record of students' work by which they are evaluated.

Formats

Electronically
Looseleaf Binder
Grade Book
Notebook
Student Folders

Criteria for Data Gathering

Class participation
Frequency of interactions with learning assignments
Quality of the work completed

Homework
Completion on time
Quality of the responses
Care and neatness of its appearance

Social Interactions
Classroom behavior
Collaboration with peers

Assessment Results
Do now
Spot quizzes
Class work
Oral presentations
Informal assessments
Project assignments
Formal assessments

When talking to others, Americans generally consider it important to make direct eye contact. American teachers may even say, "Look me in the eye when I speak to you." Students from other cultures may be confused by this request. For Latino students, the avoidance of eye contact may be a sign of respect and deference. Similarly, Asian children are taught that direct eye contact is an open show of rudeness. Children from these cultures may look away or lower their heads as a sign of respect when an adult addresses them.

Cultural influences also have instructional implications. The instructional practices of some cultures may come in direct conflict with instructional strategies practiced in American schools, such as expressing opinions, forming judgments, and solving problems. Here are some examples.

LATINO CHILDREN:

- Learn best when interacting in group situations.
- Are more comfortable with cooperative, group learning than with individual, competitive learning situations.
- Learn through observation and hands-on participation rather than through verbal interactions with adults.
- May not perform well on tasks that require repeating facts or foretelling what they will do. They may have had little experience with these activities in the home.
- Respond well to warmth, responsiveness, and frequent attention.
- Are raised to value cooperation more than individual achievement and may be embarrassed when singled out for praise.

ASIAN CHILDREN:

- May be accustomed to separate classes for boys and girls.
- Are usually taught in schools that rely heavily on rote learning and memorization.
- Are taught that conformity is more important than creativity.
- Are expected to value silence.
- Are taught to sit quietly and be respectful in class.
- May be unaccustomed to being called on in class and may even feel uncomfortable speaking or reading in front of the group.
- Are use to being told what to do and may not take the initiative in class.
- Are unaccustomed to physical contact.

MIDDLE EASTERN CHILDREN:

- May be accustomed to separate classes or schools for boys and girls.
- Are usually in classes of sixty or more.

- Are taught not to question rules.

- Have frequently been taught through storytelling.

- Are accustomed to a close protective relationship with their mothers and learn little about individualism and independence.

- Take on family responsibilities at an early age.

English-language learners bring additional language barriers even after they are able to speak English. Native speakers of English use expressions that may not be understood. Consider how confusing the statements, "I'm out of here," "You're toast," or, "Get real" may be to a new speaker of English.

While the task is far from easy, when planning instruction, effective teachers consider cultural influences and plan for students of all cultures and levels of English-language learning.

CONTENT STANDARDS

Almost every state in America has developed K–12 standards for each content area. These standards must serve to guide instruction if students are to achieve high scores on mandated tests. When planning instruction, teachers whose students are successful name the standard they are addressing through the content they have selected. They continuously review the standards to ensure that they have directed instruction to all of them.

SELECTION AND USE OF RESOURCES

Preparation for effective instruction requires the teacher to consider all of the resources available and then select those that will be most effective in delivering instruction. Here are some factors to consider.

- **Representative materials.** These are useful alternatives to the textbook and worksheet because they provide clarification of the concept being taught. Manipulatives for mathematics, cartoons, magazine articles, and pictures provide these alternatives. Teacher-made materials provide resources that may be tailored to the learning objective and the learners in the classroom.

- **Learning-style preferences.** Using oral, visual, tactile, and kinesthetic materials that match students' learning style will help each learner to more clearly understand the concepts taught. Learning-style resources may include songs, music, construction materials, audio- and videotapes, print materials, games, and organizers.

- **External resources.** The integration of external resources can often enrich the content. These include, for example, field trips to related original sites; people from the community such as the librarian, a local Holocaust survivor, the village mayor; and artifacts borrowed from the museum.

ACCOMMODATING STUDENTS WITH SPECIAL NEEDS

As inclusion programs grow in number, teachers who want all of their students to achieve at high levels with a rigorous curriculum must consider how to provide accommodations for students with special needs. The following suggested strategies result in instruction that will effectively assist students to learn.

- **Wait time.** Provide extra time between asking a question and accepting a response by waiting at least five to six seconds. Pausing after an important statement also assists by signaling that this is important.

- **Circulate.** Move away from the front of the room. Moving among the students during the teaching of a concept is one way of monitoring students' understanding and providing support and attention to individuals.

- **Group work.** Plan to use small mixed-ability groups for work in applying the concepts. This helps students to clarify their understanding and explain concepts to each other.

- **Reteach.** Group those students who require further clarification and understanding into a small group. Plan to reteach the lesson later in the day or week.

- **Extra teaching time.** Give students who are confused extra teaching time by extending the lesson to individuals or groups of two or three.

- **Encourage questions.** Make students comfortable about asking questions. Pause for questions throughout the lesson. Post a question area in the classroom.

LEARNING ASSISTS THAT ACCOMMODATE STUDENTS WITH SPECIAL NEEDS

- **Written format.** Some students become confused when they are asked to copy from the board. The transfer from distance to near vision is difficult. If homework and any other assignment is to be correctly completed, distribute the assignments in a clear written form.

- **Organizer.** Prepare and distribute an organizer that matches the content to be taught to assist students in taking notes and remembering details.

- **Varied reading levels.** Find additional print materials about the concepts being taught on reading levels appropriate for the students to support their learning.

- **Learning styles.** Introduce visual, oral, and tactile materials on the concepts under study to provide for students with varied learning styles.

- **Highlighter.** Encourage students to use a highlighter. Make it a part of the students' tools for learning. Teach the students how to appropriately use the highlighter as a learning assist.

- **Outlining.** Teach the students how to outline information read from a textbook. Clarify how to identify main ideas and details in a textbook. Teach them the clues that publishers use in books to signal important information.

- **Learning devices.** Provide learning devices that will assist students to master the information. Tools such as computers, calculators, and dictionaries are helpful.
- **Student helpers.** Establish a student help system in the classroom. Rotate student helpers each week who serve as guides for those students who need extra help. Give every student an opportunity to serve as a student helper at some time in the semester.

See Figure 2-4 for a summary of accommodation strategies.

Instruction that Fosters Learning and Achievement

There are multiple ways to instruct students. However, instruction that fosters learning and achievement has two important characteristics. First, the teacher knows and can effectively use a variety of effective instructional options. Second, the teacher matches what is to be learned with how to teach it by selecting the instructional option that will most likely result in student achievement of the learning objective. A categorized overview of options for instruction that will result in learning and achievement follows.

INSTRUCTION THAT ACTIVELY INVOLVES STUDENTS IN LEARNING

Instruction that actively involves students in learning, rather than requires them to passively receive instruction, is more likely to result in student learning and achievement. Active involvement helps students to sustain their attention on the topic and concepts being taught. In addition, actively involving students helps them to use and more fully understand what is being taught. Here is a list of some instructional strategies that actively involve students in learning.

- **Interactive lecture or recitation.** This form of instruction is used more than any other in most classrooms, especially in middle school and high school. This is probably true because many teachers consider it a means of effectively managing both time and student behavior. The interactive lecture can effectively involve students in their learning when it is truly interactive. This requires the teacher to stop every six to ten minutes to: ask a question and get a response; request students to become involved by completing an activity, writing a statement about what was presented, or asking a question of the student next to him or her (or any other strategy to actively involve the students in learning the material).
- **Demonstration.** Guidelines for viewing the demonstration and specific instructions for what to do following the demonstration must be provided to the students and fully explained before the demonstration begins.
- **Problem-based learning.** Students are presented with a problem that they are asked to solve. The problem may come from any content area. For example,

Figure 2-4

ACCOMMODATING STUDENTS WITH SPECIAL NEEDS

TEACHER ACTIONS

- Wait time
  Pause between asking a question and accepting an answer.

- Circulate
  Move to where the students are and away from the front of the room during instruction.

- Use small mixed-ability groups
  Provide opportunities for students to help each other apply the concepts taught.

- Reteach the lesson
  Teach the lesson again using a different instructional strategy to a small group of students who need clarification.

- Extra teaching time
  Give time to individual students who need more help.

- Encourage questions
  Encourage students to ask questions about what they are learning.

LEARNING ASSISTS

- Written format
  Distribute homework in a clear, written form.

- Organizer
  Create an organizer that students can use to record notes.

- Varied reading levels
  Give students reading materials about the content on their level of comprehension.

- Learning styles
  Use visual, oral, tactile, and written materials to teach the concepts.

- Highlighter
  Make the use of a highlighter a part of the student's learning tools.

- Outlining
  Teach students how to outline information from a text.

- Learning devices
  Provide students with learning devices that will assist them.

- Student helpers
  Rotate student helpers each week to serve as learning guides.

when studying about the colonial period in American history, students may be asked to resolve the problem of how to get the colonies to agree on one monetary system when each colony had its own currency. Or, students can be asked to consider the problem that the character in the story faces, and find ways to help him to resolve it.

- **Video or film viewing.** A section or part of the video selected for viewing should match the particular objective of the lesson. Viewing should be limited to no more than fifteen minutes. The entire video or film should never be shown. Before viewing the selected segment, students should be instructed about what to look for and how to record their observations. They should also be told about the task they will be asked to complete following their observation.

- **Socratic seminar.** A Socratic discussion usually focuses on a piece of information from a text or an article that presents an interesting topic or issue. The teacher designs a series of questions that assist students in understanding and interpreting the information. Students are encouraged to support what they are saying by referring to the information and/or giving examples. As the discussion progresses, the teacher moves the group to come to agreement, summary, or solution as is appropriate.

- **Debate.** Rules for the debate are first established with the class. Students must be comfortable with the way in which the debate is to be conducted prior to their involvement. Students select, or are assigned, a position they are to support and defend. They must be given time to prepare their presentation, arguments, and the way they will respond to statements from the other point of view. The class establishes guidelines for viewing and evaluating the debate that are used by members of the class who are not involved in the debate. Any topic with which the students are familiar and that can be seen from more than one point of view is suitable for a debate.

- **Role playing.** Students act out a situation by assuming the points of view of particular people in that situation. They respond and react to questions and situations as those role-played persons would.

- **Concept formation.** Students generate a random list of information on a given subject as in a brainstorming situation. All suggestions are recorded without comment or evaluation. Students are then asked to organize the random list by grouping the information in some way that makes sense to them and then give each group a label or a name.

See Figure 2-5 for a summary of instruction that actively involves students in learning.

PROCESSING THAT EXTENDS STUDENT LEARNING

Processing activities cause students to demonstrate their understanding or their ability to apply information that is being taught. The more that students are encouraged and required to process information, the greater the likelihood that the information

Figure 2-5

INSTRUCTION THAT ACTIVELY INVOLVES STUDENTS IN LEARNING

❑ **Interactive Lecture / Recitation**

Interrupt the lecture every six to ten minutes to:

Ask a question and get a response.

Request students to complete an activity.

Ask students to write a statement.

Ask students to ask a question of the student next to him/her.

❑ **Demonstration**

Provide guidelines for viewing the demonstration.

Tell students what they are to do following the demonstration.

❑ **Problem-based Learning**

Present students with a problem.

Ask them to solve the problem.

❑ **Video or Film Viewing**

Select the segment to be viewed by the students.

Tell students what they are asked to look for before they start.

Inform students about what they will be required to do following the viewing.

❑ **Socratic Seminar**

Select a piece of information from a text or written source.

Design questions that lead students to understand and interpret the material.

❑ **Debate**

Establish the rules of the debate.

Assign or allow students to select the position they support and defend.

Provide preparation time for the debaters.

Establish guidelines for those who are viewing the debate.

❑ **Role-Playing**

Students act out a situation by assuming the roles of characters.

❑ **Concept Formation**

Students generate a random list of information on a given subject.

Students organize the list by grouping the information.

Each group is labeled with a name or topic.

will be retained over time. Here are strategies that provide students with opportunities to process information.

- **Call on all students.** No student has the right to do nothing. Everyone should be able to respond to some part of the lesson. Use a random strategy that students cannot second-guess, but that you can monitor, to call on all students, not just those with their hands raised. Keep track of the students who have responded so that you can elicit a response from every student during the lesson. Students are more attentive to the question when it is asked before a student is selected for response. When the student is named first, it is a signal for everyone else in the class to relax because it is not his or her question.

- **Think pad or learning log.** Encourage students to process information by using a note pad, or a specific place in the student's notebook, on which the student records questions, thoughts, opinions, etc.

- **Wait time.** There is power in silence. Pause ten to twenty seconds following a question. This pause encourages more students to respond with more complete and complex answers by providing them with the opportunity to think about what they want to say before they are asked to respond.

- **Withhold judgment.** Students will risk giving a response that may be wrong when they are sure they will not be embarrassed. Incorrect responses must be accepted and responded to in a way that acknowledges the student but does not allow incorrect information to be transferred. Respond in a nonevaluative fashion such as: "That is interesting." "That is one way to think about it." "Let's put that idea aside for now."

- **Promote active listening.** Students are encouraged to attend to the lesson and listen to each other as well as the teacher when you do not repeat or rephrase the question, or the answers of the students; instead, ask a student to repeat the question or summarize another student's point of view. For example: "Can you summarize Mary's point?" "Can you repeat what Peter said?" "Who can repeat the question?"

- **Survey the class.** Check to determine students' understanding by doing a quick survey of the class. For example, "If you agree with Susan's answer, put your thumbs up." "If you are unsure of the answer, cross your fingers."

- **Allow for student-to-student inquiry.** Change the instructional focus from *teacher to student* and *student to teacher*, to *student to student* by asking students to call on a classmate for another idea, an explanation, or an example.

- **Questing.** Encourage students to extend their thinking beyond the specific response that they gave when a follow-up question is asked. For example, "Why do you believe that?" "Do you agree?" "Tell us more." "Give an example." "Explain your reasons for saying that." "How could that be changed?"

- **Play devil's advocate.** Challenge students to support or defend their statements. For example, "Tom does not agree with you. Can you defend your answer?"

- **"Unpack" thinking.** Ask students to think through the process they used to come to their answer and describe it for the class or the group.

- **Student questions.** Encourage students to formulate their own questions on the topic under discussion and then use their questions to challenge other students.

- **Learning pairs/squares/share.** Students state and explain their responses to a question or direction by speaking about it to the student next to him/her. Or, students may work together to formulate the response collaboratively. Two pairs of students may be asked to join into a square to compare their work. The responses of the student squares are then shared with the class.

- **Split page.** This strategy provides students with the opportunity to reflect on the lesson as it is being conducted by recording questions that occur to them on the left side of a vertically folded piece of paper. When the lesson has been completed, students attempt to respond to the questions on the right side of the paper, individually or with a peer.

See Figure 2-6 for a summary of processing that extends student learning.

QUESTIONS THAT RAISE THE LEVEL OF LEARNING

Asking questions is an integral part of the teaching process. But making those questions target the learning process is what successful instruction is all about. The level at which information is learned is directly related to the quality of the questions that teachers ask. Unfortunately, the overwhelming majority of questions usually asked by teachers are at the low levels of knowledge (questions that ask about facts) or comprehension (questions that focus on grasping the information). Students who achieve are able to use knowledge and comprehension as building blocks to help them to analyze (break down information into its components or parts), synthesize (compose something by putting information together in new ways), and evaluate (judge, rate, justify, or value information). The following sample questions illustrate how the type of question the teacher asks determines the level of learning required of the students.

- *To whom did Columbus go to get money to fund his expedition?* (**knowledge**) The response to this question can easily be found or recalled by students with little effort or understanding of the concepts involved.

- *What did Columbus do to get men to serve on his ship?* (**comprehension**) This response requires students to describe or report information without considering the factors involved.

- *Imagine you are a sailor on the Nina in 1492. Write a log of your activities for one day.* (**application**) Students are asked to generalize the new materials in a concrete situation with which they have some experience.

- *How do the dangers faced by early explorers compare with the dangers faced by modern-day explorers?* (**analysis**) In order to respond to this question, students must know and understand a great deal of information about the nature of early

Figure 2-6

PROCESSING THAT EXTENDS STUDENT LEARNING

- **Call on students randomly**

  Not just those with raised hands.

- **Think pad/learning logs**

  Each student records questions, thoughts, and opinions about the subject.

- **Wait time**

  Pause for ten to twenty seconds following a question or an interesting statement.

- **Withhold judgment**

  Respond in a nonevaluative fashion.

- **Promote active listening**

  Do not repeat a question or directions. Ask students to repeat, clarify, or summarize.

- **Survey the class**

  Check students' understanding with a quick survey of the class. "If you agree with Susan's answer, put your thumbs up."

- **Allow for student-to-student inquiry**

  Ask students to call on a classmate for another idea. "Select someone who can support your answer."

- **Questing**

  Ask a follow-up question to extend students' thinking. "Why do you believe that is true?" "What was the reason for that?"

- **Play devil's advocate**

  Challenge the student's response. "Can you defend your answer?"

- **Ask students to unpack their thinking**

  Ask students to describe how they got their answer. "Explain what you did to get that answer."

- **Student questions**

  Have students formulate and ask their own questions. "Write a question for your partner to answer."

- **Learning pairs/squares/share**

  Two minutes each of individual think time, discussion with a partner, discussion with two sets of partners, and a sharing with the class.

- **Split page**

  Students fold a paper in half vertically. On the left side they write the questions they think of during the lesson. After the lesson, they begin to answer the questions on the right side.

and current exploration. They must then analyze the information to make the comparison necessary for their response.

- *What advice would you give Columbus about how to deal with the natives who he found in the New World?* (**synthesis**) In responding to this question, students must first know and understand how Columbus dealt with the natives, and how dignity and respect are important before they can propose or design something different.

- *Should Columbus be considered a hero or a villain?* (**evaluation**) In order for students to respond with a judgment, they must consider all of the actions taken and the results achieved and then weigh their value and impact on society.

Any information source can be taught at any level depending on the type of questions the teacher prepares. Consider the following brief episode as an opportunity to ask questions that raise the level of students' learning.

Bus Hijacked

Wayne Thompson had been driving for the bus company for many years when something strange happened. He was driving his usual bus route between New York City and Chicago. Suddenly, one of the passengers got up and came over to Wayne. He demanded that Wayne stop the bus because he was going to hijack it. The passengers began to yell and scream. The hijacker turned around to try to quiet them, giving Wayne the time to contact the police on his personal cell phone. The police arrived and arrested the would-be hijacker. When Wayne returned to the company office two days later, he was told that he was suspended without pay. It seems that the bus company has a policy that says drivers cannot carry personal cell phones on their buses. "Well, how do like that," said Wayne. "I'm in more trouble than the hijacker."

Teachers usually want to be sure students know and comprehend the information, so they ask the following types of questions.

- *What was the policy of the company?* (**knowledge**) The answer is directly stated in the reading section. By correctly answering the question, students only demonstrate that they could find the answer in the paragraph, not that they understand the policy.

- *Describe how the passengers felt.* (**comprehension**) This answer is not directly stated in the passage. The behavior that the passengers demonstrated has to be interpreted into feelings.

- *Pretend you were a passenger on the bus. Write a letter to your friend about the experience.* (**application**) Students now personalize the information and express their feelings about how they might feel in that situation.

The previous questions do little to contribute to the true meaning of the passage or provide students with the opportunity to form an opinion, solve a problem, or make a decision.

Examine this next set of questions. Consider if questions at the knowledge, comprehension, and application levels are really necessary, or if they waste time in the learning process.

- *Why do you think the bus company had that policy?* (**analysis**) In order for students to respond to this question, they must first know and understand the policy. Then they must think of reasons for the company to create such a policy.

- *What new policy would you recommend for the bus company?* (**synthesis**) Students must think of something new that the bus company could do to be sure bus drivers can take positive actions and provide for the safety of passengers.

- *Wayne has a meeting with the officials of the bus company. If you were to go to the meeting with him, how would you persuade the company to give him his job back with back pay?* (**evaluation**) Students now must consider what arguments could defend the actions that Wayne took and how they could use those arguments to convince the company to give Wayne his job back.

Figure 2-7 provides a list of the levels of learning that questions can target, with sample clue words that can be used to form questions at each level.

GROUPING THAT ENHANCES INSTRUCTION

Grouping students for instruction enhances the learning process and reaps rewards in student achievement. Effective teachers routinely reorganize the class into small groups of students so that they can deliver instruction more effectively. This strategy is especially effective when students with differences in learning needs and levels of ability are in the same class.

Benefits of grouping as an instructional strategy.   Effective teachers also use student groups to enhance their instructional effectiveness. Some of the benefits of using cooperative learning as an instructional strategy follow.

- **Promotes active participation.** Every student contributes to the accomplishment of the required task. In essence, there is no place for a student to hide in a group of four or five students. Involvement of students is increased beyond what is possible with the whole class.

- **Encourages interaction.** Working together encourages respect for other students and promotes the socialization between and among students as partners in their learning. It provides an opportunity for students to experience the benefits of working together as a group.

- **Extends thinking.** The thinking process is extended and enlarged by asking students to work together to achieve a task. Students benefit from hearing the ideas of others and may use them to clarify their understanding and the development of additional ideas for the group to use.

Figure 2-7
FORMING QUESTIONS THAT RAISE THE LEVEL OF LEARNING

Level of Learning	Clue Words for Question Development		
KNOWLEDGE *Objective: Recall* Remembering or locating previously learned material	Observe Repeat Sort Record	Match Memorize Recall Label	Outline Define List Name
COMPREHENSION *Objective: Translate* Grasping the meaning of material	Recognize Locate Identify Restate Paraphrase	Tell Describe Report Express Explain	Review Cite Document Summarize Support
APPLICATION *Objective: Generalize* Using learned materials in new and concrete situations	Select Use Manipulate	Demonstrate Show Apply	Illustrate Try out Imagine
ANALYSIS *Objective: Break down* Breaking material into its parts so that it may be understood	Examine Classify Refute Map Infer	Interpret Compare Similarities Outline Differentiate	Relate Contrast Differences Analyze Conclude
SYNTHESIS *Objective: Compose* Putting materials together to form something new	Propose Design Compose	Construct Create Imagine	Plan Build Invent
EVALUATION *Objective: Judge* Judging the value of something or someone for a given purpose	Evaluate Prioritize Judge Rate Justify	Persuade Rank Value Grade Predict	Pro/Con Assess Decide Convince Argue

Strategies for grouping. Students may be grouped in a variety of ways for cooperative learning activities. Here are some strategies for grouping students.

- **Homogeneously.** Students may be grouped by similar learning style, needs, strengths, or levels of learning. The particular task the group is assigned and the materials to be used can be tailored to the style, learning need, or strength of the group.

- **Heterogeneously in mixed groups.** Students of every ability level and/or learning style are placed in each group so that learning strengths and needs are equally represented. The members of the mixed-ability group support and assist each other in the learning process.

- **Random groups.** Students are placed in groups as determined by any random strategy, such as the student next to you, pulling numbers from a hat, passing out symbols, counting off, or alphabetical order. This type of grouping provides students with the opportunity to work with everyone in the class at some time, and helps to build a sense of community.

Factors to consider. No matter how students are grouped for cooperative learning, effective teachers plan carefully so that each group will be successful. The factors that they consider are:

- **Rules and procedures.** The use of cooperative groups require some modification of the arrangement of student desks and chairs, and the movement of students themselves. In all cases, students must be taught, and then provided with opportunities to practice, how to get into and out of group configurations quickly and quietly before any cooperative strategy is used. Chaos and wasted time result when appropriate rules and procedures for moving into cooperative groups are not known and used.

- **Group size.** The sizes of the groups vary from pairs to three to six members, depending upon the task to be completed and the number of students in the class. Effective teachers match the size of the groups and the strategy they have selected for grouping their students to their instructional objective.

- **Preparation of the task.** The task the group is to complete must be specific, detailed, and clearly understood. Students should receive the task in writing, with a clear oral explanation, and have an opportunity to ask questions. A well-prepared task tells students what they are to do, how much time they have, and how they will know that they have successfully completed the assignment.

- **Provision of resources.** The resources the group will need to be successful with the task are either given to each group or readily available for them when they are needed. A variety of resources that provide the information the group needs to be successful may be used, such as text material, articles, an information sheet, a picture, or an object.

- **Assigned roles.** Each student member of the group is assigned a role that will help the group to be successful. The teacher may assign the roles or the members of the group may decide who performs which role. Some of the roles usually assigned include recorder, presenter, information seeker, timekeeper, peacemaker.

Instructional purposes.   There are a number of instructional purposes for which cooperative learning groups may be effectively used. A description of how to use cooperative groups for four instructional purposes with instructional examples are described here.

- **Master the learning ———————➤ Reteach/reinforce.** The teacher teaches a whole class lesson on a particular skill. Cooperative groups of two to four students are then formed. Students explain and reteach the new skill to each other, and then test each other's understanding. Some examples of skills that work well with this type of student grouping include finding area and perimeter, learning new vocabulary words, and identifying a sequence of events.

- **Experts ———————➤ Learn new content by breaking it into parts.** The assigned task is segmented into different parts or subtopics, each of which is important to completing the assignment. Each member of the four- or five-member group takes responsibility for learning one part or subtopic and becoming an expert on that subject. When all the groups have the same task, experts from each group, who are working on the same part or subtopic, may meet to share their information and clarify their understanding. Each group, now composed of experts on each part or subtopic, meets and each expert teaches the other members of the group. The group then collaborates on completing the task. Some examples of complex assignments that lend themselves to this type of student grouping include comparing the writing styles of various authors, and the age of exploration and discovery.

- **Gallery walk ———————➤ Review/clarify/extend previous information.** Students work in groups to review, clarify, and extend their learning of a topic. Large sheets of newsprint are posted on the walls around the room. A question or task, related to a particular topic, is placed on each posted sheet. Students are divided into six or seven groups to match the number of posted questions or topics. Students move as a group from posting to posting and help each other to contribute answers that are recorded on the sheets. Each group responds to each question or topic posted. The information that each group recorded, to answer the questions or tasks, is then shared with the entire class. Some examples of topics that can be extended by using this student grouping include environmental concerns, immigration before World War I, and characters in a novel.

- **Projects ———————➤ Application of concepts to real-life situations.** Group members work together to create a final product for a complex assignment that involves multiple tasks. The five or six members of the group determine how to approach the task, divide the work, and design the finished product. Some examples of complex projects that can be created by using this student grouping include creating a travel brochure that encourages tourists to visit a country that was previously studied by the class, and writing a newspaper (containing all the appropriate parts) that could have been distributed in 1775.

Figure 2-8 provides a summary of strategies for grouping that enhances instruction.

SUPPORTING LEARNING

Effective teachers help all of their students to learn, master information, and achieve by supporting their learning. Some specific strategies that they use to support learning are listed here.

- **Model/demonstrate.** The tasks involved in the learning of a specific skill are modeled for students or demonstrated using samples or examples. The teacher or another student can perform these demonstrations. They serve to provide a visual representation of the skill and its application to a situation for which the student is responsible. For example, a sample paragraph may be projected on the overhead and used by the teacher to model how to identify facts and details.

- **Think aloud.** Verbalizing what is being done and why it is being done helps to clarify the learning process for many students. Teachers can talk students through the learning by sharing their thinking and actions as they perform a task. For example, when teaching problem solving, teachers may talk about the steps they are using and what they are thinking as they solve a sample problem.

- **Tutors/coaches.** Some students need help at some points with understanding and mastering concepts and skills. The teacher might group students who need additional instruction or clarification and then instruct these small groups. Or, students who have mastered the information may serve as tutors for these small groups.

- **Advance/graphic organizers.** Presenting information in a visual form by using an advance organizer is an effective way to support students' learning. Learning is enhanced when the relationships among facts and concepts are visible. In addition, advance organizers help students to organize ideas, elaborate on them, relate new information to prior knowledge, and take notes. Advance organizers can be used as notes from which to study and help students to both store and retrieve information.

Design a match.   Advance organizers are designed to match the instructional objective. That is why their design begins with identifying what students are expected to learn. Each learning objective will result in the design of a particular advance organizer.

- **Spider map.** When students are expected to generate detailed responses to a topic, design a spider map that starts with the main idea in the center, and then provide lines that move out from the main idea for details and subdetails.

Figure 2-8
GROUPING THAT ENHANCES INSTRUCTION

Strategies for Grouping

Homogeneously: Students of similar learning strengths or needs are grouped together.

Heterogeneously: Students with different strengths and needs are placed in the same group.

Randomly: Students are grouped by a random strategy.

Factors to Consider

Rules and Procedures: Establish the way in which students will move desks, chairs, and themselves into a group formation.

Size of the Groups: Match instructional purpose.
Vary from pairs to between three to six members.

Preparation of the Task: Written, specific, detailed, time parameters, evaluation criteria

Provision of Resources: Readily available or distributed
Print on varied reading levels
Oral, visual, and tactile for varied learning styles

Assigned Roles: A role is assigned or assumed by each member of the group: recorder, presenter, information seeker, timekeeper, peacemaker.

Type Matches Instructional Purpose

Type	*Purpose*
Master the Learning:	*Reteaching* Students explain and reteach the information to other students.
Experts:	*Learn new content by breaking it into parts* Break complex information into parts. Each member of a group becomes an expert on an assigned part. When each group has the same tasks, experts on the same part may meet to learn together and share information. Each expert teaches that part to the other members of the group.
Gallery Walk:	*Review/clarify/extend previous learning* The number of questions or topics posted on newsprint around the room matches the number of groups formed. Each group discusses and records its answers to the posted question or topic. Each group moves to each posted question or topic until all questions or topics have been answered.
Projects:	*Application of concepts to real-life situations* Members of a group work together to complete a multifaceted task.

- **Web outline.** When students are asked to compare information to reach a conclusion, provide a web outline that enable students to separately list the information to be compared and then form a conclusion.

- **Venn diagram.** When students are asked to compare items to note how they are the same and different, design a Venn diagram. All the items that are unique to each item are placed in the left or the right circle. Those items that are the same for both items are placed in the overlapping center circle of the diagram.

- **Flow chart/sequence link.** When students are asked to learn a sequence of events or a cause-and-effect relationship, plan a design that links one box to another in a sequence or chain.

First, know the purpose of the instruction, and then plan a matching design. Figure 2-9 provides some sample designs for advance organizers that match different instructional purposes.

ONGOING ASSESSMENT OF LEARNING

Effective teachers know that if they wait for the end of the lesson or the test to check for students' understanding, they may be too late. In order to be sure that learning is taking place, teachers pause instruction periodically, throughout the lesson, to conduct a brief assessment of learning, These assessments can be conducted in a variety of ways that take very little time, but provide critical information. That information directs the teachers' actions to slow down, reteach, move on, or stop instruction. Here are some oral, written, and tactile/kinesthetic ways to assess students' learning.

ORAL ASSESSMENT

- **Tell the student next to you.** Ask students to respond to a question, give examples, or make a statement of support by speaking to another student.

- **Ask two or three students to respond orally to a question.** Ask two or three students to summarize or make a statement about what they believe, understand, or predict about the content being taught.

- **Ask the whole class for a choral response.** When a specific term, label, or name is important to the topic, use every opportunity to have the class say the word as a continuous reinforcement.

- **Ask questions at the analysis, synthesis, or evaluation level.** For example:

  "Why do you think that happened?"

  "What plan would you design?"

  "Can you predict what the outcome might be?"

- **Use questing to probe for deeper understanding.** For example:

  "Can you add some reasons?"

  "Do you agree with that answer?"

Figure 2-9
ADVANCE ORGANIZERS

Purposes: To help students organize ideas, elaborate on them, relate information to prior knowledge, and take notes that can be used to study for tests.

Design: Design advance organizers to match the instructional objective. Start with what students are expected to learn.

SPIDER MAP
To generate:
main idea,
details

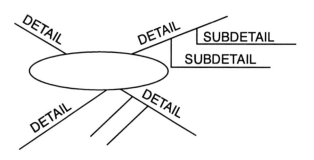

VENN DIAGRAM
To compare:
similarities and differences

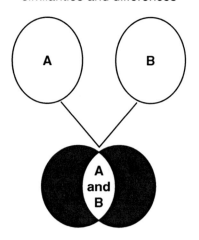

WEB OUTLINE
To compare:
points of view,
reach a conclusion

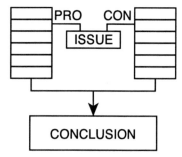

FLOW CHART/SEQUENCE LINK
To identify:
sequence of events,
cause-and-effect relationships

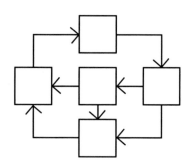

"How do you know that is true?"

"Why do you think that was done?"

- **Use interactive group role-playing and presentations.** Ask students to have a quick exchange of ideas from the points of view of the persons being studied.

- **Use buddy checkers.** Students complete a short activity, which is checked by other students.

WRITTEN ASSESSMENTS

- **Quick written check.** Ask students to place a check on a word, underline an action, or write a word that describes some aspect of the lesson.

- **Learning log.** Ask students to record something in their learning log about how they feel or what they are thinking about.

- **Think pad.** Have students write three ideas, two questions, or a sentence that summarizes the ideas on their think pad.

- **KWL.** Ask students to add to the KWL they had previously prepared. These are three separate listings about:

    What I *knew* before the lesson started

    What I *want* to learn more about

    What I *learned* during the lesson

- **Advance organizer.** Ask students to make an entry on their advance organizer.

- **Classwork assignment.** Have students complete a short classwork assignment that requires them to independently perform what has been taught.

- **Homework.** Design a homework follow-up to the lesson.

- **Self-check.** Ask students to check their own understanding of the concept by reading their notes on the advance organizer or a handout that was distributed.

TACTILE/KINESTHETIC ASSESSMENTS

- **Signaling.** Use signaling strategies such as:

    "Thumbs up if you agree."

    "Thumbs down if you do not agree."

- **Build.** Provide materials that students can use to build a structure related to the learning. For example, when teaching problem solving, distribute four playing cards to each student and ask students to use the cards to build the highest structure they can.

- **Draw.** Ask students to draw an illustration, a symbol, or an object that reminds them of some aspect of what is being taught. For example, draw a symbol to represent the global exchange of food that occurred during the age of exploration.

- **Create.** Ask pairs of students to create or invent an object that will solve a problem related to the topic under study.

- **Act out.** Ask students to act out the actions, feelings, and thoughts of someone who is being studied. For example, make your face look like King George when he received the Declaration of Independence from the colonists.

- **Role-playing.** Select a few students to role-play a poem that is being read, an action of a character in a book, or an historical action that was presented.

Figure 2-10 provides a summary of these ongoing assessment strategies.

Professionalism and Student Success

Teachers who are truly professionals demonstrate attitudes and behaviors that indicate concern for their growth as teachers through reflection on their practice, their colleagues, and their well being as well as the school and the district as a whole.

REFLECTION ON TEACHING

Reflection is a powerful way for professionals to learn and grow. In essence, we grow and gain from our experiences only when we think about them. Reflection requires the teachers to examine what they did and question how well it worked. Some questions that reflective teachers ask themselves are:

- "Did I select the correct objective for this lesson?"
- "Did the activity that I used for the groups help the students to understand?"
- "Are there better ways to group the students?"
- "Am I sure that the students really understand the concept?"

Teachers who are reflective seek to continuously learn by actively participating in the planning and delivery of professional-development sessions. They attend professional conferences and maintain active involvement in professional organizations.

Some teachers automatically reflect on their instructional practice. Others, who do not, would benefit greatly from being asked to reflect by writing a description about the effectiveness of the lesson; commenting on student work; and assessing if their intended goal was achieved.

COLLABORATION WITH COLLEAGUES

Teaching is a complex activity that is typically performed in isolation from other teachers. There is usually little incentive for teachers to explore common problems, with which they are confronted, about management, behavior, or instruction with their colleagues. Collaboration provides excellent opportunities to listen to and learn

Figure 2-10

ONGOING ASSESSMENT OF LEARNING:
CHECKING FOR STUDENTS' UNDERSTANDING

Oral	Written	Tactile-Kinesthetic
Tell a neighbor	*Quick Written*	*Signaling*
	Write a check	Thumbs up
Oral response	Underline	Thumbs down
	Write a word	
Choral response		Build a . . .
	Learning Log	Draw . . .
Questioning	How I feel . . .	Create . . .
Analysis	Reflection on . . .	Act out . . .
Synthesis		Role-playing
Evaluation	*Think Pad*	
	Three ideas . . .	
Questing	Two questions . . .	
Can you add . . .	Summary for . . .	
Do you agree . . .		
Please explain . . .	*KWL*	
How did you . . .	Add to	
Why do you . . .		
	Advance/Graphic	
Think/Pair/Share	*Organizers*	
Share	Sequence chain	
	Spider map	
Interactive	Starburst	
Group role-playing	Cause/result	
Presentations	Venn diagram	
Buddy checkers		
Decisions	*Independent*	
	Homework	
	Classwork	
	Self-check strategies	

about the experiences and point of view of another professional. Excellent teachers seek these collaborations. They find ways to speak and work with other teachers who have similar programs and concerns. Such teachers actively participate in department or grade and faculty meetings.

INVOLVEMENT IN SCHOOL/DISTRICT ACTIVITIES

Excellent teachers know and understand that activities outside the classroom are important to their development as professionals. They attend district events and meetings to be better informed about what is happening. They participate in building and district committees to contribute to the development of new and effective initiates. They also realize that school and district events are an important part of the lives of their students and they attend those events to demonstrate to their students their genuine concern for them and their accomplishments.

USE OF SCHOOL POLICIES

Professionalism is also reflected in teachers' use of and involvement with the development and improvement of school policies. Practices and procedures used in the school are known and used. Professional teachers are punctual and meet deadlines. When procedures become problematic, these teachers seek the appropriate person to speak with about the problem and may even offer suggestions for making it more effective and efficient. When the development of new policies and procedures becomes necessary, these teachers volunteer to participate on committees that will discuss the situation and make recommendations.

Parent and Community Interactions

The teacher's interaction with parents and the community contributes greatly to the success of both the teacher and the school. The value and esteem with which the school is held by the parents and the community as a whole is often the result of interactions with a teacher. Most parents know very little about the school or district aside from the perspective of their child.

ESTABLISH COMMUNICATION LINKS WITH PARENTS

Effective teachers know they are the key to positive communication links with parents, which they establish and maintain by the following actions and attitudes.

Availability. The teachers make themselves available to parents. Conferences with parents may be held before school, after school, or during the evening hours. Teachers employ every means of communicating with parents, even calling from their homes in the evening. These calls may be positive in nature, such as informing the parents of how hard the student is trying and the good work that is resulting. The calls may also be used to inform the parents about problems and concerns and ask for their involvement in a plan for improvement.

Interest.   During interactions with parents, the teachers are good listeners maintaining eye contact, an appropriate facial expression, and an interested attitude. Teachers demonstrate an interest in *all* factors that affect students' performance in school.

Helpfulness.   Teachers invite parents to participate in forming a plan to change an undesirable situation. Suggestions from both the teachers and the parents are considered and used as appropriate solutions. These suggestions often involve the joint efforts of both the teachers and the parents.

Confidentiality.   All matters discussed with parents are kept confidential. Teachers do not become involved in idle gossip. Information is shared only when and with whom it should be shared for the best interests of the students.

INTERPRET EDUCATIONAL INFORMATION

The desire and effectiveness in interpreting educational information is another way in which effective teachers target students' achievement.

Test results.   Teachers present the type of assessment being discussed and its purpose. The level of achievement demonstrated by the students toward meeting the standards set is fully explained. Teachers compare the students' progress with their prior level of achievement and identified future needs.

Student involvement in programs.   Teachers discuss and explain to the parents the particular programs in which the students are involved. Why the particular student was placed in the program, how the program will benefit the student, what results may be expected, and how those results will be communicated to the parents are fully discussed.

ENCOURAGE PARENT AND COMMUNITY INVOLVEMENT

A final item of importance to effective teachers is the value they place on parent and community involvement.

Invite parents to visit.   Parents and members of the community are encouraged to visit the classroom to observe, firsthand, how the students work and behave as members of the class and how programs operate.

Seek community interaction.   Teachers request participation from various parts of the community to enrich and enlarge the instructional resources available to students. They also pursue opportunities to display student products in the community to demonstrate excellence.

Support community efforts.   Teachers actively participate in community efforts and encourage others to participate. Teachers are sympathetic to community needs and aspirations.

Use Figure 2-11 as an outline of the standards for teaching that identify the knowledge, skills, and abilities of teachers whose students achieve. The outline of standards is intended to:

1. Provide a categorized breakdown of the standards to be used as a guide to plan for teachers' growth.

2. Be used to help teachers understand the scope of their role.

3. Provide a means of involving individual teachers in the identification of specific skills they wish to master.

Remember, the outline is *not* intended to be used as an observation checklist.

Figure 2-11

OUTLINE: STANDARDS FOR TEACHING THAT TARGET STUDENTS' ACHIEVEMENT

Areas and Components	Aspects
Classroom Environments that Enhance Learning	
Classroom Atmosphere	• Attitude and Beliefs In charge of classroom, students, and instruction High expectations • Classroom Climate Work oriented Warm and supportive
Physical Arrangement of the Room	• Aisles and passageways are clear • Furniture and space are used to enhance learning • Organized appearance • Student work is displayed
Availability of Resources	• Resources neatly arranged • Resources for learning styles • Variety of resources
Management of the Learning Environment that Maximizes Learning	
Classroom Management	• Rules and procedures are posted • Rules and procedures have been taught • Rules and procedures are followed
Behavior Management	• Expectations established and communicated • Systematic monitoring • Feedback provided • Time used productively • Actions de-escalate situations • Students use self-control strategies • Procedures used for dealing with serious behavior problems
Recordkeeping	• Appropriate format is used • Records about students are kept • Recorded information about: class participation, homework, social interactions, assessments, projects
Preparation for Effective Instruction	
Analysis of Student Needs	• Prior knowledge assessed • Skill needs identified
Cultural Sensitivity	• Knowledge of cultural differences • Knowledge of English second-language learners
Content Standards	• Knowledge of standards for content areas • Standards used in instructional planning
Selection and Use of Resources	• Representative materials are created or found • Materials include provision for learning style • External resources are integrated
Accommodating Students with Special Needs	• Actions contribute to learning • Learning assists are used

Figure 2-11 continued

Areas and Components

Aspects

Instruction that Fosters Learning and Achievement

Instruction that Actively Involves Students
- Knows varied types of instructional strategies
- Matches learning objective to the instructional strategy

Processing that Extends Students' Learning
- Strategies for student processing are incorporated into instruction

Questions that Raise the Level of Learning
- Questions address higher levels of learning: analysis, synthesis, evaluation

Grouping that Enhances Instruction
- Varied grouping patterns are used
- Rules and procedures for group work are established and used
- Group type and size match instruction
- Learning tasks are carefully prepared

Supporting Learning
- Strategies used to support learning
- Advance organizers designed to match instructional objectives

Ongoing Assessment of Learning
- Checks for student understanding are conducted throughout the lesson
- Oral, visual, and tactile strategies are used

Professionalism and Student Success

Reflection on Teaching
- Questions about instructional effectiveness are asked
- Helps to plan and attends professional development sessions
- Attends conferences and workshops
- Joins professional organizations

Collaboration with Colleagues
- Seeks to collaborate with others
- Establishes working relationships
- Participates in department/grade and faculty conferences

Involvement in School/District Activities
- Attends district events
- Participates on committees
- Attends student events

Use of School Policies
- Knows and uses established policies
- Is punctual
- Meets deadlines
- Becomes involved in policy revision or creation

Parent and Community Interaction

Establishes Communication Links with Parents
- Is available
- Is interested
- Is helpful
- Is confidential

Interprets Educational Information
- Test results
- Program involvement

Encourages Parent/Community Involvement
- Invites parents to visit
- Seeks community interaction
- Supports community efforts

Part II

How to Determine What Teachers Need to Make Students Achieve

Gathering Data about Teaching for Student Achievement

Being informed leads to making good decisions and taking correct actions. This is a daily life practice. We seek data about the weather before we decide about taking a heavy coat, boots, or umbrella. If traffic is a concern, most of us will listen to the traffic report before selecting the route to our destination. Obviously, we seek the specific data that will inform our decision. Similarly, when we strive to make students achieve, gathering specific data about the complex act of teaching and how effectively those actions result in student learning is the guide to what skills teachers need. Student achievement increases when teachers master the skills they need.

What Data to Gather

Teaching that results in student achievement is a complex activity. The data that is gathered must objectively and effectively determine teacher skill needs related to each aspect of teaching and learning.

RELATED TO TEACHING AND LEARNING

The standards for teaching that target student achievement are presented in Section 2. Helping teachers to achieve these standards helps students to achieve. Gathered data constitutes important information about the skill needs as well as the strengths of each teacher. The data is most useful when the appropriate tool is used to pinpoint specific skill needs by examining:

1. The teacher's views, concerns, and needs discussed during an overview conference.

2. What is happening, at varied points in time, in the teacher's classroom, the halls, and so forth during informal visits.

3. How the teacher's classroom operates as a total learning environment by analyzing the classroom environment.

4. How the teacher and the students use instructional time by conducting a time-on-task analysis.

5. What teachers and students produce as artifacts of teaching and learning.

6. How the teacher delivers instruction by conducting an observation.

OBJECTIVE IN NATURE

Objective data is data that has been observed and can be described. Avoid interpreting the data and making value judgments for two reasons:

1. Your interpretation may be wrong.

   For example, here is a recent classroom episode: The lesson focused on a discussion of Chapter 3 in *A Tale of Two Cities*. Five students at the back of the room did not participate in the discussion. Rather, they interacted only with each other and did not hear the discussion.

   Your observation: Five students at the back of the room did not participate in the discussion.

   The possible interpretation: Five students in the back of the room were ignored by the teacher and allowed to miss the lesson.

   Teacher's response: "Five advanced students had completed the reading of this work in a previous class. They cooperatively agreed upon a critical-thinking project related to the work. They were seated in the back of the room to permit them to begin the brainstorming activity concerned with identifying modern acts of courage."

2. Your interpretation could cause the teacher to become hostile and defense.

   For example, here is a recent classroom episode: The lesson focused on the initial presentation of division using a two-place divisor. Periodically throughout the lesson, two youngsters spoke and wrote notes to each other.

   Your observation: During this lesson, two youngsters participated, from time to time, in written and oral communication.

   The possible interpretation: Two students were continuously distracted during the lesson. They may not be motivated to learn the topic.

   Teacher's response: "One of the two youngsters is an inclusion student who was placed in the class last week. The other student is his study buddy and he helps the new inclusion student by answering his questions. I don't know how I can raise the standardized scores of all of the students and provide the special attention that inclusion students need. I thought that my class register was too high for the placement of an inclusion student. How did that happen?"

How to Gather Data

Gathered data should accurately record the date, time, place, and events objectively observed. This prevents distortion of the facts and a lack of recall when that data is later reviewed as a part of a total review of the teacher or specifically in conference with the teacher.

USING A FORMAT FOR GATHERING DATA

Using a specified format for gathering particular data sets an all-inclusive standard with which the observed data can be compared. The form may be used in four different ways:

1. To note what is not observed and missing from the standard used
2. To record what is observed, leaving blank what is not observed
3. To note an objective question or a comment about what is observed or not observed
4. To complete all specifics listed

Using a printed format, which is particularly suited to gathering specific types of data, contributes to the accuracy and ease of the collection. A specific format is presented in Part II for each of the following:

1. An observation of how a classroom functions as a total learning environment
2. An analysis of how instructional time is used by students and teachers
3. A review of teacher and student artifacts
4. A pre-observation planning form

NOTETAKING

Other types of data are more easily gathered by taking notes. However, notetaking will take different forms depending upon what data is gathered.

Verbatim notetaking.   This type of notetaking records as accurately as possible the exact words and actions of the teacher and the students. It is possible to gather data related to the sequence of the lesson, the time intervals for each segment, the interaction between the teacher and the students, and the exact questions asked and how they were answered.

Although verbatim notetaking is an excellent tool, it has several limitations:

1. It is often difficult to keep up with the actions and words.
2. Since inflection and tone cannot be recorded, an element of the delivery is lost.
3. It is sometimes difficult to hear a particular response from a student.

Informal notetaking.   Some data is best gathered through different forms of notetaking that relate to the specific activity. These include:

- Summary of a conference
- Comments recorded on requested information
- Information gathered during informal visits

VIDEO-TAPING

Making a videotape of a lesson has become a requirement for license in some states. It is also a required part of the process for achieving National Board for Professional Teaching Standards certification. The videotape serves as an excellent record of an observation for several reasons:

- It is objective, recording both audio and visual aspects.
- It can be reviewed to discuss specific actions demonstrated.
- It communicates better than words can do alone.
- It provides teachers with a means to reflect and self-assess.

Using a videotape has some limitations (listed here) and should be used in combination with written notes rather than by itself.

- The production of a good video view of the classroom throughout the observation requires someone with video-taping experience.
- The video cannot record the entire classroom all the time, so some aspects of the observation may be lost.
- Using the video takes time and additional personnel that is probably not necessary for every observation.
- Some teachers and students are not comfortable while being viewed by the camera, which may cause a change in their usual behavior.

PORTFOLIOS

A portfolio is a purposeful collection of selected artifacts that document the work of a teacher on aspects of the teaching and learning process. (See Section 8 for a discussion of artifacts.) It is a useful means for experienced teachers to gather data about themselves in any of the six areas specified in Section 2. The portfolio should contain carefully selected samples of both student and teacher work that present artifacts of the teacher's professional practice. Portfolios can be used in several ways.

1. **To determine an experienced teacher's growth need or accomplishments.** The experienced teacher identifies an area of interest and collects data about his or

her professional practice in that area. For example, suppose a teacher was interested in extending students' thinking. The teacher can collect a variety of data about the ways in which students in the class are currently asked to extend their thinking. The data collected can include plans for instruction, a record of questions asked, samples of student activities, and examples of students' work. The data collected can also focus on skills and abilities not visible in the classroom as direct actions. These may include, as examples, the ways in which the teacher communicates with parents and professional interactions with colleagues that focus on self-development. It may be used to demonstrate accomplishment of the teacher-directed growth plan, which is discussed in Section 13. The portfolio is then reviewed with the administrator to detail the specifics of the growth plan or the results accomplished in the growth plan.

2. **As documentation for the end-of-year mandated evaluation discussed in Section 1.** Portfolios have some limitations (listed below) to their use and should be carefully considered and used in combination with other data-gathering techniques and a review by another professional.

   - Portfolios take time to collect, organize, and prepare for use in professional discussions about growth plans.

   - Portfolios include only what the teacher selects and may omit other important data. Additional data should also be collected.

   - Portfolios are collected from the teacher's view and are limited by that one perspective. That is why portfolios should always require self-reflection as well as collaborative review.

See Figure 3-1 for an outline of categories for portfolio construction.

How to Use Data to Impact Teaching and Student Learning

Using the data collected to specifically guide each teacher's growth is the key to effective teaching that results in students' achievement. The data determine what skills the teacher needs. These skill needs are then targeted in a specific growth plan that is discussed with the teacher.

DETERMINE TEACHER STRENGTHS AND SKILL NEEDS

The purpose of gathering data is to determine both teacher strengths and skills needed to effectively guide students to achievement. Data is gathered through the use of six specific tools that are discussed in detail in sections 4 through 9 of Part II. Each of the six tools presented in Figure 3-2 is designed to provide information about a different aspect of teaching and learning and contributes to a comprehensive overview of the teacher.

Figure 3-1
PORTFOLIO CONSTRUCTION:
STANDARDS FOR TEACHING THAT TARGET STUDENTS' ACHIEVEMENT

Areas	Components
Classroom Environments that Enhance Learning **Definition:** Organization and climate of the classroom **Demonstrated through:** Interviews or surveys of students Observation in person or on videotape	• Sustains an environment of respect and collaboration • Arranges and decorates the physical space • A variety of resources that enhance learning are available
Management of the Learning Environment that Maximizes Learning **Definition:** Interactions and processes that are set and followed **Demonstrated through:** Review of student work Observation of the environment	• Classroom management procedures are organized/maintained • Student behavior reflects expectations • Appropriate records about students are kept
Preparation for Effective Instruction **Definition:** What to consider prior to planning instruction **Demonstrated through:** Teacher plans, records	• Analysis of student needs is conducted • Knowledge of and sensitivity to cultural differences • Content standards used in instructional planning • Appropriate resources are selected and used • Students with special needs are accommodated
Instruction that Fosters Learning and Achievement **Definition:** Active engagement of students with content Student involvement in thinking **Demonstrated through:** Observation or on videotape	• Instruction actively involves students • Strategies for student processing extends learning • Questions raise the level of learning • Grouping strategies enhance instruction • Strategies are used to support learning • Ongoing assessment of learning is conducted
Professionalism and Student Success **Definition:** Attitude toward teaching and roles assumed **Demonstrated through:** Journal entries, committee work, attendance at events, actions	• Ongoing reflection on teaching • Collaboration with colleagues is sought • Involvement in school/district activities • Use of school policies
Parent/Community Interaction **Definition:** Interest in involving parents and community **Demonstrated through:** Appointments made, body language, letters written, phone calls	• Establishes communication links with parents • Interprets educational information • Encourages parent/community involvement

Figure 3-2
DATA-GATHERING TOOLS

Tool Type	When to Use	Purpose
Exploration conference	Start of the year	• Determine teacher's plans, concerns, needs
Informal visits	Ongoing throughout the year	• Monitor instruction • Identify needs • Note progress on growth plans
Classroom environment	Early in the year in appropriate classrooms	• Assess the effectiveness of the classroom as a total learning environment
Time-on-task review	When needed	• Assess how instructional time is used by students and teachers • Analyze causes of disruption in classes
Artifacts	Scheduled throughout the year	• Determine student progress • Analyze teacher growth • Identify teacher needs
Observation	Scheduled throughout the year	• Determine teacher skill needs • Monitor progress on growth plans

Some of the tools should be a part of your routine review of teaching and learning in the school. These include the overview conference, informal visits, and the scheduled collection of artifacts. Other tools, such as a review of the classroom environment and the time-on-task review, may be more important in some classrooms than in others. You may not find it necessary to use all six tools with each teacher, but you will want to be sure that you had gathered the data you need to accurately determine what skills each teacher needs for students to achieve at high levels.

DESIGN A TEACHER GROWTH PLAN

Once teacher skill needs are determined, a specific growth plan can be designed. Part III deals with how to design the content and the process of each growth plan in detail.

COMMUNICATE WITH THE TEACHER

After using a data-gathering tool, some form of communication should be provided to the teacher. The form of this communication is directly related to the tool that was used and the type of data collected. Each data-gathering tool described in Part II is presented with a suggested means of communicating with the teacher.

Holding Overview Conferences about Student Achievement

The overview conference is an important way to start the school year with every member of the instructional staff. Each teacher, within the first four weeks of the new school term, should individually be invited to a conference.

Reasons for Conducting These Conferences

Several purposes can be accomplished by conducting overview conferences. They set the agenda for the new school year by focusing on student achievement. These conferences also contribute to building rapport with the staff by demonstrating that time has been set aside to individually communicate with each teacher. In addition, they provide information from the teacher's point of view about everything that interacts with the delivery of instruction and student achievement.

ESTABLISH EXPECTATIONS FOR THE YEAR

The teacher should be encouraged to discuss his or her plans and hopes for the year. The discussion may include personal goals that the teacher has set for him- or herself as well as the students. In addition, the teacher might be asked to talk about how new strategies or techniques that were studied will be used in instruction.

The concerns that the teacher may have about reaching these goals should be expressed. It is important to identify the possible constraints that may prevent the plan from becoming a reality.

The teacher may wish to use this opportunity to discuss some personal problems. These are usually sensitive issues, but it is important to be aware of any situation that may contribute to absence, lateness, and ineffectiveness. The trust that has been built with the teacher as well as the warm tone of the conference may contribute to the sharing of this personal information.

Some sample lead questions are:

- "How will you use the course work on writing process in your plans for instruction?"
- "How will you deal with three different preparations for instruction?"
- "You seem to be a little down. Is anything on your mind?"

PLAN FOR THE DELIVERY OF THE CURRICULUM

Standards and content.   A discussion of specific subject matter should be included in the conference. The teacher should identify the way in which standards will be targeted and the curriculum will be presented.

Meeting students' needs.   Plans to tailor instruction to address students with different needs should also be discussed. The discussion should cover all the teacher's areas of responsibility.

The elementary school teacher should present a plan for grouping students for both reading and mathematics, organizing the groups according to the levels of ability of the students in the class. The plan must include all the students for whom the teacher is responsible. Other subjects within the teacher's areas of responsibility should also be discussed. The specified plan should include the frequency and time frames for the group meetings. Provision for review and reinforcement, individual differences, and homework should also be discussed.

The secondary school teacher should present a plan for presentation of content that provides for individual differences among students and classes. The discussion should include how to provide for those students who do not appear to grasp a concept after the first teaching. A plan for the use of a variety of instructional strategies, including the interactive lecture, class discussion, group work, and individual projects, should be discussed. Plans for review and reinforcement using classwork and homework can be explored.

Students with particular needs.   The teacher should discuss and be informed about students for whom he or she is responsible. This includes the variety of academic abilities, learning needs, and special problems of the youngsters.

Some sample lead questions are:

- "How will you address the range of reading ability in your class?"
- "How will you incorporate writing skills into your social studies program?"
- "How do you plan to prepare your students for the state assessment in January?"
- "How do you plan to support your English language learners?"
- "Have you spoken with the outside counseling agency and the guidance counselor about Mary?"

IDENTIFY TEACHING RESOURCES

The teacher should specify the materials that will be used with each group or class of students. The materials should be suited to the content and the levels of ability of the students.

In addition, the materials should provide for differences in learning style to the greatest degree possible. The teacher's plans should include finding, making, and requesting the types of materials suited to the content of the subject matter. Problems concerned with a lack of appropriate materials should be stated and addressed.

Some sample lead questions are:

- "What novels have you selected for the lower-level readers?"

- "Which text do you plan to use for the new global studies curriculum?"

- "What type of manipulative materials will you use to teach those mathematical concepts?"

OUTLINE CLASSROOM MANAGEMENT AND ORGANIZATIONAL STRUCTURES

The teacher should present the way in which the classroom will be organized for instruction. This will include the seating arrangements, teacher records, student records, procedures for giving and checking homework, providing for absentees, and receiving and distributing materials and assignments.

A discussion of classroom management also includes effective use of time. The teacher's discussion should include the establishment of routines, how and where instructional groups will be formed, and how to minimize transition time.

The teacher should present the code of behavior that will be established with each class. A plan to achieve good control of the group and to deal with discipline problems should be presented.

Some sample lead questions are:

- "How and when will assigned homework be checked?"

- "What types of student information do you record?"

- "What steps will you take to control a youngster who is acting out?"

Recording the Conference Data

Taking notes about the information gathered during the overview conference will provide a record of what was discussed. Organize the notes under each item that was discussed. This will make your notetaking easier and your notes more valuable when they are reviewed at a later date. A sample form for recording the overview conference is presented in Figure 4-1.

Figure 4-1
OVERVIEW CONFERENCE SUMMARY

ITEMS/COMMENTS
Expectations:

Delivery of the Curriculum:
(standards & content, meeting students' needs, students with particular needs)

Teaching Resources:

Classroom Management & Organization:

Date: _____

Signatures: _____   _____

              Teacher   **Administrator**

Using the Conference Data

There are at least four ways in which the data from the overview conference can be used:

1. To understand the teacher's point of view
2. To determine immediate needs that impact student achievement
3. To encourage teacher reflection and analysis
4. To provide initial diagnoses of needs

UNDERSTAND THE TEACHER'S POINT OF VIEW

Data from a well-organized overview conference provides an opportunity to see the total instructional program from the teacher's point of view. It supplies an overview of all the aspects with which the teacher will deal during the year. During the conference, the teacher will reveal important information concerned with strengths and skill needs. These include:

INSTRUCTION

- How to organize for instruction
- Areas of instruction that could be improved
- How to provide for individual differences
- Sensitivity to the needs of individual students
- Understanding the problems of individuals and groups
- How to use time efficiently
- Selection and use of specific materials
- Relationship of materials to students' needs
- Dealing with a lack of materials

ORGANIZATION OF THE CLASSROOM

- Management of the classroom
- Maintaining order and discipline
- Grading students' work
- Keeping records

CONCERNS

- Items that are potential problems
- Areas in which change is desired
- Areas of insecurity

DETERMINE IMMEDIATE NEEDS THAT IMPACT STUDENT ACHIEVEMENT

The needs and problems of the teacher that require immediate attention are revealed through the conference. It is then possible to take steps to correct them as quickly as possible. Immediate needs may include:

- Students who are inappropriately placed in classes
- Instructional materials that must be ordered
- Physical needs of the classroom
- Scheduling changes

ENCOURAGE TEACHER REFLECTION AND ANALYSIS

The overview conference may serve as a source of information for teacher reflection and analysis. It provides teachers with the opportunity to analyze what they have done and to begin planning ways to improve these efforts. It is the first step in their identification of the area on which they will focus their attention. This initial analysis will later be used to develop the growth plan.

PROVIDE INITIAL DIAGNOSES OF NEEDS

The overview conference provides an opportunity to make an initial determination of teacher needs for most of the teachers on staff. It gives valuable insight about the constraints with which the teacher is faced, and what the teacher has planned as solution strategies. Moreover, a beginning understanding is provided about how each teacher functions. At this point, however, the data is incomplete. It is based solely on what the teacher says, not what the teacher does. This initial identification of needs will be confirmed, modified, or completely changed as additional data are received.

The overview conference serves as an initial source of data. Recommendations and suggestions should be minimal. However, there are two instances when suggestions should be given:

- **Items that must be changed.** For example, the teacher plans to use a piece of literature that is too difficult for the students. You should suggest some alternatives that will better serve the needs of the students. Or, the teacher proposes to work with five reading groups. You should suggest other ways to organize the reading groups so no more than three will be necessary.

- **Minor points of improvement.** For example, advising an inexperienced teacher to assign a study buddy to an inclusion student, or a source for information related to the project that the teacher has in mind, such as a list of trips, an article on cooperative learning, or the titles of novels that relate to a social studies topic.

Communicating with the Teacher

Record notes during the conference that detail the teacher's comments, ideas, and plans. Include any suggestions that were made. Ask the teacher to read the notes and sign them at the conclusion of the conference. Then give the teacher a copy of the notes.

Take time after the conference to review the notes. Make additional comments about aspects of the conference that should be remembered. Highlight particular items on your original notes or as a separate record. These notations will help you form an initial assessment of teacher strengths and skill needs.

Making Informal Visits to View Students Achieving

Informal visits are like snapshots of what is happening at a particular point in time in any area of the school. Since informal visits are unannounced, random, and frequent, they provide a means of checking the pulse of the school throughout the day. Valuable data can be gathered from all areas of the school when making informal visits. These areas include classrooms, laboratories, special program rooms, cafeteria, auditorium, gymnasium, library, computer rooms, and any other areas used by the school population.

Reasons for Making Informal Visits

Informal visits can help to accomplish a variety of objectives, discussed below.

DETERMINE WHAT IS ACTUALLY HAPPENING

A firsthand view of what is actually going on—a candid picture of the school, classrooms, teachers, and students at that point in time is provided. This view is, of course, representative but it is probably very close to the usual since it is unplanned. Look for confirmation of a schoolwide program, such as a 90-minute literacy block. Look for use of a school initiative to actively involve students in their learning. Observe students who are in the halls during the period, and say hello to teachers on hall duty. Watch student behavior during change of classes, in the restrooms, and on the staircases.

CHECK ONGOING CONCERNS

Use the informal visits as an opportunity to check areas of ongoing concern, such as a student who is new to the school, a problematic student, a new substitute teacher, a potentially disruptive classroom, the heat in the gymnasium, a construction area, and the preparation of the lunchroom.

MONITOR PROGRESS ON GROWTH PLANS

Determine if some aspects of teachers' growth plans are being implemented. For example, look for the posting of a behavior code in the classroom of a teacher who planned this strategy as a means of better managing behavior. Observe the students to determine if the strategy appears to be working. In another classroom, in which the teacher's growth plan is concerned with asking higher level questions, listen to several of the questions the teacher is asking at that time. Observe how the students respond to the questions. It may be possible to determine if the teacher is actually working on questioning skills, and if those efforts are a part of the teacher's daily activities or those reserved for observed lessons. In a classroom in which the teacher's growth plans included movement around the room as a means to better monitor student's understanding, observe where the teacher is located.

IDENTIFY TROUBLE SPOTS

The informal visits may make it possible to spot a potential problem. You may prevent a planned fight by noticing and intercepting a note passed between two students. After watching a youngster having difficulty with an exchange problem, you may note that no representative materials are available for that student's use. You may note that many of the folders of students' work are empty. You may spot some previously unnoticed loose floor tiles as you walk around the room.

BE VISIBLE

The appearance of an administrator in a classroom is regarded with fear only if it is infrequent or critical. When your appearance in and around the school is frequent and noncritical, it builds a feeling of community. It makes everyone believe that you care about the students and the staff, are interested in them, and are involved with them in student success. Both students and teachers may use the opportunity provided by an informal visit to show something of which they are very proud. Or, they may ask a question or make a complaint about something of which you were not aware. Here is an opportunity to respond immediately with praise or an assurance that you will look into the complaint and get back to them if necessary.

What to Look At and For

Informal visits can be very productive when an outline of what to look *at* and *for* is available either as mental notes or a written list. The following general outline can be modified to include the specific needs of the school. Figure 5-1 provides a summary of the outline.

Figure 5-1
INFORMAL VISITS

WHAT to LOOK AT and FOR

Where are the students and what are they doing?

Are they active or passive?

Are they working alone or with the teacher, a peer, or a group?

Are they on or off task?

Where is the teacher and what is she/he doing?

Instructing the class, a group, individuals

Conducting a lecture, discussion, demonstration, observing, assisting, correcting

Seated or standing

With students or apart

At the teacher's desk, the front of the room, a student's desk

What is the teacher's body language?

Voice level, tone, expression, actions, gestures

How is the room managed and organized?

How do students use the room?

What is the noise level and behavior?

Is the room neat and organized?

What is the seating arrangement?

What is the light quality, temperature, and general appearance?

What materials are in use?

What are the variety and type of materials students are using?

Where do you go?	EVERYWHERE
When do you go?	IN A PLANNED SEQUENCE
How long do you stay?	2 to 10 minutes
What do you record?	BRIEF NOTES AFTER YOU LEAVE
What communication do you send to the teacher?	BRIEF COMMENDATION OR COMMENT

Why do you walk around?

To check the pulse of the school

To check on a situation

To monitor a growth plan

To become a frequent presence in classrooms

STUDENT ACTIVITY: WHERE ARE THEY AND WHAT ARE THEY DOING?

Look at what students are doing in classrooms. Determine if they are passive or active participants in their learning. Note if students are working with the teacher, with a group or a peer, independently, or off task.

TEACHER ACTIVITY: WHERE IS THE TEACHER AND WHAT IS HE OR SHE DOING?

Look at what the teacher is doing, whether instructing the class, a group, or an individual. Note if the teacher is conducting a lecture, discussion, or demonstration, or observing, assisting, or correcting. See if the teacher is seated or standing, apart from students or with students, at the teacher's desk, at a student's desk, or in front of the class.

TEACHER'S BODY LANGUAGE

Note the teacher's voice level, body language, facial expression, actions, and gestures.

MANAGEMENT AND ORGANIZATION

Note how the students use the room, the noise level, behavior of the students, use of an established code or rules. Determine the neatness, organization, placement of materials, students' seating pattern, temperature and light, and the general appearance of the classroom.

MATERIALS IN USE

Note the variety and type of materials that students are using. Look for textbooks, advance organizers, media, supplementary books, or no materials in use.

SPECIFIC CONCERNS

Look at any area of interest or concern, such as confirming progress on growth plans, checking implementation of school programs, spotting potential trouble, checking student progress.

PHYSICAL PLANT

Note the general cleanliness of the building, maintenance, and the progress of scheduled repairs.

The Importance of a Time Frame
for Making Informal Visits

The objectives of the informal visits are better met if the visits are unannounced and conducted frequently throughout the year. This does not mean, however, that the visits are unplanned. Quite the contrary, the informal visit is most effective if a system or plan for its use is developed. The particular plan that is selected must fit the needs and schedule of the administrator.

HOW OFTEN TO VISIT

Every classroom should be visited every day. This may not be possible if the school is large and administrative assistance is not available. Certain busy times of the year may also make this practice periodically impossible. Visiting two to three times a week is a good alternative to the daily visit. At the very least, classrooms should be visited once a week.

WHOM TO VISIT

If visits cannot be made on a daily basis, it is important to plan whom to visit each day so that every classroom and all the areas of the school are seen. The visit plan is a matter of personal preference. Here are some suggested groupings for your visits.

- One grade — grade 10 or grade 1 classes
- One department — English or social studies classes
- Programs — English second language and bilingual classes, resource rooms, inclusion classes, computer rooms
- Clusters — early childhood classes or grade 7 interdisciplinary wing
- Building plan — classes on the top floor, classes on the first floor

TIME OF DAY FOR VISITS

Informal visits are most effective when the time of day is varied. Visits should be scheduled to take place during prime instructional time as well as during the time of day, such as late morning or afternoon, that is most difficult in the classroom.

HOW LONG TO STAY

The informal visit is intended to be brief. Keeping the visits brief will contribute to their frequency and allow everyone in the school to be seen. Between 2 and 7 (or 10) minutes are adequate. How long you stay will depend on what is seen and what is looked for. The informal visit should not be used as a lesson observation. Rather, it is a snapshot of that point in time.

Recording Data from an Informal Visit

Notetaking is the most effective way to record data gathered from informal visits. Here are some helpful hints.

- Always carry a pencil and paper when making informal visits. If possible, keep the pad out of sight. If this is not possible, you and your clipboard may become well known.

- Avoid taking notes while you are in the classroom. This activity seems to make teachers nervous. Instead, record mentally what, if anything, appears to be significant. There will be times when all you will wish to note is that you made the informal visit. An exception to this is whenever a teacher or a student asks you a question or makes a request. Be sure that person sees you write done what was asked or requested.

- Record your mental notes as soon as possible after leaving the classroom, usually in the hall. Waiting until you return to an office may result in forgetting important pieces or parts of what was seen. This is especially true when you are making several informal visits in a row.

- Have a mental outline, or a written list that is tucked away, of what to look for.

Using the Data to Improve Teaching and Learning

Record your mental notes as soon as possible after leaving the classroom. Later, when you have returned to the office, transfer those notes to a more permanent place. Be sure to record the date and the time of the informal visit. These notes become a part of the total data gathered and contribute to making a decision about the type and content of the most effective growth plan for that teacher. See Figure 5-2 for sample notes from informal visits.

Once the growth plan has been selected and implemented, the notes from future informal visits will be helpful in:

- Monitoring the teacher's progress on the growth plan

- Checking the teacher's skill development in a particular area

- Determining if the skill is mastered or more work is needed

- Identifying new skill needs

Figure 5-2
SAMPLE NOTES FROM INFORMAL VISITS

October 31   1:18–1:20 P.M.   Grade 7 Mathematics   Rm. 213

The room appears messy. Many desks are empty. The teacher is placing the aim on the board. He seems unaware that no class activity is being conducted even though the bell rang at 1:17.

November 2   1:55–1:58 P.M.   Grade 9 English   Rm. 325

The class has not ended but five students have begun to pack their book bags. The teacher is talking. No summary is visible on the board. There is no oral closure. Four more students begin to pack their book bags.

September 27   2:10–2:13 P.M.   Grade 3 Bilingual   Rm. 205

Students are silently reading from Spanish and English books. When the teacher sees me, she asks students to put their books away and meet her on the rug.

November 15   9:15–9:18 A.M.   Grade 11 Social Studies   Rm. 315

The teacher is recording notes on the board. Almost all of the students are writing in their notebooks. Three students in the back of the room are laughing at something.

October 5   8:45–8:47 A.M.   Grade 4   Rm. 331

The room is well organized and attractively decorated. Eight students were pushing each other with pencils in hand attempting to sign in on the Venn diagram in the meeting area. Three students are sitting calmly on the rug. Five students are hanging up their coats and putting their backpacks away. The teacher was in the back of the room with her back to the students.

October 18   10:45–10:48 A.M.   Grade 1   Rm. 5

All sixteen students are engaged in the lesson. They are sitting in their labeled spots in the meeting area. The teacher sits among the students. As students are told to return to their seats for independent reading, the level of noise rises. The teacher states, "Raise your hand if you think you are being loud." Three students raise their hands.

Communicating with the Teacher

Every informal visit does not require a communication with the teacher. This is especially true if:

1. Informal visits are a part of your daily schedule for all classrooms.

2. Informal visits are not new or different from what has been done in the past.

3. The staff expects, accepts, and looks forward to the informal visits.

Informal visits require communication with the teacher if:

- The visits are infrequent.

- They are a new action.

- Teachers are anxious or concerned about the visits.

- Something unusual or exceptional was seen.

- You wish to make a comment related to something that was seen.

Feedback to teachers about informal visits to their classrooms should:

1. Be objective in nature.

2. Usually communicate a commendable item.

3. Offer comments that can be acted upon quickly.

Items of a serious nature or ones that require extensive skill development are not appropriate for communications following an informal visit. Those areas of concern should become a part of the growth plan. The informal visits may speed up the selection and implementation of a specific growth plan.

When you do communicate with a teacher about an informal visit, be sure to keep a copy of the memo (see Figure 5-3). Here are some sample comments for communicating with the teacher.

COMMENDATIONS:

- "You asked questions at the analysis, synthesis, and evaluation levels during the class discussion of post World War II Europe."

- "This morning, your students demonstrated their skill and abilities in analyzing, then solving problems."

- "Your work with integrating writing into the literature program is reaping benefits."

COMMENTS:

- "Some new reference books dealing with your current topic are available from the librarian. They may be of interest to the students."

Figure 5-3

MEMORANDUM

To: _____

From: _____

Re: Informal Visit

    Date _____   Time _____

Comment

_____

_____

_____

_____

_____

_____

_____

_____

_____

_____

_____

_____

_____

_____

_____

_____

_____

_____

- "Olga seems to be acting peculiarly. Have you spoken to the guidance counselor?"
- "This afternoon I noticed several loose floor tiles in the back of your 5th-period classroom and I have reported it to the custodian. Please caution the students."

INAPPROPRIATE COMMENTS:

- "Your questioning strategies need improvement. You ask mainly 'yes' or 'no' questions."
- "Your management of the classroom is ineffective. You should better organize your room, establish a code of behavior, and try a behavior modification program."

SECTION 6

Observing Classroom Environments to Support Learning

The structure, activity, and organization of the classroom contributes in many ways to the success of students.

- **It encourages students to take pride in the work they are doing.** Everyone not only enjoys but also takes pleasure in being and working in pleasant and attractive surroundings. Working in these types of environments sends a message to students that both you and what you are doing are important.

- **It helps students to believe that educators care about them.** Students who work in structured, organized, and well-provisioned environments believe that their well being and progress are important. They believe that those who are in charge of their learning care about them and their success. These feelings contribute to a positive attitude about school, which results in good behavior and attendance.

- **It contributes to student achievement.** Students achieve at higher levels when they work in classrooms that are organized for their active involvement in instruction, and provide them with opportunities to construct, demonstrate, and manage their own learning.

How Classroom Environments Impact Student Learning

The structure, activity, and organization of the classroom can dramatically affect learning. This is obvious in early childhood education where the environment is a major part of the curriculum and instruction. For primary education classrooms, observing classroom environments to improve them is critical to effective instruction and achievement.

Effective elementary education is also dependent on the classroom environment to provide opportunities for students to review, reinforce, and extend learning. By observing elementary classroom environments, you focus on a critical element of instruction that helps teachers to design classrooms that foster student achievement.

Secondary schools rarely give attention to how classroom environments are structured or organized for instruction. This is typically true because more than one or two teachers usually share secondary classrooms during the day. The prevailing idea is that "Since the room is not totally mine, I am not responsible for it." Therefore, no one is responsible for the classroom. This attitude results in dirty, shabby, unattractive, and depressing classrooms. Just tour any urban high school to see this result. Consider the messages sent to students. "You are not important enough for any effort to be made to create classroom environments in which both you and I can take pride."

This does not have to be the case. There are middle, junior, and high schools where the classrooms are attractive, well provisioned with learning resources, decorated with students' work, and organized to extend learning. These classrooms are maintained in good order because it is expected as part of the culture of the school. Here are some ways to make that happen.

1. Reduce the number of rooms that teachers share.
2. Reduce the number of teachers who share rooms.
3. Assign each teacher the responsibility for one classroom.

Try another strategy when scheduling makes it impossible to assign one room to one teacher for the majority of his or her teaching periods. Target pride and caring. Assign each teacher the responsibility to decorate and maintain one room. Hopefully, that will be a room in which the teacher teaches at least some of the time. Then support the emphasis on attractive and educationally productive classroom environments by observing them and communicating with teachers about them. You will reap rewards in student achievement when you make this activity a priority.

Critical Aspects of the Learning Environment

Focus attention on classrooms as environments that foster learning by observing them and communicating with teachers about them. Look at three critical aspects of the classroom: (1) the roles of the teacher, (2) the activities of the students, and (3) the organization that encourages active student involvement.

ROLES OF THE TEACHER

The teacher performs three important roles in the classroom, each of which contributes to the effective and efficient performance of the classrooms as a maximum learning environment. The roles are:

- **Diagnostician of needs.** The teacher identifies the individual and group content, skills, and modality needs.

- **Instructor.** The teacher provides for instruction of skills and content in areas of need using diversified materials and strategies that meet the needs of all the students.

- **Manager of the learning environment.** The teacher organizes the total learning environment so that it helps students work effectively, comfortably, and purposefully.

A full discussion of these three roles is shown in Figure 6-1. Each role has been matched to the visible aspects of the role that can be observed.

ACTIVITIES OF THE STUDENTS

The students are involved in three areas of participation in the classroom. Each area of participation contributes to the students' success as learners. The observable behaviors show students:

- **Involved in on-task activities.** The students work with various groupings, the class, a group, a peer, or individually.

- **Using materials.** The students use materials of different modalities, levels, content, and skill needs as each requires. These materials are used appropriately and productively.

- **Managing their own instruction.** Students are responsible for completing their work, maintaining records of their progress, assisting other students, and conducting themselves in an appropriate manner.

A full discussion of these areas is given in Figure 6-2. Each area has been matched to the visible aspects of the area that can be observed.

ORGANIZATION THAT ENCOURAGES STUDENT INVOLVEMENT AND ACHIEVEMENT

There are two areas of classroom organization that encourage student involvement. Each is essential to providing an environment that offers the maximum opportunity for student learning. They are:

- **Materials.** Materials are readily available and are appropriate to the students' skill needs and modalities.

- **Appearance.** The appearance of the room is an incentive to learning.

A full discussion of these two areas is given in Figure 6-3. Each area has been matched to the visible aspects that can be observed.

Figure 6-1

A TEACHER'S THREE ROLES

Teacher Role 1: Diagnostician of Needs

In the performance of this role, the teacher:	*The visible aspects of this role include:*
tests student mastery of concepts	students' tests on display, kept in folders or in notebooks
questions students' in-depth understanding	teacher asking questions of individuals or groups of students
checks students' classwork and homework	classwork and homework in student notebooks have the teacher's initials, check, star, etc.
corrects students' classwork and homework	classwork and homework in student notebooks have the teacher's notations, comments, suggestions, etc.
observes students working in the classroom	the teacher walking around the room, looking at students' work, talking to students
groups students for instruction by skill need(s)	student groups listed on the board, on charts, in record books
moves about the room to be involved with students	the teacher walking around the room, sitting with groups and individuals

Teacher Role 2: Instructor

In the performance of this role, the teacher:	*The visible aspects of this role include:*
instructs the whole class	results of tests or informal diagnoses indicate all students need instruction in this skill
instructs groups of students	results of tests or informal diagnoses indicate students in the group need instruction in this skill
instructs individuals	results of tests or informal diagnosis indicate individual student needs instruction in this skill

Teacher Role 3: Manager of the Learning Environment

In the performance of this role, the teacher:	*The visible aspects of this role include:*
plans instruction for the class and for individuals	plans recorded in the teacher's written plans, in record books, on the chalkboard
controls the behavior of the students in the classroom	students speaking softly when allowed, sitting in appropriate areas, conducting themselves appropriately
keeps students on task	students occupied in appropriate and meaningful work
keeps records of student achievement and progress	teacher's record book containing grades, assessments, comments

Figure 6-2

ACTIVITIES OF STUDENTS

Student Area 1: Involved in On-Task Activities

When involved in on-task activities, students work:

The visible aspects of this area include:

as members of a class group

all of the students involved and attentive during a class lesson

as members of a group

groups of students involved and attentive during a group lesson

in peer groups

groups of two or three students working together

independently on assigned tasks

individual students involved and attentive to particular tasks

Student Area 2: Using Materials

In completing tasks, students use materials:

The visible aspects of this area include:

of varied modalities (oral, visual, tactile, kinesthetic) appropriate to their learning styles

students working with print, tapes, films, and manipulatives by self-selection or assignment

on different levels appropriate to their ability levels

students working with materials on different levels (on, below, above grade) as appropriate

in different parts of the classroom

students working in all parts of the classroom

in productive ways

students producing products

with respect and care

students using materials carefully, appropriately, without abuse

Student Area 3: Managing Their Own Instruction

Students demonstrate responsibility for their instruction by:

The visible aspects of this area include:

keeping records of their work and progress

students keeping samples of their work, test scores, comments made by the teacher on their work

planning the activities with which they are involved

students planning how, when, where, with what, and with whom they will complete projects

checking the work completed by themselves and peers

students checking their work and the work of classmates

giving and receiving assistance when necessary

students helping each other, giving suggestions, assistance, and clarification

showing respect for others in the classroom

students listening to each other, talking, smiling

using the established rules of the classroom

students following an established pattern for leaving their seats, leaving the room, talking, working, etc.

following a code of behavior expected of them

students speaking softly, politely, and acting in appropriate ways

moving freely but purposefully and quietly

students walking freely about the room to select, use, and return materials and work

Figure 6-3

CLASSROOM ORGANIZATION

Classroom Organization Area 1: Materials

The organization of the classroom demonstrates materials are:

visible in the classroom

varied to provide for all learning styles

neatly arranged

easily available for student use

The visible aspects of materials organization include:

visible appearance of materials

materials that are oral, visual, tactile, kinesthetic (print, film, manipulatives)

similar materials groups together, piled, arranged, stacked

placement of materials on levels and in areas that students can reach

Classroom Organization Area 2: Appearance

The appearance of the classroom's organization demonstrates:

furniture arranged to suit instruction

instructional areas available

student work on display

cleanliness

an attractive setting

adequate lighting

comfortable temperature

The visible aspects of the classroom's appearance include:

student chairs and desks are grouped for class, group, and individual work

space set aside for teacher/student groups, student groups, individuals

bulletin boards filled with current student products

teacher and student desks are free of excess paper, floors free of paper and dust

an appealing and cheerful total arrangement of the furniture, materials, and display

all light bulbs are working, shades are open or drawn to suit need

windows are open or shut, students closer or farther away from the heat as desired

Recording the Data Observed

Data about the classroom environment is easily recorded using a printed form. (See Figure 6-4.) This form contains all the items discussed as contributing to an effective and efficient classroom learning environment. The items on the form may be modified to suit particular classrooms and students' needs. For example, the classrooms of disabled pre-primary students may have additional requirements that should be added.

Some of the items may be observed in action, such as the teacher walking about the room or students working in groups. Other items, such as teacher comments on students' work, materials and furniture arrangements, and bulletin board displays, can be observed as the result of past actions. It is advisable to become familiar with the printed form before using it in a classroom environment so that you know what to look for.

When using the form, keep these points in mind:

- Check the items observed (both current and past actions).
- Qualify the teacher roles and organization areas by using this code:
  5 = outstanding, 4 = excellent, 3 = good, 2 = fair, 1 = poor.
- Qualify student areas by using this code: A = all of the students, M = most of the students, S = some of the students, N = none of the students.
- Account for items lacking by leaving the spaces blank.
- Record specific observations next to each item, if necessary.
- Make additional comments in the lower right corner, if necessary.

See Figure 6-5 for a completed sample environment observation.

Analyzing and Using the Data to Improve Teaching and Learning

The data gathered from the "Classroom Environment Observation Form" contains valuable information about classroom structure, activity, and organization. The information contributes to a growing body of knowledge that helps to specify the skill needs of each teacher. See Figure 6-6 for an analysis of the sample data.

Both you and the teacher should sign and receive a copy of the "Classroom Environment Observation Form." It will prove valuable as you:

- Refer back to comments and impressions.
- Request the teacher's reflection on the data.
- Relate environment needs to the teacher's other skill needs.
- Develop the growth plan.

Figure 6-4

CLASSROOM ENVIRONMENT OBSERVATION FORM

Scale: 5 = outstanding, 4 = excellent,
3 = good, 2 = fair, 1 = poor

Scale: A = all, M = most,
S = some, = N none

TEACHER ROLES

Diagnostician of Needs
Observations

ACTIVITIES
___ tests
___ questions
___ checks classwork
___ checks homework
___ corrects classwork
___ observes
___ groups for instruction
___ moves about
___ instructs whole class

Instructor
Observations
___ instructs groups
___ instructs individuals
___ plans instruction

Manager of the Environment
Observations
___ controls behavior
___ keeps students on task
___ keeps progress records

ORGANIZATION OF THE CLASSROOM

Materials
Observations

ACTIVITIES
___ visible
___ varied for learning style
___ different levels of ability
___ neatly arranged
___ easily available
___ furniture arranged to suit
___ instructional areas
___ students' work displayed

Appearance
Observations
___ clean
___ attractive
___ adequate lighting
___ comfortable temperature

STUDENT AREAS

On-task Activities
Observations

ACTIVITIES
___ class group
___ group
___ peer group
___ independently
___ varied modalities
___ different levels
___ productively
___ with respect/care

Using Materials
Observations
___ keep records
___ plan activities
___ check work
___ give/get help
___ respect others

Managing Own Instruction
Observations
___ use rules
___ follow code of behavior
___ move freely when told
___ move quietly

Teacher _____ Class _____ Date _____

Comments:

_____   _____
Teacher's Signature   *Supervisor's Signature*

Figure 6-5

CLASSROOM ENVIRONMENT OBSERVATION FORM

Scale: 5 = outstanding, 4 = excellent,
3 = good, 2 = fair, 1 = poor

Scale: A = all, M = most,
S = some, = N none

TEACHER ROLES

Diagnostician of Needs

Observations

ACTIVITIES
- _2_ tests
- _2_ questions
- _1_ checks classwork
- _1_ checks homework
- _1_ corrects classwork
- _3_ observes
- _1_ groups for instruction
- _3_ moves about

Instructor

Observations

- _4_ instructs whole class
- _2_ instructs groups
- _2_ instructs individuals

Manager of the Environment

Observations

- _1_ plans instruction
- _3_ controls behavior
- _2_ keeps students on task
- _1_ keeps progress records

ORGANIZATION OF THE CLASSROOM

Materials

Observations

ACTIVITIES
- _4_ visible
- _3_ varied for learning style
- _2_ different levels of ability
- _2_ neatly arranged
- _1_ easily available
- _3_ furniture arranged to suit
- _2_ instructional areas
- _3_ students' work displayed

Appearance

Observations

- _3_ clean
- _5_ attractive
- _3_ adequate lighting
- _4_ comfortable temperature

STUDENT AREAS

On-task Activities

Observations

ACTIVITIES
- _A_ class group
- _S_ group
- _M_ peer group
- _M_ independently
- _M_ varied modalities

Using Materials

Observations

- _M_ different levels
- _A_ productively
- _A_ with respect/care

Managing Own Instruction

Observations

- _N_ keep records
- _N_ plan activities
- _S_ check work
- _M_ give/get help
- _A_ respect others
- _A_ use rules
- _A_ follow code of behavior
- _A_ move freely when told
- _A_ move quietly

Teacher _Ms. Ortega_ Class _1-102_ Date _3/21/01_

Comments:

*Please review this form
before our conference.*

L. Ortega
Teacher's Signature

J. Metz
Supervisor's Signature

Figure 6-6
ANALYSIS OF DATA COLLECTED IN FIGURE 6-5

The room is set up for small-group instruction. The mathematics area contains manipulatives and is well defined. The classroom also has defined areas for science, dramatic play, listening, library, blocks, computers, and writing. All of the areas serve multiple purposes. For example, the rug in the library area becomes the space for small-group instruction.

The students are engaged in a cut-and-paste activity. At first glance the students seem to be working in small groups on different activities. At closer inspection, students are working on different parts of the same activity.

One student informs me that they are allowed play time. The block, mathematics manipulatives, and dramatic play areas are considered play areas. Some students are engaged in the play area.

Administrator's Reflections	Questions for Discussion
• More structured activities could be incorporated into the play area.	How can you use the play area to further your learning objectives?
• All areas should have pencils and paper available for students to use.	How could placing paper and pencils in all areas contribute to students' learning?
• Structures built in the block area should have a sign indicating who built the structure and a story about it. Pictures could serve as models.	How can you give students pride of ownership for what they create? How can you extend their learning? Is there a way to provide models when they build structures?
• Newspapers, magazines, and paper for students to prepare a grocery list should be available in the dramatic play area.	How can students' learning be enhanced in the dramatic play area?
• The manipulatives in the mathematics area should have activity cards for students to complete in pairs.	How can mathematics objectives be incorporated into students' work with manipulatives?
• Records should be kept about what students do in the areas.	How do you keep track of what the students do in each area?
• Small-group instruction should be planned.	How do you plan for small-group instruction?
• Teacher should keep records of student progress.	What do you record as indicators of student progress?

Communicating with the Teacher

Review the data gathered during the classroom environment observation with the teacher. It is important for the teacher to think about and understand how the overall effectiveness of his or her classroom contributes to or detracts from students' achievement.

Focus the discussion first on items that can easily be improved, such as techniques for checking classwork and homework; strategies for maintaining student records of work, selection, organization, and student use of materials; furniture arrangement; neatness and cleanliness of the classroom; and displaying student work.

Other items that require more extensive assistance should be presented as items that will be incorporated into the growth plan. These may include teacher diagnosis of student skill needs, preparing learning centers that extend learning, grouping for instruction, and planning for instruction.

Conducting a Time-on-Task Review to Observe Learning in Progress

Educational research confirms the ancient wisdom that attending to the task makes you better able to do it. There is a direct relationship between achievement and continuous focused attention to the tasks involved in learning. The time-on-task review provides an opportunity to focus on each student within a particular class, during a short time frame, to determine what each individual student is doing during that instructional time frame.

Time-on-Task and Teaching, Learning, and Achievement

The purpose of the time-on-task review is to observe each student in the classroom over a fifteen- to thirty-minute time frame to determine four factors that have an impact on learning and achievement.

1. **The engagement rate:** The number of students on task (appropriately involved in activities) and the number of students off task (involved in nonacademic-related activities).

2. **Productive instruction:** The quality of the tasks with which the students are involved and their appropriateness for the learners.

3. **Teacher's ability to monitor and adjust:** The changes in instruction, direction, and explanation made by the teacher as a result of monitoring student actions.

4. **Off-task incidences:** The nature and frequency of off-task behaviors exhibited by the students and when they occur.

WHEN TO CONDUCT THIS REVIEW

The time-on-task review is intended to assess a fully functioning learning environment. It is, therefore, more effective to delay conducting the review until classroom routines and procedures have been established and implemented.

Every teacher could benefit from the type of analysis that the time-on-task review offers. However, when time does not permit a review of every class, it will prove helpful to conduct the review in the following situations:

- *In classes that are disruptive.* Such classes may be noisy as you pass the room. Students may often be out of their seats, in the halls, or make frequent use of the bathrooms.

- *In classes where large percentages of the students receive poor test scores over a period of time.*

- *In classes that have undergone some problem or change.* For example, the teacher has been absent for a period of time or several new students have been admitted within a short period of time.

- *In classes where the teacher appears anxious, depressed, exhausted, or distressed.*

- *When there has been a complaint from a responsible source,* such as teachers in neighboring classrooms or groups of parents.

A WORD OF CAUTION

Classrooms reflect the personality of the teacher and are usually different from each other in organization and management. Each time-on-task review should be individual, without comparison to others.

Before you begin to record data, take a few minutes to become familiar with the flow and tempo of the classroom. For example, teachers who employ cooperative learning, project-centered work, or discovery learning usually have much greater student movement within the room than classrooms that are more traditional in nature.

Be aware of factors that may prevent the review from being informative. For example, distracting factors that may contribute to students' off-task activity include a coming school holiday, construction work, or an accident. Some classroom activities in progress may not provide sufficient scope of student involvement for an informative review. These may include, for example, student presentations, viewing a videotape, or testing. In these cases, postpone the review for a future time.

Remember that this telescoped analysis of student actions covered one very short period of time during one day of the school year. The actions observed during the time-on-task review may be representative of what usually happens in that class. On the other hand, it may be an unusual day. That determination can only be made over time.

Recording the Data as It Is Gathered

The time-on-task review is best recorded using a printed form. (See Figure 7-1.) The form provides a space to note the type of activity in progress during each time frame. The form also contains a list of areas of student participation. These areas represent on-task and off-task student actions. The list of areas of participation may be modified to suit particular class situations.

ACTIVITIES IN PROGRESS

Use the space above each numbered time segment to indicate the activity in progress at that time. These notes will be useful when analyzing the review to relate high and low numbers of on-task or off-task behavior to the activity being conducted. A brief note about the activity—such as motivation, distribution of materials, lecture, discussion, read aloud, question and answer, cooperative groups, think/pair share, worksheet, advance organizer, transition, homework check—can be made. Or, create a code to record the activity. For example: L (Lecture); D (Discussion); C (Circulating); QA (Question and Answer); H (Homework); TPS (Think/Pair/Share); T (Transition); AO (Advance Organizer).

ON-TASK STUDENT PARTICIPATION

The on-task areas on the form are coded with a single asterisk, and include student actions that are:

- **Teacher-directed.** All students who are involved with the teacher in any type of activity. This may include whole-class lessons, group lessons, individual student instruction, or discussion.

- **Group assignment.** All students working in groups of any size without the teacher.

- **Individual assignment.** All students working by themselves.

- **Recordkeeping.** All students involved in notation of any kind related to their work. This may include students correcting their work, copying a homework assignment, recording test scores, handing in completed work, and so forth.

OFF-TASK STUDENT PARTICIPATION

The off-task areas on the form are coded with a double asterisk and include student actions identified as:

- **Transition.** All students between activities. This may include students coming from or going to a group lesson, looking for a book, looking for homework, returning materials, sharpening a pencil, turning pages, and so forth.

- **Discipline.** All students involved in disruptive behavior to any degree. This may include fighting, pushing, yelling, acting out, and so forth.

- **Unoccupied.** All students off assignment. This may include students who are doing nothing; looking out the window; looking around the room; playing with a toy, game, or cards; and so forth.

- **Out of room.** All students who are not in the classroom for any reason.

You will rapidly become familiar with the listings and their relationship to student actions observed in the classroom. You determine in which area to place each student's actions. Use your own judgment to determine if a particular student action is on or off task, but be consistent in that judgment.

ACCOUNT FOR ALL STUDENTS

Every student in attendance that day must be accounted for in a particular area of participation, for each time segment. This means that if thirty students are attending school on that day, there must be a total of thirty accounted for in each time segment.

As previously discussed, the areas of participation represent student actions that are on task and those that are off task. Therefore, all the on-task actions plus all the off-task actions must also agree with the total number of students in attendance that day for each time segment.

Figure 7-2 shows a sample recording of student actions of one time segment for a class with thirty students attending.

During the first time segment of the time-on-task review, each student's action was observed, assigned to an area of participation, and recorded in the appropriate box.

- *teacher-directed:* Ten students worked in a group with the teacher.

- *group assignment:* Six students were working together to plan a newscast format for presentation to the class of their individual current events reports.

- *individual assignment:* Eight students worked separately on various tasks.

- *recordkeeping:* One student copied a homework assignment from the board, and one student placed some completed work on the teacher's desk.

- *transition:* One student returned a reference book to the bookcase, and one student turned pages looking for a specific piece of information.

- *unoccupied:* One student drank water from the fountain.

- *out of room:* One student was missing and counted as out of the room.

- *Total On Task:* Twenty-six students were involved in on-task areas of participation.

- *Total Off Task:* Four students were involved in off-task areas of participation.

- *Total Attending:* Thirty students were in attendance on that day, so thirty students were accounted for in the first time segment.

Figure 7-1

TIME-ON-TASK REVIEW

Class _____ Teacher _____ Date _____ Attendance _____

Time Began _____

Teacher Activity _____

Student Activity

Time Segment	1	2	3	4	5	6	7	8	9	10	11	12	13	14	15	Total
*teacher-directed																
*group assignment																
*individual assignment																
*recordkeeping																
**transition																
**discipline																
**unoccupied																
**out of room																
Total On Task*																
Total Off Task**																
Total Attending																

Engagement Rate: $\dfrac{\text{Total On Task}}{\text{Total Attending}}$ = _____ = _____ % On Task

Comments:

_____
Teacher's Signature

_____
Supervisor's Signature

95

Figure 7-2

SAMPLE TIME SEGMENT

Time Segment	1	2
*teacher-directed	10	
*group assignment	6	
*individual assignment	8	
*recordkeeping	2	
**transition	2	
**discipline		
**unoccupied	1	
**out of room	1	
Total On Task*	26	
Total Off Task**	4	
Total Attending	30	

TIME SEGMENTS

There are a total of fifteen time segments to complete during the time-on-task review. Each time segment should take between one and two minutes to complete. The difference in time is dependent upon the amount of activity and action in the classroom. You will have a good idea of how much time is needed after you have completed the first time segment. Then, use that time frame consistently.

The time segments are recorded sequentially using the time frame you have set. When there is a great deal of activity in the classroom and you must watch a number of students individually, it may be helpful to use tally marks to record each student's actions correctly. The tally marks in each box can be counted and recorded as a numeral later.

Analyzing the Data Gathered to Impact Achievement

There is a large amount of information to be gathered from the time-on-task review. This information contributes to a growing fund of knowledge available to guide you in the development of a growth plan that will help each teacher improve the effectiveness of his or her instruction.

The first task following the time-on-task review is to analyze the data. There are four categories to consider in this analysis:

1. Engagement rate

2. Types of off-task actions noted

3. Types and quality of on-task actions noted

4. Number of students involved in each time segment

ENGAGEMENT RATE

The first category to consider is the engagement rate, that is, the percentage of students considered on task during the time the review was conducted.

To calculate the engagement rate, first add the total number of students marked as on task during each time segment. Record that total in the last column of the score sheet. Then multiply the number of students in attendance that day by fifteen, the total number of observations that were made. Enter that attendance total in the last column of the score sheet. To find the percentage of students on task, divide the total number of students on task by the total number attending that day. Here is a sample engagement rate calculation:

$$\frac{\text{Total on task for the fifteen time segments}}{\text{Total number of students attending } (30 \times 15)} = \frac{375}{450} = 83\%$$

Eighty-three percent of the students in that class were on task during the time that the time-on-task review was conducted. Approximately five students were off task during each time segment. In order to aim at a higher percentage of on-task activity, analyze what types of off-task actions were noted.

TYPES OF OFF-TASK ACTIONS NOTED

Calculate the total number of students engaged in each type of off-task action observed during the fifteen time segments. Record the total for each type of off-task actions in the total column.

Analyze the types of off-task actions that were observed:

- *Were students slow to move from one activity to the next?* The numbers recorded on the transition line extend through several time segments.

- *Were students in transition confused about what to do next?* Several students coded as in transition asked others what to do or were observed trying to determine what others were doing.

- *Did transition periods lead to discipline problems?* The number of students coded as discipline increased during the transition segments.

- *Were particular students consistently disruptive?* The students coded as discipline are the same students or the same core of students throughout the segments.

- *What was the nature of the disruptive activities?* Students were talking or pushing or acting out.

- *Did unoccupied students appear tired, bored, confused?* Students had their heads down on the desk, gazed out the window, looked around the room.

- *How frequently did students leave the room?* At least one student was coded out of room during each or most time segments.

- *How long were students gone from the classroom?* The number of time segments during which the same student was recorded as out of room.

TYPES AND QUALITY OF ON-TASK ACTIONS NOTED

Calculate the total number of students engaged in each type of on-task action observed during the fifteen time segments. Record each total of on-task actions in the total column.

Analyze the types of on-task actions observed:

- *Was the teacher actively involving students in the lesson?* Students raised their hands, responded to questions, took notes, interacted with other students.

- *Did the student-directed groups work productively?* Students talked about the task at hand and worked together to complete the assignment.

- *Were the individual assignments understood by the students?* Students were able to complete the assignment on their own without assistance.
- *What types of records did the students attend to?* Placing writing drafts in writing folders. Signing out a resource for a report. Recording a task completed and placed in the finished work box.

Next, analyze the quality of the on-task actions you observed:

- How many students in the teacher-directed group were not attentive and therefore recorded in the unoccupied category?
- What types of group activities were conducted? Were they meaningful, important, of value?
- Were the individual assignments of value, important, productive? Were students merely copying or actually engaged in thinking?
- Were the records kept by the students necessary, of value, important to their progress?

NUMBER OF STUDENTS INVOLVED IN EACH STUDENT ACTIVITY

Review the numbers in the total column. Consider the number of students involved in each activity. Analyze the proportion of students in each area.

- How many students were unoccupied during each time segment? Was there a larger number of unoccupied students during particular time segments? What was the teacher activity during these segments?
- How many students were in transition for each segment and for the total review? What directions did the teacher give for the transition?
- Did the number of students who left the room increase during a particular part of the lesson?
- How many students were involved with recordkeeping? How long did the recordkeeping take? Were some students finished before others? How many and for how long?

Using the Data to Increase Achievement

The analysis of the time-on-task review may result in comments and raise questions. Record these in the comment section of the form or on a separate piece of paper. Highlight the data in the areas that relate those comments and questions. The highlighted data, together with the comments and questions, will be useful in guiding the discussion with the teacher.

Both the teacher and you should sign and keep a copy of the time-on-task review. Those copies may be useful for:

- Adding to the data collected about the teacher
- Identifying specific areas to be included in the growth plan
- Providing data for the teacher's portfolio
- Reviewing at a later date to note progress made
- Documentation to include with the end-of-year growth plan summary

Communicating with the Teacher

The time-on-task review should be discussed with the teacher. The information is important to the teacher as he or she seeks to become more effective. The conference also provides an excellent opportunity to involve the teacher in a professional activity by asking him or her to review the data, and reflect on causes, interpretations and solutions. Here are some sample observations from a review and the possible causes for them.

SAMPLE OBSERVATIONS	POSSIBLE CAUSES
Six students were in transition for four time segments.	Students may not have understood the directions given about what to do or how to proceed.
Three students sat unoccupied with individual assignments opened on their desks.	Students may not understand the material well enough to complete the assignment independently.
Two students were consistently inattentive during the lesson.	These students may have gaps in their learning that made the lesson difficult or they may require more attention during the lesson.

Skill areas that require extensive assistance should be incorporated into the growth plan. In this case, these may include questioning techniques, strategies to assess students' learning needs, and motivation techniques.

See Figure 7-3 for a completed sample time-on-task review and Figure 7-4 for an analysis of the data with comments for the discussion with the teacher.

Figure 7-3

TIME-ON-TASK REVIEW

Class __Algebra__ Teacher __Gina Medina__ Date __October 2, 2001__ Attendance __16 + 1 (late student)__

Time Began __11:35 A.M.__ **Teacher Activity Key: L (Lecture), D (Discussion), C (Circulating), QA (Q&A), H (Homework)**

Teacher Activity

Student Activity	1	2	3	4	5	6	7	8	9	10	11	12	13	14	15	Total
Teacher Activity	H	H	D, C	L, D	L, D	L, D	L, D	L, D	L	L, D	L, D	L, D	QA	L	L	
Time Segment	1	2	3	4	5	6	7	8	9	10	11	12	13	14	15	Total
*teacher-directed	5	9	14	9	12	10	5	1		8	6	12	9		6	106
*group assignment																
*individual assignment																
*recordkeeping	2	2		6	4	6	11	15	15	5	11	2	3	16	10	108
**transition	7	5	1													13
**discipline																
**unoccupied			1	1					2	4		3	5	1	1	18
**out of room	2															2
Total On Task*	7	11	14	15	16	16	16	16	15	13	17	14	12	16	16	214
Total Off Task**	9	5	2	1	0	0	0	0	2	4	0	3	5	1	1	33
Total Attending	16	16	16	16	16	16	16	16	17	17	17	17	17	17	17	247

Engagement Rate: $\dfrac{\text{Total On Task}}{\text{Total Attending}} = \dfrac{214}{247} = 86.6\%$ On Task

_____ *Teacher's Signature*

_____ *Supervisor's Signature*

Figure 7-4

ANALYSIS OF DATA COLLECTED IN FIGURE 7-3

The on-task engagement rate of 86.6% is less than desirable when one considers that 13.4% of the students were not engaged. The most effective way to use this data is to ask the teacher to review and analyze the information and come up with solutions.

Observations for Discussion	Comments and Questions to be Discussed/ Solutions to be Proposed by the teacher
All activities were teacher directed. Students were involved only in answering the teacher's questions and taking notes.	Actively involving students in their learning helps students to better understand the material. How could you do that?
Thirteen students were in transition during the first three time segments.	The way the lesson begins is critical because it serves to focus students on the content. How do you plan to open a lesson?
	A strong beginning also helps students to understand how the information is useful in the real world and important to them. How could you incorporate a relationship to the real world in your lessons?
A total of eighteen students were unoccupied during eight time segments.	Attending throughout the lesson is difficult for many students. How can a lesson be organized so that students can spend time attending to the lecture followed by time for them to use the information?

Reviewing Artifacts to Document Learning

Artifacts may be defined as what are left to document past human actions. The artifacts of teaching and learning include any materials or actions employed by the teacher to help students to learn. A visit to any school will show that most students in K–12 classrooms are involved in as much, if not more, time with the stuff the teacher generates as they are with direct interactions with the teacher. Artifacts therefore become important sources of verification about what was proposed by the teacher and what the students learned, remembered, and incorporated into their growing store of information. Here is a way to estimate how effectively teachers are facilitating students' learning and how successfully students are learning.

Teacher portfolios are a purposeful collections of artifacts selected by the teacher. They serve to document the work of a teacher on aspects of the teaching and learning process. Refer to Section 3 for a discussion of portfolios.

Artifact Sources

Teachers and students are sources for artifacts that interact between what was proposed and what was actually achieved. Both sources provide valuable information about four areas that are critical to achievement.

1. **The quality instruction.** Determine the nature of instruction that was planned, and the quality of the related materials that were prepared to enhance and support learning by reviewing teachers' plans, worksheets, advance or graphic organizers, and classwork and homework assignments.

2. **The achievement of students.** Consider how well students are performing as a result of instruction as demonstrated by their classwork, homework, test results, and report cards.

3. **The implementation of school and district programs and initiates.** Determine how the teacher has incorporated specific elements of the school or district program into instruction and assessment. For example: Are the teacher's plans for

the mandated 90-minute literacy block in evidence? representative of reading, writing, listening and speaking? and diversified in activities that will engage students for that block of time?

4. **Progress with the objective stated in the teacher's growth plan.** Look for evidence of growth in those areas that have been agreed upon for improvement. For example, look at the quality of the questions that are included in the lesson plans and support materials of teachers who are working on higher-level questioning strategies. Determine if they target analysis, synthesis, and evaluation. Look for strategies that will involve students as active participants in the plans and support materials prepared by teachers working on student participation.

Teacher Artifacts

The teacher is the sole source of some artifacts. These artifacts relate to the plans, records, and communications with which the teacher has been involved.

REVIEWING TEACHER PLANS

Planning for instruction is an essential requirement for every teacher. Even in districts such as New York City that have regulations about teacher plans, teachers are not removed from this professional responsibility.

Teacher plans should contain the following indicators of quality:

- **Comprehensiveness.** The plans should include all the areas for which the teacher is responsible.

- **Organization.** The plans should be written in an easily understood manner. They should be neat and appropriate for the teacher's reference.

- **Detail.** There should be sufficient detail about the content of the material to clarify what, how, and when each is intended to be presented in the instructional program.

- **Pace.** The planned instruction should reflect progress at an appropriate pace through the established curriculum. The scope of the curriculum for the grade or the course is usually outlined by state standards, sometimes with benchmarks for different grades and time periods. Monitoring progress through the curriculum becomes essential to students' success with the reality of high-stakes testing and the need for them to be ready for higher levels of content.

- **Differentiation.** The plans should specify how provisions are made for students with different abilities and needs. These provisions become essential as inclusion programs increase the numbers of students with handicapping conditions who are mainstreamed.

- **Diversified instructional strategies.** Plans should include variety in instructional presentation, including interactive lecture, demonstration, student discussion, small-group interaction, student-to-student interaction, and individual tasks.

- **Variety of materials used.** Plans should indicate variety in instructional materials used to reach objectives. This variety includes texts, reference materials, periodicals, newspapers, worksheets, advance or graphic organizers, technology, media, and manipulatives.

- **Provision for student processing.** The plans should specify when and how students will be asked to think about the content and construct meaning for themselves.

- **Monitor progress on the teacher's growth plan.** Areas of concentration decided upon for the growth plan should be included in the teacher's plans, such as a listing of the specific questions that will be asked, the details for setting up cooperative group work, stated "sets" or motivations for various lessons, or specific grouping practices.

COLLECTING TEACHER PLANS

The method and manner of collecting and reviewing teacher plans will vary with your situation. The responsibility for specific teachers can be assigned in schools in which there are assistants and/or department chairs. Several methods are described here.

Plans of all teachers are collected every week.   This strategy may be very desirable but not too practical if you are the only administrator in charge and you have a large staff. A great deal of time will be taken up with reviewing all these plans and little else will be accomplished.

Rotation.   The plans of different groups of teachers are collected every two or three weeks. Each teacher's plans for the two- or three-week interval are then reviewed. There are two advantages to this strategy: (1) a smaller number of plans are reviewed, and (2) it is possible to see a two- or three-week sequence of activities.

Teacher plans may be grouped for rotation by whatever system is most convenient, such as grade level, subject area(s), teams, department(s), or location in the building.

Differentiation.   It may be desirable to further provide for teacher needs by collecting the plans of inexperienced or weak teachers each week and collecting the plans of master and outstanding teachers once a month.

Be sure to communicate the collection strategy selected to the staff. They should be informed about both *when* and *how* their plans will be reviewed.

Here are two important rules to consider when collecting teachers' plans.

1. **Never collect plans you will not read and comment on.** If teacher plans are not important enough to be read, why should teachers spend time writing them? Teachers know if their plans are read. You may find notes to you in the plans, or a teacher may ask your opinion about a particular technique that he or she has planned. It is also possible that a teacher whose plans were poorly written, in great haste, will be left with the impression that what was done is perfectly acceptable.

2. **Never keep teacher plans more than one day.** Teachers use their plans to implement instruction. If this is not true, then there is little reason for teachers to plan! If you are slow in returning teacher plans, how can teachers use them?

RECORDING PLANNING DATA

A printed memo is both an easy and effective way in which to record data gathered when reviewing teacher plans because:

- The memo serves as a comprehensive list of what should be included in the plans.
- Areas and specifics omitted from the plans can be checked.
- A copy of the annotated printed memo can be kept.
- The annotated original can be sent to the teacher when the plans are returned.

The sample printed memos are intended to be a suggested list of what should be included in teacher plans. Modify the list to fit the specifics of your school program. Figure 8-1 suggests a printed plan memo for elementary schools. Figure 8-2 suggests a printed plan memo for secondary schools.

USING THE DATA TO IMPROVE INSTRUCTION

Keep a copy of the notations on the printed plan memo. When areas are checked, or specifics omitted or questioned, the teacher is expected to respond. It is helpful to add the teacher's response to your copy of the plan memo. Or, if the teacher returns the original with comments, substitute the original for your copy.

The plan review memos should be kept sequentially for each teacher. They will serve three useful purposes:

1. It will be possible to refer back to former comments when you review future plans.

2. You will be able to establish a pattern of weaknesses in both planning and instruction, such as extensive use of texts, lack of variety in instructional presentation, or frequently omitted content areas.

3. Through informal visits to the classrooms, you will be able to verify that what is planned is what is actually being done.

Figure 8-1
ELEMENTARY: PLAN REVIEW MEMO

To: _____ (initial & return)

From: _____

Re: Your plans dated _____

TOTAL AREAS OF RESPONSIBILITY (Items checked are omitted on your plans.)

____ communication arts (_____ reading _____ writing _____ listening _____ speaking)

_____ groups _____ frequency of instruction

____ mathematics instruction _____ groups _____ frequency of instruction

____ social studies

____ science

____ art ____ music ____ physical education

SPECIFICS (Items checked are missing or not clear on your plans.)*

_____ Standard Targeted (see #   written on your plans)

_____ Lesson Objective(s) (see #   written on your plans)

_____ Instructional Strategy (see #   written on your plans)

_____ Grouping for Instruction (see #   written on your plans)

_____ Instructional Materials (see #   written on your plans)

_____ Technology Integration

_____ Homework _____ (subject)

COMMENTS

____ plans are late   ____ plans are not clear   ____ plans lack detail

____ please see me _____

____ other _____

_____

*For your reference a number has been written on your plans related to the item(s) checked.

Figure 8-2
SECONDARY: PLAN REVIEW MEMO

To: _____(initial & return)

From: _____

Re: Your plans dated _____

TOTAL AREAS OF RESPONSIBILITY (Items checked are omitted on your plans.)

_____ all courses taught   course(s) missing _____

_____ administrative responsibilities

SPECIFICS (Items checked are missing or not clear on your plans.)*

_____ Standard(s) Targeted (see #   written on your plans)

_____ Lesson Objective(s) (see #   written on your plans)

_____ Instructional Strategy (see #   written on your plans)

_____ Grouping for Instruction (see #   written on your plans)

_____ Instructional Materials (see #   written on your plans)

_____ Technology Integration

_____ Homework _____(course)

COMMENTS

_____ plans are late   _____ plans are not clear   _____ plans lack detail

_____ please see me _____

_____ other _____

_____

*For your reference a number has been written on your plans related to the item(s) checked.

COMMUNICATING WITH THE TEACHER

Initial, date, and write a comment, if appropriate, directly on the teacher's plans. Only commendable comments should be written directly on the plans; other types of comments should be recorded on the printed plan memo. There are few things more demoralizing for a teacher than to see negative comments written on his or her lesson plans.

Just as negative comments are demoralizing, positive comments written on teacher's plans are encouraging. Comment on the plan about the implementation of a new idea, or a strategy discussed during the growth planning conference, or movement as agreed upon toward meeting growth plan objectives. For example:

- "The plan you have presented for cooperative group work on the science topic is exciting. Please keep me posted on how it is going."

- "The interdisciplinary approach to World War II planned with teachers from the English department appears comprehensive and effective. Please invite me to see the program when it is up and running."

- "The manipulative materials you have selected to teach subtraction with exchange should work well. Please let me know the results of your efforts."

The annotated plan memo is used only for teacher plan correction and/or improvement. When a teacher receives a plan review memo, the teacher must initial and return the memo with:

1. Revised, corrected, improved plans,

2. An explanation, or

3. A request for a conference.

REVIEWING TEACHERS' RECORDS AND REPORTS TO PARENTS

The data in teachers' records or grade books and reports to parents about student progress provide important information about the instructional process and its effectiveness. What is assigned and what is graded demonstrate the type of instructional program conducted by the teacher. Look for the areas that the teacher has included:

- grades that are given for work other than tests
- grades on tests
- participation in classwork activities
- homework completion and its quality
- attendance and lateness
- cooperation/discipline
- indication that a parent contact was made by note or phone

These data will provide information about how well instruction is impacting all members of the class over time. Look for a large number of students who are not completing homework or receiving low or failing grades. Become aware of individual students who appear to consistently receive low grades. The records will direct attention to the individuals and small groups of students who may need additional help in achieving instructional objectives. These students should be receiving extra help and that information should be indicated on the teacher's plans.

These records are the source of information used to determine student grades on reports to parents. Reports to parents should provide a comprehensive summary of how the students are progressing. Serious problems may be avoided if every student's report to parents is read before it is sent home. This is especially true for comments that teachers are required to write. Review all of the comments to ensure that they are appropriately stated and reflective of the grades that were given.

COLLECTING TEACHERS' RECORDS AND REPORTS TO PARENTS

Teachers' records or grade books should be collected and reviewed periodically. The frequency of their collection will depend upon the availability of your time and personnel. Ideally, teachers' records should be collected each month, or at least once during each quarter.

Reports to parents should be collected and reviewed prior to their distribution to parents.

RECORDING RECORD DATA

Taking notes, which are dated, is the most effective way to record data about teacher records. Create a separate section of a looseleaf binder, with an individual page for each teacher, to record these notes about teacher records and reports to parents that you have reviewed.

USING THE DATA TO IMPROVE INSTRUCTION

The data provided by the review of teacher records should be used in combination with the data from teacher plans to suggest areas in which to help the teacher raise student achievement. Any areas of a serious nature should be immediately acted upon with a communication to the teacher followed by a meeting.

COMMUNICATING WITH THE TEACHER

A brief note should be sent to each teacher about the review of his or her records. The note may commend the teacher. For example:

- "Thank you for the care you have taken in maintaining comprehensive records of your students."

- "You provide many opportunities for your students to succeed by giving them grades for extra-credit projects that you add to failing test grades. Thank you for your efforts."

- "Your individualized comments clarify the reports sent to parents. Your efforts are noted and appreciated."

The note may inform the teacher about a concern. For example:

- "Sally Hanson and James Wand in your third-period class seem to be having difficulty with Earth Science. Please meet with me to plan some strategies to help them."

- "Lateness appears to be a concern in your period-one Spanish class. Let's meet to talk about strategies to encourage all the students to be on time."

Student Artifacts

Student artifacts should be viewed from two perspectives.

1. **The appropriateness and the quality of what teachers have prepared for students to complete.** Consider if and how students are required to use the content to process the information rather than merely memorize the information. These experiences for students are critical in preparing them to score well on new tests, including the SAT, which require students not only know the content, but also be able to use the content to analyze and evaluate information.

2. **The level of achievement of the students in completing these assignments.** Consider what is graded, the type of grades they are given, the way in which teachers give feedback to students, and how successful students are with the tasks.

Any and all examples of student work are indicators of student progress. Select those for review that are the most important indicators for your program. Student artifacts cover a wide spectrum of work. The following is a partial list of student artifacts to consider with criteria for their review from the two perspectives.

REVIEWING STUDENT ARTIFACTS

TEACHER-MADE TESTS

- *From the students' perspective,* review the grades to consider the level of student achievement of the class. Look at the range of scores and the numbers of students who passed or failed.

- *From the teacher's perspective,* consider the quality of the test. Examine the test questions to identify the types of questions that were constructed by the teacher. In other words, what were students required to do on this test? Were they asked to respond true or false, fill in responses, and/or select from choices? Were they asked to write an essay that required them to analyze content, make comparisons, solve a problem, make a decision, and/or apply the information to their own experiences in the real world?

WRITING SAMPLES

- *From the students' perspective,* estimate the quality of the writing. Consider the number of errors made by the students. Determine if the students achieved the stated writing objective.

- *From the teacher's perspective,* consider the appropriateness of the stated writing objective and its relationship to the standard indicated. Review the data from former writing samples to determine if there is diversification in writing objectives over time. Observe the feedback given to students by looking at how corrections are indicated and the types of comments, if any, made. Review the teacher's plan to follow up on the results and the next steps in instruction.

CLASSWORK

- *From the students' perspective,* consider their ability to correctly complete the assignment. Determine if this was an individual or group assignment.

- *From the teacher's perspective,* consider the quality of the assignment and its relationship to the stated objective. Look for indicators of higher order thinking. Look for how feedback was given to students and if corrections and/or comments were made on the work.

ADVANCE/GRAPHIC ORGANIZERS

- *From the students' perspective,* determine their ability to use the organizer correctly and completely. Determine if this task was completed individually, in pairs, or in small groups.

- *From the teacher's perspective,* determine the appropriateness of the organizer selected to the objective of the task required. Was this the optimum organizer for the objective? Look for how feedback was given to students and if corrections and/or comments were made on the work.

HOMEWORK ASSIGNMENTS

- *From the students' perspective,* determine their ability to complete the assignment correctly, neatly, and with care.

- *From the teacher's perspective,* consider the quality of the assignment and its appropriateness to the topic. Did the assignment require students to broaden their understanding, apply their knowledge, and/or contribute to the development of skills? Look for feedback given to students, corrections, and/or comments made on the work and if grades were given.

STUDENT PROJECTS

- *From the students' perspective,* clarify if this project was completed individually, in pairs, or in small groups. Determine the quality of the work and its completeness related to the teacher's instruction.

- *From the teacher's perspective,* consider the appropriateness of this use of students' time related to the objective and the standards stated. Look for how feedback was given to students and if corrections and/or comments were made on the work. If this was a cooperative group project, determine how group grades were calculated.

Figure 8-3 provides a summary of student artifacts with criteria for their review.

HOW AND WHEN TO COLLECT THE ARTIFACTS

The following criteria should be considered when developing the guidelines for collecting student artifacts.

- **The availability of administrative time.** Do not collect artifacts when you do not have the time to review them and respond to the teacher. Every artifact that is collected must be read and analyzed. In addition, the teacher will expect a response.

- **Availability of the artifact.** Certain artifacts are available only at given points in time. These include, for example, summary tests, unit projects, and so forth. Be sure the artifacts you request are available. Other types of artifacts should be continuously available, such as classwork, homework, and teacher-made tests.

- **Diversity of artifacts.** Consider the variety of student artifacts that are available for review and the information that each can provide about the effectiveness of instruction and the achievement of students. Select a varied group of artifacts to review over the course of the year.

- **Standards previously set.** When guidelines for reviewing student artifacts have been established, it is important to maintain them. For example, each class or department may be required to submit samples of student writing each month as part of a schoolwide effort to focus on writing and improve student performance in this area.

- **Whole-class sets or selected samples.** It may not be necessary to review whole-class sets of every artifact that is collected. Consider if a review of selected samples of student artifacts will be just as informative. For example, request the five best, worst, and/or average papers. Or, request the class set but make it clear that you will review a random sample of work.

After determining which student artifacts to review, determine the time schedule for their collection. The collection frequency must match time constraints, available personnel, and the purpose of the review. Some suggested frequencies follow.

Figure 8-3
REVIEWING STUDENT ARTIFACTS SUMMARY

Artifact	Student Perspective	Teacher Perspective
Teacher-made tests	Level of student achievement The range of the scores Numbers that passed/failed	Test quality Types of questions asked: true/false, fill in, select from choices, essay, analysis of content, comparison, problem solving, decision making, application to student experiences
Writing samples	Quality of writing Number of errors made Achievement of objective	Writing objective (diversified over time) Feedback given to students Manner of correction and comments Future plans based on results
Classwork	Students' ability to complete appropriately Individual or group assignment	Quality of the assignment Relationship to objective and standard Requirement for higher-order thinking Feedback given to students Corrections and comments
Advance/Graphic organizers	Students' ability to use appropriately Individual or group assignment	Appropriateness of the organizer selected related to the assignment Feedback given to students Corrections and comments
Homework assignments	Students' ability to complete correctly, neatly, and with care	Quality of the assignment related to the topic Feedback given to students Corrections, comments, grades
Student projects	Individual or group work	Appropriateness of the task Quality and completeness Feedback given to students Group grades for cooperative groups

COLLECTION FREQUENCY	PLUSES AND MINUSES
once per week	permits continuous review
	time-consuming
	appropriate for new or marginally effective teachers
twice per month	effective for continuous monitoring
	time-consuming
	appropriate for small schools
once per month	effective overall
	vary artifact requested each month, for example:
	September—classwork samples
	October—homework samples
	November—test papers
every other month	practical for large schools
rotate the collection schedule among grades	reduces the number of student artifacts to review at one time, for example: artifacts due once per month could be collected on different weeks from different grades or departments

Here is an example of a rotation schedule:

- First week: grades 5 and 6 / students in grade 9 courses from all departments
- Second week: grades 3 and 4 / students in grade 10 courses from all departments
- Third week: grades 1 and 2 / students in grade 11 courses from all departments
- Fourth week: kindergarten and pre-K / students in grade 12 courses from all departments

RECORDING THE DATA

Student artifacts should be submitted with a top sheet. (See Figure 8-4.) The information completed by the teacher on the top sheet provides guidelines to use in reviewing the artifacts.

The teacher should first specify the type of student artifacts that have been submitted. Next, the teacher states what his or her objective was and which standard(s) is being addressed in asking students to complete this work.

Figure 8-4
TOP SHEET FOR STUDENT ARTIFACTS REVIEW

Teacher _____ Class _____ Date_____

Artifact Type: _____ teacher-made test

_____ writing samples

_____ classwork

_____ advance/graphic organizer

_____ homework assignment

_____ student projects

_____ other _____

Standard Addressed: _____

_____

_____

Objective: _____

_____

_____

Evaluation of Results: _____

_____

_____

_____

_____

Future Plans: _____

_____

_____

_____

_____

_____

Reviewer's Comments: _____

_____

_____

_____

_____

The teacher then states his or her evaluation of the student artifacts that have been submitted. This evaluation should relate to the stated objective and standard. Last, the teacher specifies future plans that will be implemented based on the results of the student artifacts submitted.

The top sheet provides a space for comments after having reviewed the teacher's statements and the students' work.

USING THE DATA TO TARGET ACHIEVEMENT

The review of student artifacts adds to the growing body of information about the effectiveness of the teacher. Growth in areas previously identified can be monitored and new needs can be identified.

Department heads, assistant principals, coordinators, directors, or lead teachers in large schools may most effectively review student artifacts. In those cases, time should be set aside to communicate the outcomes of the review with the administrative staff responsible for teacher evaluation.

A copy of the top sheet submitted by the teacher, with the comments of the reviewer, should be kept. The original is returned to the teacher with the student artifacts that have been reviewed.

The top sheets should be kept sequentially for each teacher. They may be used to:

1. Refer back to previous top sheets at a later date.

2. Monitor the teacher's growth in particular areas.

3. Monitor student progress.

4. Compare current comments with those made in the past.

COMMUNICATING WITH THE TEACHER

Initial, date, and comment directly on the top sheet. Comments may take the form of commendation or questions to be considered.

SAMPLE COMMENDATION COMMENTS

- "The students have made excellent progress in their writing ability."
- "Your stated objectives have been met."
- "This was a very motivating project for the students."
- "Your future plans show a deep understanding of the students' needs."
- "Your evaluation of the students' work demonstrates your insight and concern for their continued motivation and success."

SAMPLE QUESTIONS AND COMMENTS

- "How will the results of this test be used in your plan for instruction?"
- "Did the students clearly understand the objective and directions?"
- "Please meet with me to discuss the correction of students' writing."
- "How will your analysis of why so many students failed the test influence your instructional plans?"
- "Please meet with me to discuss alternative formats for students' reports."

Observed needs of a serious nature and ones that require more extensive assistance and support may become part of the growth plan. A particular teacher's needs and the selection of the growth plan objective may be confirmed by several of the data-gathering tools that have been used. For example, a teacher's use of lower-level questions may have been observed during informal visits, seen in teacher plans, and asked on teacher-made tests.

Artifacts as Sources of Learning Targets for Student Achievement

Student artifacts document the achievement of students in reaching instructional goals. These goals are directly related to the standards set and should be reflected in the objectives teachers target in their plans. Collecting and reviewing student and teacher artifacts will also provide information about specific school and district learning targets.

LEARNING TARGETS TO LOOK FOR

The specific learning targets to address when reviewing student artifacts relate to what has been established for the school and district. These targets are usually addressed in professional-development sessions.

Look for documentation of students' work in the established learning targets when reviewing student artifacts. For example, cooperative learning as an instructional strategy may be a learning target for the school year. Determine if student projects and/or classwork employ cooperative learning as the instructional strategy. Look for cooperative learning as the instructional strategy in teacher plans. As a second example, differentiating instruction to provide for varied abilities may be a district learning target as programs for inclusion grow in number. Look for differentiated instructional strategies in teacher plans and student artifacts.

Figure 8-5 presents some learning targets to look for in student and teacher artifacts with questions to ask if the targets are not in evidence.

Figure 8-5
LEARNING TARGETS TO LOOK FOR

WHAT TO LOOK FOR	QUESTIONS TO ASK
Content standards	"Where are the student objectives?"
	"Which standards are targeted?"
Thinking skills	"How are thinking skills incorporated?"
Learning skills	"Which learning skills are developed?"
Student collaboration	"How are students encouraged to work together?"
Provision for varied abilities	"How are differences in ability provided for?"
Monitoring student progress	"How is student progress monitored?"
Student feedback	"What feedback is given to students?"
Student assessment	"How are students assessed?"
Authentic tasks	"How do the tasks required of the students represent the real world?"
Extended learning	"How is student learning extended?"
Interdisciplinary focus	"What disciplines are included?"

Conducting Observations to Raise Student Achievement

Observation provides the teacher with a mirror view of the classroom as seen through the eyes of the observer. Teachers can use these images to help them understand what is happening in their classrooms, and then use that information to improve their practice. Research has shown that teachers are more open to changing their instructional behaviors after an observer objectively describes their classrooms to them. The mirror view is often the incentive needed for change.

Five Phases of Observation

Each phase of the observation process contributes to raising student achievement as teachers grow in their abilities to plan and deliver effective instruction.

Phase 1: Plan for Instruction

The teacher completes a plan for instruction as the first phase of the observation process. This plan provides the observer with an overview of the lesson that will be observed. It also provides the information that will be discussed during the pre-conference. Figure 9-1 provides an outline for the teacher's observation plan.

THE DESIGNING INSTRUCTION PLANNING FRAMEWORK

This framework is a guide to planning instruction. It is used to build an effective lesson that will enhance students' learning. Not all aspects of the framework need to be included, nor should they be included if they do not contribute to the effectiveness of the lesson.

Identify the standard to be addressed. The teacher consults state or local guides for the content area to select the appropriate standard(s) that will be addressed in the lesson.

Figure 9-1

OBSERVATION PLAN

Teacher _____ Class _____ Pre-Conference Date _____

Requested Observation Date _____ Requested Time for the Observation _____

Please respond to the following questions in preparation for our pre-conference.

Which standard(s) will you address?

What is the objective of the lesson?

How will you open the lesson? (the set or motivation)

How will students be asked to reflect on (think about) the content?

What instructional strategy has been selected?

In what ways will students work together during the lesson?

How will you check for understanding?

Will guided practice be used? How?

What independent practice will be required of the students?

What closure strategy will be used?

What other information do you wish to share?

Define the learning objective.   The teacher defines the objective of the lesson. Defining the learning objective is the essential first step to student achievement. Students who clearly know what they are to learn in the lesson are better able to focus their attention and follow the materials presented. The learning objective includes the content to be learned and the level of difficulty that is appropriate for the learner. Researchers tell us that anything can be taught to anyone provided that the correct level of difficulty is selected. For example, geometry can be taught in the kindergarten and in high school. Obviously, the content to be mastered by the students will differ radically.

The teacher also specifies the ways in which the students will process the content. For example, will they compare, map, rank, solve a problem, make a decision? See Section 2 and Figure 2-6 for strategies that extend student processing of content.

Set the stage for learning.   The teacher plans an opening set for the lesson that serves two important purposes. First, it focuses the students and raises their interest in what is to be learned in today's lesson. Second, it provides a means of helping students to relate the new learning to their prior knowledge. For example, when teaching Newton's law that every action has an immediate and opposite reaction, begin by asking students to close their eyes and visualize themselves in a pool. Ask them to simulate the swimming strokes that they are taking. Then ask them to visualize the direction in which the water is being pushed by their arms and the resulting direction in which their bodies are moving. Other sets may ask students to brainstorm about the topic under study or complete a KWL: K *(what I know)*, W *(what I want to learn)*, and L *(what I learned)*, which should be used as the closure activity.

As important as the opening set is, it may not always be necessary. For example, when lessons in which students are involved carry over to the next day, students may be excited about continuing their work and do not need to be motivated. In essence, the work itself is the motivation.

Select the instructional strategy.   The teacher selects an instructional strategy that involves the students as active participants in their learning, and contributes to their understanding of the learning objective. This is what students will do during the lesson. Good instructional strategies provide for learning style preferences and employ strategies for accommodation. See Section 2 and Figure 2-4 for a discussion of accommodation strategies.

There are a variety of instructional strategies that can be used in the teaching process. Skillful, experienced teachers know and can use a large number of strategies. In addition, they know how to match the strategy to the learning objective. For these reasons, focusing on the instructional strategy, as a means of enlarging the teacher's instructional options, will help teachers to more effectively achieve student success. See Section 2 and Figure 2-5 for a discussion of diversified instructional strategies.

Match the strategy to the plan for grouping.   The teacher selects how students will be grouped for at least part of the time during the lesson. The most commonly used grouping strategy, especially in high schools, is whole-class instruction.

This strategy may work well for some learning objectives some of the time, but should not be used exclusively all of the time. The interaction between and among students that results from working with a peer or in a small group contributes to students' thinking about the material and understanding the content. See Section 2 and Figure 2-8 for a discussion of grouping strategies.

Check for understanding.   The teacher uses strategies throughout the lesson to check for students' understanding. Using overt and covert responses, the teacher seeks to find out "Are they with me? Do they understand?" Based on the information the teacher receives from conducting a check for understanding, the teacher may adjust instruction by slowing down the lesson, speeding up, continuing as planned, or ending the lesson. If the teacher waits for the end of the lesson to check for understanding, it may be too late to do anything about it. See Section 2 and Figure 2-10 for a discussion of strategies for checking for understanding.

Guide student practice.   The teacher plans specific periods in the lesson for students to practice the skills being taught under the guidance and direction of the teacher. Guiding student practice is especially important when skills are being taught, such as in mathematics. For example, the teacher may use guided practice periods to be sure students can perform the operations they have been taught with sample examples. Or the teacher may use the guided practice periods to be sure students can use outlining strategies taught with a sample paragraph. Guided practice always comes before independent practice when students are asked to use the new understanding without guidance. These practice periods may not be necessary for lessons that target conceptual understandings or relationships.

Provide independent practice.   Teachers plan for students to practice or extend their knowledge by using the new content and understanding on their own. Independent practice is effectively conducted through homework assignments.

Close the lesson.   Every lesson should have a closure. The bell is not an appropriate way to close a lesson. Closure serves two important purposes. First, it enables students to clarify their thinking about what they have learned in the lesson. Second, it helps the teacher to evaluate if the learning objective has been met. Closure can take many forms. For example, the teacher may ask each student to state one new learning from the lesson. Or, the teacher may ask each student to write a question based on the lesson to be used in the next exam. Or, the teacher may turn the learning objective into a question and ask students to respond. Or, the teacher may ask the students to complete the L *(what I learned)* portion of the KWL they worked on during the set. Every lesson should end with a planned closure. Teachers must be sure to leave two to three minutes at the end of the instructional time to conduct the closure.

Figure 9-2 provides a summary of the Designing Instruction Planning Framework. This framework is useful to teachers as they plan instruction. It may also prove useful to observers when they analyze the lesson that was observed.

Figure 9-2

DESIGNING INSTRUCTION
PLANNING FRAMEWORK

A. DEFINE THE LEARNING OBJECTIVE.

1. Identify the *standard*.
2. Specify the content at the *level of difficulty*.
3. Identify the way students will *process information.* (level of complexity)

B. SET THE STAGE FOR LEARNING.

1. Focus the students.
2. Relate new learning to *prior knowledge*.

C. SELECT THE INSTRUCTIONAL STRATEGY.

1. Make students *active participants*.
2. Provide for *learning style*.
3. Incorporate *accommodations*.

D. MATCH THE GROUPING PLAN TO THE OBJECTIVE.

1. *Large* group instruction
2. *Small* work group
3. Peer learning *supports*
4. Individual *processing* strategies

E. CHECK FOR UNDERSTANDING.

1. Elicit *overt* responses.
2. Elicit *covert* responses.
3. *Adjust* instruction based on student responses.

F. GUIDE STUDENTS' PRACTICE.

1. Sharpen directions.
2. Relate practice to skills.
3. Provide *assistance*.

G. INDEPENDENT PRACTICE.

1. Establish the *purpose*.
2. Define the *process*.
3. Be sure of student success.

H. CLOSE THE LESSON.

1. Students *process* learning.
2. Teacher *evaluates* learning.

P L A N   A H E A D

Phase 2: Pre-Conference

The pre-conference can serve three purposes based on the skills and needs of the individual teacher: communicating with the teacher, assessing the growth needs of the teacher, and developing the teacher's skills. Each provides an opportunity to build rapport and trust with the teacher. To achieve this, the teacher should be in control of the pre-conference and it is the teacher's voice that should be heard. The teacher should also specify the date and time for the observation.

COMMUNICATE WITH THE TEACHER

The teacher establishes the purpose and direction of the lesson to be observed. During the discussion, the teacher reveals his or her level of teaching excellence as he or she provides information about what the students will learn, the plan for delivering instruction, how the students will be involved in their learning, and how the teacher will know that students are learning. The observer may need to ask questions to better understand the teacher's plan. The teacher may be asked to explain or clarify the instructional strategy he or she plans to use. The teacher may also be asked to specify what should be seen or heard to indicate that students are learning. Some sample language follows.

- "When you say students will complete a comparison chart, what do you mean?"
- "Could you clarify how using the chart will lead to meeting the objective?"
- "What should I see students doing to demonstrate their understanding?"

The teacher specifies or is asked to specify the specific type or kind of feedback that would be of interest. For example, the teacher may be interested in how clearly directions are given, or how quickly the students move into and out of groups. The observer clarifies what data to collect to provide this feedback and reaches agreement with the teacher about the form in which it will be collected.

ASSESS GROWTH NEEDS

By listening carefully to the teacher's plan for instruction, the observer is able to get an initial assessment of the teacher's growth in skill areas that are or have been the focus of a growth plan. When a growth plan is in progress, the pre-conference provides an opportunity for the teacher to demonstrate these skills. For example, if a teacher is working on behavior management, the pre-conference should include how positive behavior will be maintained throughout the lesson. The pre-conference also provides the observer with the opportunity to note changing needs and areas of growth for future plans. For example, the instructional strategy planned by the teacher may not provide sufficient involvement of the students in their own learning. Learning additional instructional strategies may be a focus for a future growth plan.

DEVELOP SKILLS

The pre-conference provides an opportunity for skill development, as the teacher is encouraged to conduct a mental or simulated rehearsal of the lesson. During this time, the observer should assist the teacher in rethinking, refining, or even changing the original plan. For example, when a teacher is working on a growth plan that includes dealing positively with students' wrong answers, the observer may provide an opportunity for practice. The observer and the teacher may engage in a simulation of some of the questions that the teacher plans to ask of the students. The observer answers the questions incorrectly, providing the teacher with the opportunity to practice positive response strategies. As a second example, for teachers working on asking higher-order questions during the lesson, the observer and the teacher may review the questions planned and determine their level.

Figure 9-3 provides a summary of the objectives that can be accomplished during the pre-conference based on the teacher's level of excellence and growth plan focus.

Phase Three: Observation

The purpose of observation is to gather detailed, objective information about the teaching and learning process in classrooms, that will help teachers to view and improve their practice. The type of observation conducted is always related to the purpose to be achieved, and is either used to determine the objective of the growth plan or indicated as a part of the growth plan.

OVERVIEW OBSERVATION

The purpose of the overview observation is to consider all aspects of the lesson that were designed by the teacher. The observation data provides an overview of the instructional process planned by the teacher and the results achieved by the students. This makes it a powerful tool in determining the needs and skills of individual teachers in teaching for student achievement.

The district may require the overview observation for every teacher at some time during the school year. There are at least two instances when the overview observation should be a first priority:

1. *When little is known about the teacher.* The teacher may be new to the school or new to teaching.

2. *When the teacher has been identified as marginally competent or close to unsatisfactory.* In this case, there are so many areas in need of improvement that the overview observation is needed to prioritize the focus of the growth plan.

Figure 9-3

Pre-Conference:

BUILDS TRUST AND RAPPORT

PURPOSES

1. COMMUNICATION

Establish purpose and direction for the observation.
Elicit teacher's request for specific feedback.
Decide what and how data is to be collected.

2. ASSESS GROWTH

Determine how identified skill needs are being mastered.
Check the progress of the growth plan.
Identify the teacher's abilities and changing needs.

3. DEVELOP SKILLS

Teach needed skills and abilities that will contribute to
the teacher's effectiveness.

RECORDING OVERVIEW OBSERVATION DATA

Taking verbatim notes, sometimes called a script, is the best way to record the data observed in an overview observation. All of the verbal and visual actions and interactions taking place in the classroom during the observation are recorded or described. In addition, verbatim notes record only what was heard or seen without interpretation or value. Taking verbatim notes can be an arduous task. In order to record more efficiently, the observer should abbreviate words and leave out words that do not add meaning to the script or help to clarify the instructional process.

The script should include a timeline. These are notations of the time as the lesson proceeds, recorded in the left-hand margin of the notepaper. The first time note is made at the start of the lesson. The time continues to be recorded about every 5 to 10 minutes, or whenever the activity changes. This information allows the observer and the teacher to review how time was used during the lesson to accomplish the learning objective. For example, did students have enough time to complete the task in small groups? Was there enough time to conduct a closure? Did the time used for the set limit the amount of time left for instruction?

TOPIC-SPECIFIC OBSERVATION

The purpose of the topic-specific observation is to consider a particular aspect of the teaching and learning process that is either requested by the teacher or the observer. These aspects may be a part of the teacher's growth plan, or they may be areas of particular interest to the teacher.

There are several reasons to conduct this type of observation:

- The teacher is working on a growth objective specified in his or her growth plan. This growth objective may have been observed as a teaching skill need during a previously conducted overview observation. Both the observer and the teacher want to determine if the teacher has mastered the previously identified skill need.

- The teacher has recently attended a seminar on a particular strategy—for example, providing opportunities for students to construct their own learning—and is interested in getting information about how well the strategy is being used in the instructional process.

- The teacher is working on raising the level of questions asked and wants some feedback.

- The teacher is interested in a particular instructional concern—for example, the number of students called on during the lesson—and wants specific information about it.

- The teacher is interested in how effectively he or she deals with incorrect student answers.

RECORDING THE OBSERVATION DATA

The format for recording the data from the topic-specific observation depends on what data is being collected. It will be helpful to talk with the teacher about ideas for collecting the data, or, if the teacher does not have an idea, suggest a data-collection strategy and ask the teacher if that sounds like something that will help to gather the requested data. Here are some examples.

Instructional strategy specified in the growth plan. Depending on the strategy selected and used by the teacher, the observer may record the data through selective verbatim notes. These notes record only the specific instructional strategy. As a second example, when focusing on student achievement of the lesson objective, recording the directions given to students and their use of an activity sheet or advance/graphic organizer, and asking the teacher to collect them after the lesson, will provide valuable information.

Strategy presented in a recent workshop or seminar. If, for example, the teacher attended a workshop on constructionist learning, the teacher may be interested in implementing strategies that help students construct their own learning. It may be helpful to record the specific instructive statements that the teacher makes through selective verbatim notetaking, and the nature of the activities with which students are involved. Look for open-ended questions and assignments that students complete in pairs or small groups and that ask students about how the content relates to the learning objective. The teacher working on helping students to construct their own learning should avoid providing students with responses, or solutions to the problems and/or decisions being developed by the students. Keeping a selective verbatim script of the teacher's statements and looking at completed student artifacts will provide valuable information for discussion with the teacher. (Refer to Figure 2-6 for processing that extends student learning.)

Raising the level of questions asked. Record all of the questions asked by the teacher and some sample responses of students that were at the high end or the low end of the taxonomy. The teacher and the observer can review the questions during the conference to determine the level of thinking asked of students. (Refer to Figure 2-7 for question prompts at each level of the taxonomy.)

The number of students called on during the lesson. This data is most easily collected using a student seating chart. List the students by name or number. Record with a slash each student called on during the lesson. Both the observer and the teacher will begin to see patterns. Are more students called on from the front of the room and the middle of the room than from the left or right sides of the classroom and the back of the room? Are more girls called on than boys? These are important areas to discuss. See Figure 9-4 for a sample seating chart record.

Figure 9-4

SEATING CHART FOR RECORDING STUDENTS CALLED ON

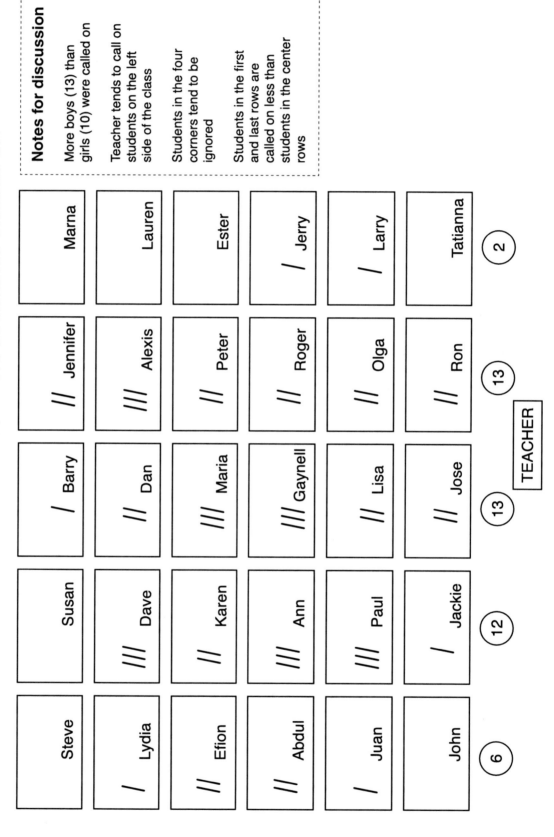

Notes for discussion

More boys (13) than girls (10) were called on

Teacher tends to call on students on the left side of the class

Students in the four corners tend to be ignored

Students in the first and last rows are called on less than students in the center rows

Steve	Susan / / /	Barry /	Jennifer / /	Marna
Lydia /	Dave / / /	Dan / /	Alexis / / /	Lauren
Efion / /	Karen / /	Maria / / /	Peter / /	Ester
Abdul / /	Ann / / /	Gaynell / / /	Roger / /	Jerry /
Juan /	Paul / / /	Lisa / /	Olga / /	Larry /
John	Jackie /	Jose / /	Ron / /	Tatianna
6	12	13	13	2

TEACHER

Phase Four: Analysis and Reflection

The data gathered during the observation is used to raise student achievement. The selective verbatim or verbatim notes are first reviewed and analyzed by the observer. All aspects of the teaching and learning process, including how time was used, should be considered. It may be helpful to refer to the designing instruction planning framework discussed earlier in this section, and the standards for teaching that target students' achievement in Section 2, as the script is reviewed.

The observer forms initial impressions and assessments about the lesson observed and finds data from the script to support them. Here are some questions that observers ask themselves as they review and analyze their scripts.

- "What was the general climate of the classroom and how did students behave?"
- "Was the learning objective at the correct level of difficulty for the students?"
- "Did the students understand? Were they challenged to grow?"
- "Were students asked to reflect on the information presented?"
- "Did the set at the start of the lesson focus and engage the students?"
- "Did the instructional strategy used actively engage the students in the lesson?"
- "Was there a closure for the lesson?"
- "Was the stated learning objective reached?"
- "Did the students provide evidence of their learning?"
- "How was time used?"
- "How was the teacher's plan changed during the lesson?"

Phase Five: Conference with the Teacher

There are two simple rules that contribute to building trust and encouraging the teacher to reflect on how to grow professionally.

1. **Ask, don't tell.** To the greatest possible extent, involve the teacher in a dialogue that encourages him or her to speak openly and professionally about instruction and its improvement. Continuously seek to ask questions that will help the teacher to focus and reflect. The responsibility for improvement belongs to the teacher and ideas for improvement should, to the greatest possible extent, come from the teacher. Giving suggestions closes down discussion in three ways. First, if you have all the answers, the teacher will think his or her ideas have no value and so why bother. Second, the teacher becomes dependent upon your ideas rather than growing and developing as a professional with his or her own ideas. Third, you really do not have all the ideas. The teacher may have some valid and creative ideas.

2. **Avoid criticism.** Criticism leads to defense. When people are told that what they did was not very good, or really bad, instead of looking for solutions they will spend their time justifying their actions and finding ways to move the blame they feel to someone or something else. This is not only a waste of time; it is counter-productive to helping teachers to improve.

The conference provides the vehicle to review the objective data recorded with the teacher, and talk about the various aspects of the lesson. For example, the observer and the teacher may explore: the learning objective selected, how students were active participants in the lesson, the instructional strategy selected, the level of the questions asked by the teacher, the grouping strategy that was used, how the teacher checked for understanding, how the lesson was closed, and how time was used during the lesson.

Be careful not to overload the teacher with so much data that true reflection by the teacher is not possible and a general feeling of defeat results. Instead, ask the teacher what aspects of the lesson are of interest to him or her. Or select an aspect of high priority that can contribute to improving instruction. Part IV will discuss specific strategies and techniques for communicating during the conference.

CONFERENCE PLAN

Preparing a plan will help you to conduct an effective conference. The plan should always encourage the teacher to reflect upon the lesson and provide his or her point of view. (See Figure 9-5.)

1. **Select a tentative goal for the conference.** Although you may have specific areas in mind to focus on, the teacher's concerns and areas of interest should always come first. The conference should start by asking the teacher about the lesson. Ask specific questions that encourage discussion rather than global questions, such as, "What did you think of the lesson?" which encourage a one-word answer—good, fine, or okay. Here are some sample questions.

   • "What went particularly well?"

   • "What surprised you in the lesson?"

   • "What did not go so well as you would have wanted?"

2. **Identify data from the script to use for reflection.** These are objective statements recorded during the lesson that you may wish the teacher to hear and talk about. These data may also be the feedback that the teacher requested. Here are some sample statements.

   • "Let's look at the script to talk about the specific questions you asked."

   • "Here are my script notations about how the students formed the groups. What is your analysis of the process?"

   • "I recorded all of your directions to the students as you requested. Let's review them to see what you think."

Figure 9-5

CONFERENCE PLAN
GOAL: TEACHER REFLECTION

1. **Select a tentative goal for the conference.**

    Focus first on the teacher's concerns and areas of interest.

2. **Identify data from the script to use for reflection.**

    These are objective statements recorded during the lesson.

    These data may also be the feedback that the teacher requested.

3. **Involve the teacher in reflection to propose solution strategies.**

    If the teacher cannot suggest solutions, provide some alternatives from among which the teacher can select.

4. **Form a growth plan to help the teacher learn the strategies agreed upon.**

    The plan should include the specific skills that the teacher will work on and how the teacher will be helped to develop those skills.

5. **Confirm understanding.**

    Be sure there is complete understanding about both what will be worked on and how assistance will be given.

3. **Involve the teacher in reflection to propose solution strategies.** Discuss the teacher's concerns and ask the teacher to suggest solutions. If the teacher cannot suggest solutions, you may have to provide some alternatives from among which the teacher can select. Here are some sample questions.

   - "What do you think you would like to do about selecting the level of difficulty of future lessons?"
   - "How can you help students form groups quickly?"
   - "Would you like to hear about some strategies that I have seen other teachers use?"
   - "Which of these strategies sounds like something you might like to try?"

4. **Form a growth plan to help the teacher learn the strategies agreed upon.** The plan should include the specific skills that the teacher will work on and how the teacher will be helped to develop those skills. The growth plan also specifies how the observer will assist the teacher and a timeline for those activities. When there are no specific skills to be focused on, the teacher should be asked to develop a teacher-directed growth plan. The specifics of forming growth plans are discussed in Part III.

5. **Confirm understanding.** Before the conference ends, be sure there is complete understanding about both what will be worked on and how assistance will be given. The observer can provide confirmation by paraphrasing. Or, the observer can ask the teacher to state what the plan includes. For example,

   - "Here is my understanding of the growth plan. Let's see if this is your understanding, too."
   - "Could you state your understanding about the growth plan so we can see if we both agree?"

The Write-up

PREPARE A GROWTH PLAN

The best way to provide a written account of the observation cycle conducted and the conclusions reached during the conference with the teacher is to prepare a growth plan. Part III presents four growth plans. They are directed, collaborative, teacher-directed for the individual, and teacher-directed for peers. The plan selected should match the skill development needs of individual teachers.

OBSERVATION WRITE-UP

Some districts require a specific format for the observation write-up which may include a completed checklist. When this is the case, prepare an objective, proactive narrative that focuses on the aspects of instruction that were discussed and the plan for growth that has been developed. Avoid criticism and negative comments. Remember that you wish the teacher to be an active and enthusiastic participant in the growth plan. Having negative statements on record does not inspire anyone to strive toward excellence.

Figure 9-6 suggests an outline for a required narrative summary of the observation and conference.

Objective Requirements
of Recording Observation Data

Observation is a very natural and normal three-way process of viewing, interpreting what is seen, and making a judgment. The brain automatically processes a visual image, searches for previously stored connections related to what is good and bad, and assigns a value or meaning to that observation. For example, when we observe a classroom in which students stare out of the window, we interpret this to mean that students are bored and not involved. When we observe students and teachers shouting at each other, our judgment registers that the teacher is losing control.

Any or all of these interpretations may be correct. But if the goal is change, rather than excuses or justifications, focusing on descriptions without interpretations and judgments will more likely lead to change. It is more likely that the teacher can and will want to work on changing the behavior of the students and him- or herself than that he or she will want to deal with the out-of-control label.

The observer must always be aware of recording and discussing objective descriptions rather than interpretations and value judgments. Teachers are not so open to change when the view of their classrooms include interpretation of their actions and the value judgments that result. Their focus moves from change to defense of their actions.

Figure 9-6

OBSERVATION WRITE-UP

Teacher _____ Class _____ Date _____

Lesson summary

Area of focus selected for the observation

Areas discussed during the post-conference

Growth activities planned

Methods of assessment

Time frame

Part III

How to Match Growth Plans to What Teachers Need to Make Students Achieve

Matching the Growth Plan to What Each Teacher Needs

If instruction is to improve so that all students achieve, then an organized and active structure must be in place to help each teacher grow in instructional effectiveness. Section 2 presented the standards for teaching that target students' achievement. How can all teachers be helped to meet those standards? Part II presented six tools that can be used to provide data about what teachers need to make students achieve. The route to helping teachers to meet these needs is directed by three elements:

1. *What* to work on (the growth objective)
2. *How* to work on it (the growth plan type)
3. Matching both *what* and *how* to the individual teacher

Using these three elements to guide your work with teachers will make those efforts both effective and efficient.

Why Matching Growth Plans to Teacher Needs Results in Student Achievement

Giving you instruction in driving a long ball across the green, for example, will not improve your putting game. Obviously, when you receive instruction in the specific area where you demonstrate need you are going to improve. That is why the selection of the growth plan objective is critical. But, the selection of the growth plan type is also critical because it becomes the vehicle to reaching the objective. Two other factors should also be considered when making a match between the teacher and the growth plan objective and type. They are effective use of time and teacher preference.

EFFECTIVE USE OF TIME

Administrative time is subject to varied demands. That is why efficient use of time to work with teachers is essential if effective results are to be accomplished.

For administrative time to be both productively and efficiently used, it must be allocated by need. The question to answer is, "How can I achieve the best teacher growth for the time expended?"

This is a difficult question to answer. Consideration must be given to both teacher needs for assistance and the nature of those needs. Obviously, teachers with the greatest need for assistance should be given the largest allocation of time. This group of teachers usually includes those new to teaching as well as those new to the school. Teachers who are marginal in teaching performance or barely satisfactory also fall into this group.

The teachers who require extensive assistance may lack many essential teaching skills. Teachers with few or no significant skill needs usually require less time. However, these better-performing teachers may not be self-directing and may require time to help them to solve problems or set new directions. Even teachers with no skill needs who are seekers of perfection in their teacher role may demand time. These master teachers may prefer working directly with the administrator to any other involvement.

The allocation of limited assistance time is therefore a difficult but important decision. Try to balance the greatest need with the anticipated best result.

TEACHER PREFERENCE

It is always a good idea to involve the teacher in decisions about the selection of the growth objective and the growth plan. Teachers may have some preferences about what they want to work on and how that work should be conducted. Consideration of teacher preferences could lead to greater motivation and a commitment to succeed on the part of the teacher.

The conditions under which a teacher should be given either total selection preference, preference to select from among alternatives, a collaborative selection preference, or no selection preference is dependent on several factors and will be discussed.

Selecting the Growth Objective

The selection of the growth objective, this is, *what to work on,* is the result of the needs determined by the collection of data, discussed in Part II.

ADMINISTRATOR SELECTS THE GROWTH OBJECTIVE

For the teacher who demonstrates many teaching skill needs, especially in critical skill areas, the administrator makes the selection. Where there are many critical needs, the skill areas may need to be prioritized. The teacher is given little opportunity to determine what skill needs are included in the growth objectives. If possible, the teacher could be involved by selecting which of the first two or three priority skills to work on first.

TEACHER SELECTS FROM STATED ALTERNATIVES

When the data gathered to determine teacher needs reveals several skill needs of equal importance, it is advisable to involve the teacher. First present the data gathered by the tools, and then ask the teacher to state or confirm skill needs demonstrated. Present those skill needs as the growth objectives and ask the teacher to select the order in which these skills should be addressed. This involvement of the teacher provides for his or her areas of greatest interest or concern.

TEACHER AND ADMINISTRATOR COLLABORATIVELY SELECT THE GROWTH OBJECTIVE

When the data gathered for the determination of skill needs reveals minor areas in need of teacher skill development, none of which is critical, both you and the teacher should collaboratively select the growth objective. Skill areas in this group include those needing refinement or modification. The teacher's selection of the growth objective, in consultation with you, can contribute to motivation and interest, which are the prime considerations in achieving growth.

TEACHER SELECTS THE GROWTH OBJECTIVE

When the determination of teacher skill needs reveals few, if any, areas in need of skill development, the teacher should select the growth objective. This selection reflects the teacher's area of interest for professional self-development of new ideas and fresh approaches to instruction, and represents the teacher's personal route on the road to excellence. This approach may be especially effective at the secondary level where teachers consider themselves content experts. Their need to be recognized, admired, and consulted should be acknowledged.

Selecting the Growth Plan

The selection of the growth plan, this is, *how to work on the objective,* is directly related to the following four factors.

- **The teacher's level of expertise.** Consider how much the teacher knows about instruction and learning. Is there a foundation upon which to work? Can the teacher contribute to a discussion about the instructional strategies and modifications?

- **Awareness of obstacles to the learning process and knowledge of alternatives.** Can the teacher identify the individual needs of the students and the gaps in skills that may be preventing some students from learning? Does the teacher know how to provide for these individual differences?

- **Awareness of problems.** Think about the teacher's ability to recognize a problem that has developed, or is developing. If the teacher recognizes that there is a problem, is the teacher able to suggest alternative ways to deal with the problem? Or, can the teacher suggest even one way to solve the problem? Can the teacher implement the solution strategy and then evaluate its effectiveness?

- **Inclination to learn, grow, and develop.** Assess the level of the teacher's interest in growing as a professional and willingness to put forth both the time and effort required.

Teachers demonstrate these characteristics in the way in which they plan, conduct their classes, move students through the halls, and interact with colleagues and parents.

DIRECTED GROWTH PLAN

The directed growth plan is intended for teachers who have a low level of teaching expertise. They generally have difficulty seeing problems and/or finding solutions for them. These teachers know, understand, and can use few instructional strategies to assist students in the learning process. Although they may be motivated and have a high interest in learning and growing professionally, they lack essential knowledge about how to do that. This population of teachers usually includes those new to teaching. Unfortunately, teachers who are marginally effective or barely satisfactory fall into this population as well, and usually lack the inclination to learn, grow, and develop.

COLLABORATIVE GROWTH PLAN

Teachers who work well in a collaborative growth plan usually have a background of successful teaching experience. These teachers are generally aware of problems, sometimes before they start, and know some alternative solutions to try. The teachers are highly motivated with an interest in improving their current level of performance. They seek a professional collaboration with the administrator as a means of learning, growing, and developing into master teachers.

TEACHER-DIRECTED GROWTH PLAN

This population of teachers usually has a wealth of teaching experience, is self-motivated, and truly professional. This group comprises the excellent, outstanding, and master teachers on the staff. The growth plan is directed by these teachers who are capable of and interested in guiding and directing their own professional growth.

These master teachers may select to work with a colleague, who is also a master teacher. Or, these teachers may prefer to work on their own. The only choice that master teachers do not have, however, is the choice *not* to grow. No one ever knows everything that there is to know. True professionals know and understand that the field of research and information is continuously growing and providing us with new input.

Figure 10-1 provides a summary overview of the growth objective and plan selection process.

Figure 10-1

GROWTH PLAN OVERVIEW

GROWTH PLAN	GROWTH OBJECTIVE	WHO SELECTS	FOR WHOM
Directed	Critical skill needs	Administrator	New teachers
	Teaching expertise		Unmotivated teachers
	Seeing and solving problems		
Collaborative	Some noncritical needs	Administrator and Teacher	Teachers with knowledge and motivation
	Refinement/modification needs		Successful teaching experience
			Aware of problems
			Knows some solutions
Teacher-Directed	Teacher interest	Teacher	Master teachers
Collegial			Excellent teachers
Self-directed			

Communicating the Growth Plan

When the determination of needs has resulted in the selection of the growth objective to work on and a decision about the growth plan to be used has been made, it is time to invite the teacher to a conference. At this conference, the growth process begins with a full discussion between you and the teacher of the data gathered and both the growth objective and the growth plan. Any changes that are indicated either in the objective (to provide for teacher preference) or in plan type (because new information becomes available) can be made during the conference. (See Part IV for a comprehensive discussion of how to conduct conferences to communicate for student success.)

Using a Directed Growth Plan

The directed growth plan requires your maximum involvement and total control. This plan is, therefore, extremely time-consuming, and should be undertaken only after careful consideration of the obligations involved.

The plan involves a step-by-step approach to assistance. It begins with the identification of one area for skill improvement. The teacher then works with the administrator to develop a specific and detailed plan for improvement, a time frame for its completion, and assessment criteria. The plan is then put into action under your direction and observation. After you analyze the results, both the teacher and you confer on the analysis. Those results form the direction for the next step in the process.

As each result identifies a new need or required approach, a specific and detailed plan must be developed, implemented, analyzed, and assessed. This process continues in a cycle until such time that both you and the teacher are confident that the targeted skills have been developed and will continue to be practiced. At this point, a directed approach is either suspended for a time, by mutual agreement, or redirected to a new skill target.

The goal of all administrators is to have a staff of capable, enthusiastic, and self-directed professionals. For this reason, devoting time to raising the professional capabilities of the least able members of the staff to a point where they can function in a less directed and more collaborative growth plan is of tremendous benefit to the students, the staff, and you. (See Figure 11-1 for an overview of the process on page 147.)

Which Teachers Will Benefit from a Directed Growth Plan?

A directed growth plan is a powerful and effective skill-development process that requires the time and energy of a knowledgeable and confident administrator. There are three factors to consider when determining which teachers are most appropriate candidates for this process.

- The teacher is functioning at a fairly low level of effectiveness in the classroom. Such teachers possess little knowledge about instruction and its delivery. They feel confused or at a loss about what to do.

- The teacher believes the administrator is both willing and able to provide information and assistance that will help the teacher be successful.

- The situation demands that immediate action be taken and quick and specific solutions be put into place.

How to Use a Directed Growth Plan

The determination of the teacher skill needs discussed in Part II should result in the identification of specific areas of critical need. This information is now used to prepare the directed growth plan.

THE PLANNING MEETING

The objectives to be accomplished during the planning meeting are:

1. To identify the growth objective
2. To develop a directed growth plan to meet that objective
3. To specify how and who will provide the needed assistance
4. To determine the time frame for the directed growth plan
5. To specify the assessment criteria

During the initial meeting, the data you gathered in determining the teacher's skill needs is shared. Care should be taken not to overwhelm the teacher or contribute to feelings of inadequacy. It may be helpful to group the critical needs evidenced in the data gathered. For example, needs related to instruction, organization, and classroom management may be placed in separate groups. The specific area of critical skill needs that is to be the growth objective is suggested. The teacher should be involved, to the largest extent possible, in providing feedback and in setting the sequence for addressing the skill needs by stating his or her priorities. The directed growth plan is developed and agreed upon. Since this group of teachers is among the least able or least willing to improve on the staff, they may have minimum input and you may need to take total control. See Figure 11-2 for a sample directed growth plan.

A specific plan for helping the teacher to learn those skills is implemented. When an additional person, who can act as a coach, is available, he or she should be incorporated into the plan with specific responsibilities. A time frame for completion of the learning activities and specific criteria for assessing the teacher's growth in performing the skill are also established.

Figure 11-1

DIRECTED GROWTH PLAN: FLOW CHART SUMMARY

DETERMINE
APPROPRIATE
CANDIDATE

IDENTIFY ONE AREA
OF FOCUS FOR
IMPROVEMENT

PLANNING MEETING
Discuss the data gathered
Establish the plan:
activities specified
time frame established
assessment specified

INTENSIVE
ASSISTANCE
WITH SKILL
DEVELOPMENT

ASSESSMENT
CONDUCTED
AND ANALYZED

Plan completed
Plan not completed
To be continued
New plan developed
Growth plan is suspended

Figure 11-2
DIRECTED GROWTH PLAN

Teacher: __Norma Kalin__ Assignment: __Grade 2__ Date: __October 6, 2001__

Growth Objectives *(What behaviors, skills, and abilities are to be developed?)*

The improvement of questioning techniques.

- a. Eliminate or reduce "yes/no" questions.
- b. Eliminate fill-in questions.
- c. Eliminate multiple-choice questions.
- d. Develop critical-thinking questions at the level of analysis, synthesis, and evaluation.
- e. Encourage questions that ask *how, why, what.*

Specific Activities *(How will the skills and abilities be developed?)*

1. The teacher will receive:
   - a copy of Forming Questions that Raise the Level of Learning
   - two journal articles on the subject of questioning for higher levels of thinking
2. The principal and the teacher will:
   - Review the teacher's questions recorded on the most recent script of an overview observation and help the teacher to rewrite the questions at a higher level of thinking.
   - Work together to plan a new lesson using questions at high levels of thinking.
   - Work together every morning to review and improve the questions planned for lessons to be conducted during the next two weeks.

Time Frame *(When will the plan begin, be monitored, be completed?)*

- a. The plan will begin on October 6 and be completed by October 20.
- b. The principal will monitor the teacher's progress in asking questions that require higher levels of thinking during the two-week work period by conducting daily informal visits.

Evaluation Criteria *(How will the plan be evaluated? What student achievement data will be collected?)*

- a. The principal will conduct an observation with selected verbatim scripting of the questions the teacher asks and the responses students make to those questions.
- b. The teacher and the principal will review the script at a conference.

Future Areas in Need of Growth

- Use of manipulative materials in mathematics instruction.
- Creating learning centers in each content area.

_____   _____
Administrator's Signature   Teacher's Signature

THE LEARNING PROCESS

The learning process you select includes those activities that have a high probably of achieving the goal. In this instance you are the expert—as a doctor or an attorney might be in other circumstances—directing the growth plan. The activities may involve skill-development sessions conducted by you and/or the coach, visitation to classrooms that offer good examples of the skill to be developed, printed materials, and workshops on the topic.

Even if a coach is involved in implementing the plan, you are also continuously involved in teaching, modeling, monitoring, and assessing the teacher's progress during the time frame established. The plan may be modified based on results.

You conduct an assessment at the point when the teacher believes the skill has been developed or at the end of the time frame established.

ASSESSMENT OF RESULTS

The assessment used to confirm the results of the plan should match the criteria stated in the growth plan. In this way, the teacher is aware of how his or her development of the skill will be assessed. Depending on the skill that was targeted and the activities conducted, the results of the plan can be confirmed in a variety of ways. Most skills can be confirmed by an observation. Select the appropriate observation form for the assessment. Here are some examples.

- The skill to be developed was designing and delivering an instructional plan. *Conduct an observation cycle and record verbatim notes.*

- The skill was related to student attention during the lesson. *Conduct a time-on-time review.*

- The skill was preparing a rich learning environment for a lower grade class. *Conduct an environment review.*

- The skill involved using instructional strategies that actively involve the students in their learning. *Conduct an observation cycle and record selective verbatim notes.*

- The skill involved management and organization of the classroom. *Conduct informal visits at different times of the day.*

ANALYSIS OF ASSESSMENT

Analyze your objective observation notes to determine the degree of the teacher's success in learning and using the skill. If you are not sure of the results, conduct a second observation and compare the results with the first one.

Now consider what the next step should be. If the teacher has not developed the ability to use the targeted skill, consider developing a second directed plan. If the teacher has demonstrated the ability to use the targeted skill, look at the original growth plan to review the future areas needing growth. Determine if a new plan with a new skill, or set of skills, should be developed. Or, should the directed growth plan process be suspended for a time? Or, is the teacher now able to move to a collaborative plan? You are ready to meet with the teacher when you have reached a conclusion.

CONFERENCE WITH THE TEACHER

Meet with the teacher to discuss the plan and its results. Share the data you gathered during the assessment. Involve the teacher in reflecting on what was learned and how these skills have contributed to his or her professional growth. Explore next steps by eliciting the teacher's ideas and sharing yours. Then confirm what the next step will be.

WRITING THE REVIEW OF THE DIRECTED GROWTH PLAN

The written review of the directed growth plan should confirm what was discussed and agreed upon during the conference. (See Figure 11-3.) Begin with a statement of the area of focus. Next, summarize the assessment that was conducted and the results. For example: "This directed growth plan has successfully been completed. The teacher has demonstrated the following skills."

Complete the write-up with a statement anticipating future plans, such as:

- A statement about when a new directed growth plan will be developed with a new area of focus.
- A statement that a new directed growth plan will not be conducted.
- A statement that the teacher will continue in a collaborative growth plan.

Both you and the teacher should sign the review. It becomes a part of the teacher's permanent record and should be used in the end-of-year assessment required by the district.

Coaching as a Directed Growth Plan

The availability of a coach can add tremendously to the achievement of the growth plan in several ways.

1. The coach may be more continuously available than you.
2. The teacher may actually be more comfortable speaking about his or her limitations with the coach than with you.
3. The coach may have materials and experiences with the topic that you have not had.

Figure 11-3
DIRECTED GROWTH PLAN: REVIEW AND SUMMARY

Teacher: _____   Class: _____   Date: _____

Area of Focus:

Assessment Conducted:

Results of the Assessment:

Future Plans:

_____   _____
Administrator's Signature   Teacher's Signature

Although the coach may take a lead role in working with the teacher on the specific details of the plan, the plan should not completely be turned over to the coach. You should always be a part of the picture for several reasons:

1. You should be in charge of the directed growth plan. It is your responsibility to ensure that the activities planned are those that have the best possibility of achieving the goal.

2. You should monitor what is being done and how it is being done to be sure the plan is being accurately followed.

3. You are in the best position to determine if progress is being made and what else needs to be done for a successful result.

4. By maintaining a visible and active interest in the directed plan, you confirm the importance of the work and your commitment to its success.

5. Ongoing involvement will be of help to you when the results are analyzed and assessed.

See Section 21 for a full discussion of the coaching process.

Eavesdropping on a Planning Meeting for a Directed Growth Plan

Figure 11-4 allows you to eavesdrop on a planning meeting for a directed growth plan. Determine if all of the objectives for the planning meeting discussed above have been met. Note the language used by the principal and compare it with the language used in the planning meetings for collaborative and teacher-directed growth plans.

Figure 11-4

EAVESDROPPING ON A PLANNING MEETING
FOR A DIRECTED GROWTH PLAN

PRINCIPAL: Good to see you. I'm glad you are right on time so that we can have the maximum amount of time to work together.

TEACHER: I am very excited about the opportunity to work with you and learn.

PRINCIPAL: That's wonderful, so let's get started. At our exploration conference, you said you were concerned about the inattentiveness of the students during your lessons. Have you found out why that is happening and how to solve the problem?

TEACHER: Not really. I keep trying to vary the time of the lesson and the topics as well as the materials I use, but nothing seems to be of much help.

PRINCIPAL: I have been able to see you in active involvement with the students on several occasions. I have made many informal walk-in visits, and we had one overview observation.

TEACHER: Yes, I am aware that you have been observing me. I learned a great deal about designing lessons at our conference after the overview observation. I hope you have found the reason for my major problem.

PRINCIPAL: I believe there are several areas we could work on to help students to be more attentive.

TEACHER: I am very interested in hearing what you believe some of the solutions may be.

PRINCIPAL: I think there are three areas that we could work on. The use of manipulative materials in mathematics instruction, creating learning centers in each content area, and the types of questions you ask during the lesson. Which one is of greatest interest to you for our first growth plan?

TEACHER: We began to discuss questioning techniques at our conference after the overview observation.

PRINCIPAL: If this is the area you select for our first growth plan, we will have time now to fully discuss the growth plan focused on your questioning techniques.

TEACHER: That would be my first choice.

PRINCIPAL: Good. Since our conference, have you had an opportunity to consider the types of questions you ask during a lesson?

TEACHER: I have begun to evaluate my questions, but I really need some help.

PRINCIPAL: We can explore that now. Let's talk about some of your questions that I have recorded in my observation script. Let's discuss them one at a time to discover what they require from the students. Let's start with these four questions:

1. In our community we have lots of _____.
2. What are they? Why are they important? Who uses them?
3. Do you think they will stay the same, increase, or decrease?
4. Do these services make our lives better?

153

Figure 11-4 continued

TEACHER: I think I understand question one. It requires the students to guess the one exact word I want as an answer. The selection of that exact word may be a problem for them. Question four requires a "yes" or "no" answer. I guess that's not a very interesting question. I am not sure about the other two questions.

PRINCIPAL: Question two is composed of three different questions. Students may become confused trying to answer all three since each question may be answered differently. What I think you were doing was trying to improve your question.

TEACHER: You're right. I was not satisfied with the question, so I kept trying to make it better. I would have been better off just waiting for a response and then restating it.

PRINCIPAL: Question three is a multiple-choice question. Why is that not a good type of question to ask in a discussion situation?

TEACHER: First of all, the students have to remember the question and then the choice of answers. In addition, I am preventing the youngsters from expressing themselves in their own words.

PRINCIPAL: I am in total agreement with your analysis of the questions. Now, let's discuss how to design questions that challenge students to think.

TEACHER: I have been reading the articles you left in my letterbox about higher order questions. Thank you for sharing them with me. I understand that one way to be sure your questions require students to think is to start with why, how, or what.

PRINCIPAL: That's a good beginning. Also consider using the Forming Questions that Raise the Level of Learning outline as a guide. Here is a copy we can use for this discussion. Another factor to consider is that when students are required to think about forming their answers to a question, they are more likely to respond in a complete sentence.

TEACHER: I never thought about that. I certainly would like to encourage better language development with my students.

PRINCIPAL: Do you have any ideas about how we can assess your growth in asking questions that make students think?

TEACHER: Well, after I have gained some skill in writing high-level questions, perhaps you could observe me to see if I can ask those questions during the lesson.

PRINCIPAL: That is the exact assessment strategy I would select. At the end of the time frame we select, we will have an observation cycle. But I will script only the questions you ask and the students' responses to those questions. We can then review the script to determine if you can write and ask high-level questions.

TEACHER: Good. I am sure I can master this skill and use it effectively in my lessons.

PRINCIPAL: The last item to establish for our plan is the time frame for the growth plan. I am suggesting a two-week interval from October 6 to October 20.

TEACHER: I think that should work.

PRINCIPAL: Great. Now just to be sure we both have the same understanding about the growth plan we are working on, could you tell me your understanding of the growth plan?

Figure 11-4 continued

TEACHER: Sure. We are going to work on improving the level of the questions I ask the students. I am going to work with you to learn how to plan questions that will get students to think and, I hope, pay attention to the lesson. I also like the idea of being able to use the Forming Questions that Raise the Level of Learning outline as a guide.

PRINCIPAL: I will place the growth plan in your letterbox. Please review the plan and then sign it and return one copy to me.

TEACHER: Okay.

PRINCIPAL: We have time to start the growth plan right now. Let's plan another lesson. Look at your plans for next week and select a topic that you will teach.

TEACHER: I was planning to introduce a new unit about the types of homes in which families live.

PRINCIPAL: Good, we can begin your personalized growth plan right now. Before this meeting ends, we will review the entire process that the growth plan will cover. Let's start by spending some time now designing the first lesson of the new unit. Then, together we can write the questions that will launch an exciting unit. After that, we can role-play the lesson.

The learning process has begun.

SECTION 12

Using a Collaborative Growth Plan

The collaborative growth plan requires the teacher and you to interact in positive and productive ways. The plan provides opportunities for the teacher to begin to assume responsibility for directing his or her professional growth. The success of this plan is based on mutual respect, trust, and interest in the professional development of the teacher. A collaborative growth plan requires a time commitment, but it is usually not so extensive as for a directed growth plan.

You share the responsibility for decision-making with the teacher. In truth, collaboration is participation by equals. When a difference of opinion arises, each participant must try to convince the other of his or her point of view. A compromise is reached in the end. Some teachers may have difficulty understanding and accepting this responsibility, especially if this is their first involvement in a collaborative growth plan. Teachers who have recently moved from a directed growth plan to a collaborative growth plan, due to their growth in professional skills, may also have some difficulty in understanding the collaborative role required of them. There are two actions you can take.

1. Encourage teachers to offer their own ideas and thoughts on the topic. Ask open questions such as:
   - "What do you think about . . . ?"
   - "What similar experiences have you had with . . . ?"
   - "How do you think this might work?"
   - "How could you get that result?"

2. Be sure no decision is made without the feedback and input of the teacher.

If you are not actively seeking the full involvement of the teacher in stating ideas and providing feedback about suggestions, then no matter what you call the plan, it is not collaborative. If the teacher has no ideas to contribute and does not have feedback to offer about the suggestions, the teacher is not ready for a collaborative growth plan.

The development of a collaborative growth plan begins with the mutually agreed-upon selection of the growth objective, an area of growth to be targeted. The discussion then focuses on the specifics of the plan to be implemented, the time frame for completion of the plan, and the assessment criteria to be used. The growth plan is then put into action.

How, or if, you participate in the growth plan is specified in the description of the plan. Your expertise with the topic, along with your available time, usually determine the level of your participation. However, you are always involved in monitoring the progress of the plan in ways that are appropriate. For example, you may monitor the plan's progress by reading the teacher's plans, reviewing samples of students' work, or conducting informal visits to the classroom.

After the agreed-upon time period has passed, you and the teacher review the results of the plan. The discussion of these results will then determine if additional efforts are to be undertaken, or if the growth plan has been completed. You and the teacher collaboratively make that decision.

Which Teachers Will Benefit from a Collaborative Growth Plan?

A collaborative growth plan draws its power from the position of respect and esteem in which the teacher is placed. Teachers involved in this type of growth plan believe they are skillful and committed to student achievement. They consider themselves bright and resourceful enough to collaborate in the development of a growth plan focused on their professional development. These beliefs contribute to the development of confidence and motivation that are characteristic of outstanding teachers.

However, there are three factors to consider when determining which teachers are appropriate candidates for a collaborative growth plan.

1. *The type of skill needs the teacher demonstrates as a result of the data gathered using the tools discussed in Part II.* Teachers who demonstrate basic, critical skill needs require the intensive and immediate assistance of a directed growth plan to master those skills. These skills might include, for example, management of the classroom and designing instruction. On the other hand, collaborative growth plans work better with teachers who have refinement and enhancement needs, such as:

   - Improving adaptation for students with individual needs
   - Learning new instructional strategies
   - Raising the level of questions asked
   - Learning to use more strategies that require student thinking
   - Refining and enlarging the use of graphic/advance organizers

2. *A background of successful teaching experience.* A collaborative growth plan requires that the teacher be an active and equal participant in the discussion by presenting a point of view, feedback, and input. The teacher must be able to bring ideas, suggestions, and experiences to the identification of the growth objective and the development of the growth plan.

3. *The level of motivation.* Teachers in a collaborative growth plan are usually highly motivated. They have an interest in improving their current level of performance. In addition, they seek a professional collaboration with the administrator as a means of learning, growing, and developing into master teachers.

How to Use a Collaborative Growth Plan

The success of a collaborative growth plan is dependent upon you and the teacher participating as equals in making joint decisions about the teacher's growth objective and the growth plan. Figure 12-1 provides a sample collaborative growth plan.

THE PLANNING MEETING

The objectives to be accomplished during the planning meeting are to:

1. Jointly identify the growth objective.
2. Develop a collaborative growth plan to meet that objective.
3. Establish the administrator's involvement in the plan.
4. Determine the time frame.
5. Specify the assessment criteria.

The planning meeting should begin with a presentation of the data you gathered. You and the teacher review and discuss the data. The teacher provides input and feedback on the data as well as particular needs and areas of interests.

Jointly identify the growth objective. The data you gathered may result in the identification of particular skills that would be valuable for the teacher, and you may suggest these for the growth objective. The teacher, however, may have a different set of skill needs and interests that are of immediate concern, so these may be preferred by the teacher for the growth objective.

Discuss both points of view when you and the teacher differ in the selection of the growth objective. Participate as equals, each explaining the reasons for the selection of the specific growth objective. Both you and the teacher try to convince each other about the other person's point of view. The discussion ends when one individual convinces the other of his or her point of view or a compromise is reached.

Figure 12-1
COLLABORATIVE GROWTH PLAN

Teacher __Michael Hale__   Assignment __Social Studies 9th grade__   Date __October 11, 2001__

Growth Objective (What behaviors, skills, and abilities are to be developed?)

To develop and refine the use of cooperative learning strategies by examining the ways in which rulers of distinct cultures seek to exercise power and authority.

Specific Activities (How will the behavior, skills, and abilities be developed?)

1. The teacher will review written materials on the subject of cooperative learning as an instructional strategy and speak with two teachers in the department who have used the cooperative learning strategy successfully.

2. The teacher will design the course of study around cooperative learning strategies using the theme of absolutism in distinct cultures.

3. Students will be placed in groups representing diverse ability levels.

4. The members of each group will be assigned specific roles including: minutes keeper, resource finder, timekeeper, organizer of work, resolver of conflicts.

5. The work of each member of each group will be totaled to form an average grade for the group.

6. The administrator will introduce the concept and logistics for cooperative learning groups to the class.

Time Frame (When will the plan begin, be monitored, be completed?)

• The unit will begin on October 30 and be completed by November 17.

• The administrator will review the teacher's plans throughout the growth plan.

• The teacher will invite the administrator to view the cooperative groups in action periodically throughout the growth plan.

Assessment Criteria (How will the plan be assessed?)

• Students will be assessed by a series of short quizzes, a unit test, and the projects produced by each cooperative group. The grades achieved will be reviewed.

• Samples of students' work will be examined.

• The teacher will keep a journal of positive and negative student interactions to determine how cooperative learning influenced these interactions.

_____   _____
Administrator's Signature   Teacher's Signature

Two factors are important to keep in mind about reaching agreement on the growth objective.

1. You must take care not to appear manipulative or directive when explaining your point of view about the preferred growth objective. Be sure the tone of equality in decision-making is maintained in the discussion.

2. Remember that the single most important factor in the improvement of teacher skills is the *teacher's* motivation to improve. To continue to press for your objective over the teacher's strongly felt needs or interest could be counterproductive. Unless you can convince the teacher that your objective will offer appreciably greater benefits to him or her, postpone your selected objective to another time.

Develop a collaborative growth plan to meet that objective.   Once the growth objective has been agreed upon, you and the teacher develop the plan. This discussion is characterized by brainstorming; sharing ideas, suggestions, and resources; and exploring alternatives. The specific plan that is developed is now recorded in detail.

Establish the administrator's involvement in the plan.   Your specific involvement is also identified, the details of which are recorded and confirmed. You might take various roles in the plan, such as:

- **Resource person:** to secure materials, arrange for involvement with other personnel, or make arrangements for a visitation
- **Facilitator:** to modify schedules or programs
- **Participant in the plan:** to teach a model lesson or provide an orientation for the students
- **Active observer in the plan:** to interact with the teacher and the students in the classroom
- **Passive observer in the plan:** to watch teacher actions

Determine the time frame.   A time frame for the expected completion of the plan should be set and recorded. The time frame may be modified at a future date, but specific actions are more likely to take place when they have a specified date.

Specify the assessment criteria.   Finally, determine how the results of the plan will be assessed. The form of the assessment should fit the plan to be implemented. Assessment criteria include:

- Observation of student actions
- Review of student products
- Observation of teacher actions
- Conference between the administrator and the teacher
- Comments of parents
- Comments of other teachers
- Written presentation of the plan's results

MONITORING THE PLAN

Your first obligation in the collaborative growth plan is to fulfill your role commitment. You must complete whatever action and involvement has been specified as soon as possible. Your actions or inactions are related to the success or failure of the growth plan.

Be aware of the time frame and the amount of time that has passed. Rather than wait until the specified time has passed to check with the teacher, check periodically along the way to remind, encourage, and ensure that the teacher is progressing with the specified plan. Periodic checks include:

- A review of teacher plans
- Short notes sent to the teacher
- Informal visits
- Informal review of students' work

No further action is necessary if the plan is proceeding as specified. However, you must intervene if the plan is delayed, in trouble, stalled, or inoperative. It is important to determine exactly what is happening, or not happening, and why. Interventions include:

- A conference with the teacher
- Informal observations
- Review of students' work

The information you gather from the interventions taken will guide your further actions. These include:

- The plan is proceeding in a positive way and no further action is necessary.
- Additional resources are needed and must be provided.
- A meeting with the teacher is necessary because the plan should be modified or changed, or cancelled and a new plan developed.

ASSESSING THE RESULTS WITH THE TEACHER

The criteria for assessment, specified in the growth plan, should be used to conduct the assessment when the time frame has been completed. The exact date may be modified to provide for unforeseen events such as teacher absence, snow days, district priorities, etc.

The assessment data gathered should be collaboratively reviewed with the teacher. Both you and the teacher should analyze the data and come to an agreement about the success of the collaborative growth plan. At that point, you should determine, together, if the growth objective has been successfully met through the collaborative plan. If no new immediate needs are apparent, the plan is completed. If further action is needed on the growth plan, a new or modified objective may be set. This new or modified objective must be accompanied by a specified plan.

WRITING THE REVIEW OF THE COLLABORATIVE GROWTH PLAN

Your written review of the collaborative growth plan should confirm what was discussed and agreed upon with the teacher during the meeting to assess the results. (See Figure 12-2.) Begin by stating the growth objective, and note whether it was accomplished totally, partially, or not at all. Next, list the plan specifics and whether they were implemented successfully, unsuccessfully, or not implemented. Then specify the assessment criteria, noting the degree of success. The actual time frame used should be stated. Last, state whether there is a future collaborative growth plan that has been mutually agreed upon or that no new growth plan will be conducted at this time. Both you and the teacher should sign the review. It becomes a part of the teacher's permanent record and will provide valuable information for the end-of-year assessment required by the district.

Eavesdropping on a Planning Meeting for a Collaborative Growth Plan

Figure 12-3 allows you to eavesdrop on a planning meeting for a collaborative growth plan. Determine if all of the objectives for the planning meeting discussed above have been met. Note the language used by the administrator and compare it with the language used in the planning meetings for directed and teacher-directed growth plans.

Figure 12-2
COLLABORATIVE GROWTH PLAN: REVIEW AND SUMMARY

Teacher _____ Assignment _____ Date _____

Growth Objective (accomplished totally/partially/not at all)

Plan Specifics (implemented successfully/unsuccessfully/not implemented)

Assessment Criteria (high/moderate/low success degree)

Time Frame

Future Growth Plan

_____   _____
Administrator's Signature   Teacher's Signature

Figure 12-3

EAVESDROPPING ON PLANNING MEETING FOR A COLLABORATIVE GROWTH PLAN

ADMINISTRATOR: I am delighted to have the opportunity to speak with you. I have been thinking about our collaborative growth plan.

TEACHER: I have been looking forward to this. Working collaboratively with you is a wonderful opportunity for me.

ADMINISTRATOR: As you know, I have been in your classroom several times this semester. I would like to commend you on your management and organization of the learning environment as well as your well-designed lessons. We discussed that at the conference following the overview observation.

TEACHER: Yes, I enjoyed speaking with you about your observations in my classroom.

ADMINISTRATOR: At the conference you said you had some thoughts about an area that you wished to focus on for the growth plan.

TEACHER: I have been thinking about developing cooperative learning as an instructional strategy. It adds another dimension to the instructional objectives I am currently using for these ninth graders.

ADMINISTRATOR: That is a very interesting idea. I had another one I would like to share with you. I was thinking about infusing writing into your social studies curriculum. The new state tests include writing essays in response to content questions and original documents.

TEACHER: Infusing writing into the social studies program is certainly an area in which I am interested. But I am very excited about trying cooperative learning as a way to both extend the learning strategies that I use and promote the interaction of the students.

ADMINISTRATOR: Cooperative learning is a powerful learning strategy. Perhaps we can postpone the writing objective for next time. Have you given any thought to how you will develop the plan to use cooperative learning?

TEACHER: I have some beginning ideas that I would like to explore with you and get your feedback about.

ADMINISTRATOR: That would be great.

TEACHER: I have been reading some articles about cooperative learning and I think that I understand the basic structure. I have also spoken with two teachers in the department who have had successful experiences using cooperative learning.

ADMINISTRATOR: Sounds like a wonderful start. What are your ideas?

TEACHER: I want to use cooperative learning to study how rulers in distinct cultures seek to exercise power and authority. The cultures in this unit are Ming and Qing China, Tokugawa Japan, Russia under Peter the Great, and France under Louis XIV.

ADMINISTRATOR: Do you have a particular way in which students will approach these diverse cultures?

TEACHER: I know what I want them to do in the cooperative groups and I have planned the specific lessons I will teach about each culture. Now I need some help in planning how the cooperative groups will work together to achieve these ends.

Figure 12-3 continued

ADMINISTRATOR: Let's start with how you will form the groups. Will you group them randomly or by some selection criteria?

TEACHER: I am not really sure. The two teachers I asked use different strategies. What do you think?

ADMINISTRATOR: There is research that supports grouping by ability as well as mixed groups. However, with challenging content such as this, I suggest mixed-ability groups. In that way, weaker students can be helped and supported by more able students.

TEACHER: What is the incentive for the more able students to help the less able ones?

ADMINISTRATOR: What have you read about grading the work of the cooperative groups?

TEACHER: Here again, there are differences of opinion on the subject. I wanted your point of view about giving a group grade. I mean, will that really work?

ADMINISTRATOR: Well, it supports the idea that each member of the group is responsible for the success of every other member of the group.

TEACHER: In that case, mixed-ability groups receiving a group grade really does provide an incentive for students to help each other. It certainly works well with my objective of promoting greater student interaction. Does the group grade include everything in the unit, projects as well as quizzes and tests?

ADMINISTRATOR: Yes, it includes everything that is graded in the unit. In that way, not only do students help each other with the tasks and projects to be accomplished, but they also help each other with taking notes, studying, and mastering the content.

TEACHER: Wow. I didn't realize how comprehensive this was. I really want to try mixed-ability groups but I am a little unsure about group grading.

ADMINISTRATOR: If you are really using cooperative learning, not some adaptation of the method, then both mixed-ability groups and group grading should be used. What is your concern?

TEACHER: I am worried that some of the high-achieving students may be angry if their grades are lower because of a less able or less willing student in the group. That could lead to parent complaints.

ADMINISTRATOR: You can count on my support. In addition, you are not the first teacher in the school to use this method. We have done very well with it so far. A lot depends on how the process is introduced to the students. Have I convinced you?

TEACHER: Yes, I would like to go with both ideas.

ADMINISTRATOR: Now, have you given some thought to the specific roles that the students will take within the group?

TEACHER: I was thinking about the following roles: keeper of the minutes of group meetings, resource finder, timekeeper, organizer of the work, conflict resolver. That makes five roles which match the size of the group.

ADMINISTRATOR: That sounds fine. After the first cooperative task has been completed, you will know if you have the right roles. What time frame have you selected for the unit?

Figure 12-3 continued

TEACHER:	The unit will begin on October 30 and be completed on November 17. I am providing more time than I normally would for the topic, but I want to be sure the cooperative learning tasks will work.
ADMINISTRATOR:	That sounds reasonable. How should we assess the plan?
TEACHER:	I would like the grades achieved by each individual student on quizzes, tests, and cooperative projects to be used in the review. I hope that the grades will be high because the students learned so much through this strategy. I would also like to keep a journal of student interactions, both positive and negative. I am looking for positive ways to encourage all of the students to work together.
ADMINISTRATOR:	I like your assessment plan. We should have a great deal of interesting data to discuss. What do you want me to do to help you with this plan?
TEACHER:	I would like you to introduce the purpose and the process of cooperative learning to the students. I heard you say how important that is. I would also like to invite you to see the cooperative groups in action periodically through the unit. I also know that I can come in to speak with you at any time that I may have some questions.
ADMINISTRATOR:	Let's plan the date for my introduction of cooperative learning to the class. I would like to use a whole class period so that I can have the students participate in simulations. Properly preparing the students for what they are being asked to do is very important. I want to also establish how they move their chairs both quickly and quietly into groups.
TEACHER:	I will take notes so that next time I will know how to do that.
ADMINISTRATOR:	I look forward to your invitation to watch the cooperative groups in action. That will be a real treat. And, of course, come and tell me what is going on with the plan at any time you wish.
TEACHER:	I am really excited about this plan and ready to go. Could you do the introduction on October 27 so that we will be ready to go that Monday?
ADMINISTRATOR:	Great. That's a date. Now just to be sure that we both have the same understanding about the growth plan, could you explain the growth plan to me?
TEACHER:	Sure. I will design a course of study using cooperative learning strategies around the theme of absolutism in distinct cultures. Students will be placed in groups representing diverse ability levels. The members of each group will be assigned specific roles. The work of each member of each group will be totaled to form an average grade for the group. You will introduce the concept and logistics for cooperative learning groups to the class.
ADMINISTRATOR:	I will have the growth plan in your letterbox by the end of the day. Please look it over, sign it, and give one copy to me. This is a very exciting plan. I look forward to our collaboration.

Using Teacher-Directed Growth Plans

The teacher-directed growth plan encourages the teacher to take responsibility for his or her growth and development. This teacher has the ability, confidence, and incentive to act on his or her own. The responsibility to successfully develop and complete the plan is in the hands of this teacher.

Your role in a teacher-directed growth plan is to assist the teacher in the process of thinking through his or her planned activities. You communicate with the teacher in ways that keep the teacher focused on the topic, its implications, problem identification, and problem solutions. You do not interject ideas into the discussion unless asked to do so. You provide feedback or ask questions that are intended to extend the teacher's thinking, not influence the teacher's plan. Your purpose is to help the teacher come to his or her own conclusion.

Which Teachers Will Benefit from a Teacher-Directed Growth Plan?

The data gathered to determine needs demonstrates the outstanding abilities of this teacher in all areas of the standards. It is therefore appropriate that this teacher be involved in a teacher-directed growth plan, which allows the teacher to control and direct his or her growth and development. The teacher involved must be an outstanding professional who is motivated by intrinsic incentives to improve, refine, and create for the development of self, peers, and the profession.

The topic of the growth plan is a special need or interest selected by the teacher. Some examples of topics are:

1. Developing approaches for English language learners

2. Creating approaches to instruction that will work effectively with inclusion students

3. Designing curriculum that integrates content areas

4. Using current research to identify instructional strategies that will help less successful students to be more successful

Appropriate candidates for self-directed growth plans should be selected with care because they are truly on their own. The following criteria should be considered:

- A high level of instructional knowledge and experience
- A professional attitude about teaching and a devotion to the work
- The professional ability to consider a problem from many perspectives and generate alternative solutions
- The ability to fully consider each step in the plan, follow-through, make adjustments and changes to the plan as needed, and take full responsibility for its completion
- Knowledge and expertise about the topic intended for the growth plan
- The teacher's interest in working without the guidance of the administrator

Teacher-directed growth plans are most successful with those teachers who are interested in improving themselves. For these master teachers, teaching is more than a job—it is a calling. It is the way in which they are able to mold the future.

Types of Teacher-Directed Growth Plans

There are two ways in which teachers may select to work on a teacher-directed growth plan: (1) The teacher may select to work alone, or (2) the teacher may select to work with a colleague. A discussion of each type of teacher-directed growth plan follows.

TEACHER-DIRECTED GROWTH PLAN FOR THE INDIVIDUAL

These teachers may select an individual involvement in the teacher-directed growth plan for various reasons. They may find working alone more productive. Others may find an individual teacher-directed growth plan more challenging because they will not have feedback from a peer. They may have needs or interests that are unique and not shared by other master teachers on the staff.

Teachers who become involved in teacher-directed growth plans as an individual should possess both the ability and the habit of reflecting on their practice. They should be able to analyze what they have done and the results of those actions. This is an attribute of a master teacher. Figure 13-1 provides a sample teacher-directed growth plan for the individual.

TEACHER-DIRECTED GROWTH PLAN FOR PEERS

These teachers may select a peer involvement in the teacher-directed growth plan for various reasons. They may find working together more productive than working alone. They may find working with a peer on a teacher-directed growth plan more challenging because they will have feedback from a peer. They may share mutual needs or interests.

Figure 13-1
TEACHER-DIRECTED GROWTH PLAN FOR THE INDIVIDUAL

Teacher __Peter Fletcher__   Assignment __English Grade 8__   Date __November 1, 2001__

Growth Objective (What behaviors, skills, and abilities are to be developed?)

To develop and refine the use of visual representations that enable students to better understand content, concepts, relationships, and results.

Specific Activities (How will the behavior, skills, and abilities be developed?)

1. The teacher will review written materials and the latest research about using nonverbal representations, such as graphic and advance organizers, as a means of enhancing instruction and student achievement.
2. The teacher will design graphic and advance organizers for the unit on the novel *Lord of the Flies* by Golding.
3. The organizers that will be developed include: topic and related facts, time sequence patterns, cause-and-effect patterns, episode and persons patterns, principles and examples patterns.
4. Students will use organizers throughout the unit individually and in groups representing diverse ability levels.
5. Students will use the organizers for notetaking.
6. Students will use organizers in completing homework assignments.
7. Students will use organizers as sources for writing assignments.
8. Student groups will use organizers to complete projects.
9. Students will use organizers as information references for studying for tests.
10. The teacher will introduce the use of organizers in general to the class.
11. Each new organizer will be explained and discussed as it is used in the unit.

Time Frame (When will the plan be completed?)

The unit will begin on November 8 and be completed by December 6.

Assessment Criteria (How will the plan be assessed?)

- A series of short quizzes, homework assignments, assigned essays, and a final examination will be used to assess students' mastery of the unit.
- The level of achievement demonstrated by the students will be used in assessing the success of the growth plan.
- Projects completed by student groups will be reviewed to determine how organizers contributed to students' understanding and application of the concepts.
- Samples of students' completed organizers will be reviewed as a part of the assessment.

_____   _____
Administrator's Signature   Teacher's Signature

Whether the teacher elects to become involved individually or with a peer in a teacher-directed growth plan is an individual decision. However, when peers express a desire to work together, be sure they are well suited to the task. In general, teachers who do not get along well for whatever reasons should not be paired. The result of such a union may be increased hostility. On the other hand, teachers who are close personal friends should also not be paired for teacher-directed growth plans. Close friends may have problems providing each other with constructive criticism. If no constructive criticism takes place, little professional growth can take place. The best peer grouping for this growth plan is between teachers who have a positive professional relationship. The teachers should have mutual respect for and appreciation of each other's work.

The following factors should be given careful consideration:

- The teachers' abilities to observe, analyze, and share constructive suggestions with a peer
- The teachers' desire to work with a peer in this type of relationship
- The teachers' mutual interest in the identified area

Teachers working in a teacher-directed growth plan for peers should possess, or be interested in developing, observation and analysis skills. They should possess the ability to analyze what they do as well as what they see others do. Indeed, this is another indicator of master teachers. Figure 13-2 provides a sample teacher-directed growth plan for peers.

Constructing a Teacher-Directed Growth Plan

THE PLANNING MEETING

The same objectives should be accomplished in the planning meetings for the individual or peers in teacher-directed growth plans. Be sure all the objectives have been accomplished before the meeting is concluded.

The objectives to be accomplished during the planning meeting are to:

- Identify the growth objective.
- Outline the activities for achieving the objective.
- Determine the time frame.
- Specify the assessment criteria.
- State how the results will be reported to the administrator.

Identify the growth objective.   The growth objective is identified by the individual teacher or the peers. The idea for the growth objective may come from any source. It may come from a felt need, interest, or new idea that has been suggested as a result of reading professional journals or articles on current research or attending a conference.

Figure 13-2

TEACHER-DIRECTED GROWTH PLAN FOR PEERS

Teachers __Maria Polaris__   Assignment __Grade 5__   Date __November 1, 2001__

__Esta Homes__   __Grade 5__

Growth Objective (What behaviors, skills, and abilities are to be developed?)

To develop and refine an interdisciplinary unit that includes: science, geography, mathematics, language arts, and social studies.

Specific Activities (How will the behavior, skills, and abilities be developed?)

1. The teachers will review written materials and the latest research about developing interdisciplinary units.

2. The teachers will plan an interdisciplinary unit based on the social studies topic: Regions of the United States.

3. Students will use the theme of Regions of the United States to work on standards in each content area.

4. The interdisciplinary unit will include a study of: climate, products, map study, novels about various regions, essays, graphs, charts, calculations, and problem solving.

5. Students will work individually and in pairs and small groups.

6. Student products include: classwork, homework, essays, group projects, quizzes, and tests.

7. Resources include: textbooks, information from appropriate web sites, videos, maps, charts, novels, and teacher-created materials.

8. The teachers will combine their classes to introduce the interdisciplinary unit. Classes may also be combined for viewing videos and sharing projects.

Time Frame (When will the plan be completed?)

The unit will begin on November 8 and be completed by December 6.

Assessment Criteria (How will the plan be assessed?)

• A series of short quizzes, homework assignments, class assignment, small-group projects, assigned essays, oral presentations, and a final examination will be used to assess students' mastery of the unit.

• The level of achievement demonstrated by the students will be used in assessing the success of the growth plan.

• Samples of students' completed work will be reviewed as a part of the assessment.

• The principal will be invited to hear the oral presentations.

_____
Administrator's Signature

_____
Teacher's Signature

_____
Teacher's Signature

Outline the activities for achieving the objective.   Once the growth objective has been selected, a plan of activities is discussed in detail. The teacher(s) who identified the objective may have also designed a plan for its achievement. The plan is then reviewed with you and specific details are worked out. You assist the teacher(s) in thinking through all of the aspects of the planned activities by asking questions to clarify or explore points that have not been included in the teacher(s)'s discussion. You do not contribute ideas, no matter how wonderful they may be, unless asked to do so by the teacher(s). The teacher(s) design the plan and make all the decisions about how the activities will be conducted. You may help peers reach conclusions about differences of opinion. You may also provide needed support in time and resources that may be requested by the teacher(s).

Determine the time frame.   The teacher(s) select a time frame for the completion of the growth plan. The time frame selected may well be an estimate, so it is used flexibly. But the establishment of a time frame sets an expectation for the teacher(s) and gives you a guideline as to when results should be expected. When the time frame is changed, you should be notified so that modifications to the plan can be made.

Specify the assessment criteria.   The assessment criteria selected should match the growth objective and the plan. Usually, the criteria selected are the results expected from the successful completion of the plan. The teacher(s) should determine which assessment criteria are most suitable. Some examples of assessment criteria include:

- Observation of student actions
- Review of student products
- Review of a teacher product
- Teacher demonstration

State how the results will be reported.   The results are always presented to you within the established time frame. It is also a good idea to share the results with other professionals on staff. Teachers in teacher-directed growth plans may be asked to demonstrate for other teachers, conduct a discussion, or present at a staff-development session.

MONITORING THE PROGRESS OF THE PLAN

The teacher(s) should be allowed to work on the plan without intervention. Monitoring efforts are best accomplished by encouraging the teacher(s) and confirming your continued interest and confidence in the efforts being made. Assess progress informally by asking how things are going and making yourself available when solicited. A review of the teacher(s)'s plans and informal visits will keep you informed about the progress of the growth plans.

JOINT ASSESSMENT OF RESULTS

The results of the teacher-directed growth plan should be presented to you within the designated time frame. Schedule a meeting to jointly review the results at the end of the time frame if the teacher(s) have not done so.

At the assessment meeting, the teacher(s) present the results in the form specified in the plan. You and the teacher(s) jointly analyze the results and reach a mutual conclusion about the level of success that has been achieved. The decision to conclude or continue the growth plan is jointly decided. When the teacher(s) wish to continue to work on the plan to further improve it, the original plan specification should be reviewed to determine if it is still appropriate and needs only to have the time fame altered. If the original plan specification is no longer appropriate, the teacher(s) should determine how it should be modified or rewritten.

WRITING THE REVIEW OF A TEACHER-DIRECTED GROWTH PLAN

Your written review of the teacher-directed growth plan should record what was discussed at the plan review meeting. (See Figure 13-3.) Record the conclusion jointly reached about whether the growth objective has been accomplished totally, partially, or not at all. Record the conclusion jointly reached about the degree to which the plan specifics were followed and achieved: successfully, unsuccessfully, or not implemented. Record the conclusion jointly reached about the degree of success evidenced in the assessment criteria. The actual time frame used should be recorded. Last, detail the decision reached to continue the growth plan, alter the plan specification, or conclude the plan.

Eavesdropping on Planning Meetings for Teacher-Directed Growth Plans

Figure 13-4 allows you to eavesdrop on a planning meeting for a teacher-directed growth plan for the individual. Figure 13-5 allows you to eavesdrop on a planning meeting for a teacher-directed growth plan for peers. Determine if all of the objectives for the planning meeting discussed above have been met. Note the language used by the administrator and compare it with the language used in the planning meetings for directed and collaborative growth plans.

Figure 13-3
TEACHER-DIRECTED GROWTH PLAN: REVIEW AND SUMMARY

Teacher (s) _____ Assignment _____ Date _____

_____ _____

Growth Objective (accomplished totally/partially/not at all)

Plan Specifics (implemented successfully/unsuccessfully/not implemented)

Assessment Criteria (high/moderate/low success degree)

Time Frame

Future Growth Plan

_____ _____
Administrator's Signature   Teacher's Signature

Figure 13-4

EAVESDROPPING ON A PLANNING MEETING FOR A TEACHER-DIRECTED GROWTH PLAN FOR AN INDIVIDUAL

ADMINISTRATOR: I have been looking forward to this meeting and hearing about your ideas for a growth plan.

TEACHER: I have been thinking about this for some time and now I am ready to share my ideas with you.

ADMINISTRATOR: Go on.

TEACHER: I have been very impressed by the research about how student learning can be enhanced through using visual representations. It makes so much sense. You know we spend so much time talking to students and telling them things. But showing them how that information looks when it is organized visually can really help them to understand the material.

ADMINISTRATOR: Seeing ideas visually represented is helpful for everyone.

TEACHER: Yes, and that is what my plan is about. I am in the process of developing visual representations that students can complete and then use to understand the content, concepts, relationships, and results of what they are learning. I am going to use the novel *Lord of the Flies* for my first attempt. I will teach this novel through visual representations.

ADMINISTRATOR: Help me to understand what you mean when you say visual representations.

TEACHER: What I mean are a series of graphic and advance organizers that will visually represent each of the major concepts that I am using to work on the standards.

ADMINISTRATOR: Tell me more about your plans.

TEACHER: I am in the process of developing graphic and advance organizers that will help students to visually understand: relationships, time-sequence patterns, cause-and-effect patterns, how episodes and persons fit together, and the relationships between principles and patterns.

ADMINISTRATOR: How will you use the organizers?

TEACHER: I intend to introduce each organizer just before it is used. The construction of the organizer will guide the students to focus their attention on gathering and recording the information on the organizer.

ADMINISTRATOR: *(Nods head and smiles.)*

TEACHER: Besides contributing to the gathering and organizing of information, the organizers will also be used to extend students' understanding.

ADMINISTRATOR: So you also plan to use the organizers to extend students' understanding.

TEACHER: Yes. The organizers will be used for several related activities. For example, three student essays will be assigned. The information recorded on the organizers will be essential to writing the essays. In addition, there will be three group projects. Each

Figure 13-4 continued

project will require the use of the information recorded on the organizers. One last piece. The organizers will be used to complete homework assignments and as study notes for the end-of-unit exam.

ADMINISTRATOR: It sounds like you have an exciting plan. What time frame have you selected for this plan?

TEACHER: I will begin the introduction on November 8 and I plan to complete the last activity by December 6.

ADMINISTRATOR: What assessment criteria of the plan are you considering?

TEACHER: Here is what I am planning to review with you. First, the grades students receive on quizzes, homework assignments, essays, and the final. I would like to see if using organizers have helped students to be successful. Second, the projects completed by student groups. Again, I am looking for how organizers contributed to students' understanding and application of the concepts. Last, I would like to review some samples of completed student organizers so we can determine the quality of the students' work.

ADMINISTRATOR: The plan is very clear to me. Let's just check my perception. Here is what I heard. You will design graphic and advance organizers for the unit on the novel *Lord of the Flies* by Golding. The organizers that will be developed include: topic and related facts, time-sequence patterns, cause-and-effect patterns, episode and persons patterns, principles and examples patterns. Students will use organizers throughout the unit individually and in groups representing diverse ability levels. Students will use the organizers for notetaking, in completing homework assignments, as sources of information for writing assignments, to complete projects, and as references for studying for tests. You will introduce the use of organizers in general to the class and each new organizer will be explained and discussed as it is used in the unit.

TEACHER: I think you got it all.

ADMINISTRATOR: Is there any role you would like me to play?

TEACHER: Not really. I would like to try this out on my own. I will be making changes and adjustments as I go along to be sure that the organizers are clear, usable, and effective. You will be able to see exactly what I am doing when you review my plans.

ADMINISTRATOR: I will have this growth plan written up and in your letterbox by tomorrow. Please review the plan, sign it if you agree, and return one copy to me.

TEACHER: Fine. I will do that.

ADMINISTRATOR: This plan has tremendous implications for improving instruction. Perhaps after the plan is completed, and we have reviewed the results, you might consider conducting a professional development session on the subject.

TEACHER: That is an idea that I will keep in mind. I first want to see how it works.

ADMINISTRATOR: Fine. I look forward to reviewing the results with you.

Figure 13-5

EAVESDROPPING ON A PLANNING MEETING FOR A TEACHER-DIRECTED GROWTH PLAN FOR PEERS

PRINCIPAL: Well, here you are. I have been most anxious to speak with you about your ideas for a peer growth plan.

TEACHER 1:   We are also excited about our plan.

TEACHER 2:   We have been working on this for a long time and now we think we have it ready to share with you.

PRINCIPAL: I am ready to listen to your ideas.

TEACHER 1:   We want to develop and teach an interdisciplinary unit that will encompass five content areas. As a matter of fact, the unit will drive all of our plans for the month.

PRINCIPAL: So you are saying that your total curriculum and instructional plans for the month will be devoted to teaching this interdisciplinary unit.

TEACHER 2:   Yes, that's right. The unit will encompass the five content areas of social studies, geography, science, mathematics, and language arts. Each content area will be specified according to the standards that will be taught.

TEACHER 1:   Of course, we have a theme that will drive the interdisciplinary unit.

TEACHER 2:   That's right. We want students to be able to make connections. In life, everything is connected. It is only in school that we separate content for the purposes of teaching. Now we want to show students how everything connects.

PRINCIPAL: Uh huh. I see your point. Tell me more.

TEACHER 1:   The theme that we have selected, Regions of the United States, is taken directly from the social studies curriculum. We have been working on integrating science, geography, mathematics, and language arts with that social studies content.

TEACHER 2:   The more we worked on the idea, the more sensible it became. For example, if students are learning about regions of the United States, they should be reading novels that are set in different regions of the United States to help them understand how the people live.

TEACHER 1:   And, they should be writing about those regions and the people in the novels who live there.

TEACHER 2:   Similarly, if students are learning about regions of the United States, they should be learning about related science concepts such as climate and rock formations.

TEACHER 1:   Geography and map reading become important to understanding where the regions are and provide the students with a visual understanding of their locations.

TEACHER 2:   Mathematics became another way to tie in the study of the regions as we realized that students could compute mathematical equations based on numerical values that came out of the novels, the study of climate, and so forth. In addition, we could write problems related to the information.

TEACHER 1:   The problems could be of two types. There could be mathematical problems related to the information. But there could also be problems to discuss related to the study of the regions, the problems of the characters in the novel, or regional problems that are in the news.

Figure 13-5 continued

PRINCIPAL: Have you designed your instructional strategies?

TEACHER 2: We are planning a range of diversified instructional strategies. They will include lessons that we have developed as well as paired learnings for reflection and small-group projects.

TEACHER 1: We also have writing assignments and oral presentations, such as a debate about which is the best region of the country.

TEACHER 2: Of course, we have also prepared short quizzes to monitor student understanding as well as a longer examination in the format of the state test. In addition, homework assignments and classwork assignments will be required.

PRINCIPAL: Have you located the resources that you need?

TEACHER 1: Pretty much so. There are two videos on order that we have not yet received. The trip we are planning to the museum is awaiting district approval.

PRINCIPAL: Call on me if you need help. Have you thought about how you could collaborate in the classroom?

TEACHER 2: We have decided to bring the two classes together for the first introduction to the interdisciplinary plan. We thought it would be useful for the two of us to do that presentation together. There are certain activities that we may also conduct together, such as viewing the videos and taking the trip.

TEACHER 1: We are considering having the group projects presented to the two classes.

PRINCIPAL: What do you see as the advantages?

TEACHER 1: Well, we thought that if both classes were working on the same unit at the same time, it might be interesting to see what each produced.

PRINCIPAL: Are there any disadvantages?

TEACHER 2: Space may be a problem and so we thought we would reserve the multipurpose room for that activity.

TEACHER 1: Another problem could be the amount of time required for the groups in two classes to present. We worked that out by deciding that the presentation would be conducted over the course of a week using one hour a day. We have also prepared a format for a listening and reflection guide so that students have a specific task to complete and hand in as they listen to the presentations. The guides are not finalized because we want to involve the students in developing some of the specifics of what to look for and think about as student groups present.

PRINCIPAL: I know you said you will use a month for this interdisciplinary unit. What is your time frame?

TEACHER 2: We plan to begin on November 8 and end by December 6. The sharing of group projects may continue past that date. We are not sure how much time will be needed.

PRINCIPAL: *(Nods head and smiles.)* What assessment criteria will you review with me?

TEACHER 1: We plan to review all of the work produced. It is probably more than you want to see but we plan to show you selected samples of the best and poorest work submitted.

Figure 13-5 continued

TEACHER 2: That will include classwork, homework, quizzes, essays, the group projects, and the final exam. The only piece that is missing are the oral presentations.

TEACHER 1: We could invite you to see the oral presentations. Then you would have a comprehensive overview of the unit for our review.

PRINCIPAL: That would be great. Is there anything you would like me to do to assist your efforts?

TEACHER 2: Not that I can think of at this time. You will be able to see what we are doing when you review our jointly developed plans. If we get into trouble, we will come asking for help. What do you think, Maria?

TEACHER 1: The only thing I can think of is help with getting the videos and permission for the trip if there is a problem.

PRINCIPAL: Now, just to be sure we are on the same page, here is my understanding of your peer growth plan. You will work together to plan an interdisciplinary unit based on the social studies topic Regions of the United States. Students will work on standards in each of the content areas of language arts, social studies, science, and mathematics using the theme Regions of the United States. The interdisciplinary unit will include a study of: climate, products, map study, novels about various regions, essays, graphs, charts, calculations, and problem solving. Students will work individually and in pairs and small groups. Student products include classwork, homework, essays, group projects, quizzes, and tests. Resources include textbooks, information from appropriate web sites, videos, maps, charts, novels, and teacher-created materials. You will combine your classes to introduce the interdisciplinary unit. Classes may also be combined for viewing videos and sharing projects. The unit will begin on November 8 and be completed by December 6. I have a list of the assessment criteria. Do I have it right?

TEACHER 1: Yes, you do.

TEACHER 2: I agree. You really are a good listener.

PRINCIPAL: That's because I am really interested in your growth plan. I will have a copy of the growth plan in your letterboxes by tomorrow morning. Please read it over and, if you both agree, please sign one copy and return it to me.

TEACHER 1: Could you please give each of us a copy for our reference?

PRINCIPAL: Of course. Well, then, you are on your way to an exciting effort. After the review, let's consider a joint presentation for a professional development session.

TEACHER 2: Okay, we will keep that in mind.

PRINCIPAL: Thank you.

Building a Learning Community for Student Achievement

Growth plans target the development of effective teachers and the building of a learning community that can support, extend, and enhance these efforts. When teachers form communities to learn and grow professionally, the total impact on student achievement is greater than the sum of the parts. Each teacher's engagement in the discussion, to advance individual knowledge and understanding of actions and events, contributes to a collective that adds to the knowledge and understanding of the learning community.

How Professionals Learn

There are at least four factors that contribute to professional learning. These are reflecting on practice, personal inquiry, collaborating, and supporting.

REFLECTING ON PRACTICE

Reflecting on practice is an essential activity for professional learning. The experience we had is not so important to growth as the reflection on that experience. In this process, teachers wonder about their practice and ask themselves such questions as "Do I really know if the students understand the concept I taught?" "Did I provide enough time for the students to interact?" "Did I allow the students to construct their own understanding for the event?" This reflective practice leads to self-assessment of areas in need of growth.

Some teachers engage in reflection as a natural outgrowth of their teaching. However, many do not. This critical activity can be included as a part of the observation cycle. It can also become a planned activity of a learning community.

PERSONAL INQUIRY

Teaching is a complex act and few teachers are experts at all aspects. Teachers know the areas in which they are more as well as less capable. As professionals, teachers wish to improve all the areas of their practice. When teachers feel safe and respected, they will choose to work on areas in which they have needs. Selecting one's own growth objectives generally leads to greater enthusiasm and energy for the work than when someone else has chosen for you. The collaborative and teacher-directed growth plans become excellent vehicles for fulfilling these needs. Sharing needs and ideas for growth can also become an important activity of a learning community.

COLLABORATING

As important as reflection on practice is, it is twice as effective when shared with others. Teacher isolation and the demands of teaching provide few opportunities for teachers to explore problems, hear different perspectives, and share new ideas with other teachers. These professional conversations that are characteristics of learning communities contribute immeasurably to teacher growth as wisdom about practice is shared.

SUPPORTING

Few people can sustain enthusiasm, confidence, and effort in isolation. Everyone needs to be supported and encouraged. This is especially true of the stressful and exhausting work of professional teachers. A learning community provides teachers with colleagues who will listen and respond to their concerns, celebrate their efforts and successes, and foster each other's development as professionals of the highest caliber.

How to Build a Learning Community

Learning communities do not happen by themselves. Their development requires effort and sustained support. The first step in building a learning community is not convincing teachers that it is a good idea—teachers will jump at the chance. Rather, it is convincing teachers of your sustained support. The second step is providing varied opportunities for teachers to become an active part of a learning community.

SUSTAINED SUPPORT

Providing the sustained support for learning communities to thrive requires resources sometimes achieved through creative use of funds.

Time to meet.   A learning community must have a regularly scheduled time to meet free from assigned duties. Teachers may select to meet during the lunch hour or before or after school. Some learning communities consider their work so important that they meet in the evening or on weekends. Providing time during the regular school day for these meetings demonstrates not only your support, but also your belief in the importance of their work. The teachers will positively receive any time that can be given to the work of the learning community. For example, release teachers whenever possible from administrative assignments such as hall duty. Encourage teachers to use professional periods as a time to meet. Use grade, department, and/or faculty meeting time for learning community activities. Section 20 presents eight low-cost meeting strategies.

Substitute teachers. The learning community may be given the opportunity to watch each other teach, search for resources, or meet with a colleague when their teaching assignment is covered by a substitute teacher.

Professional meetings. Finding ways to send members of the learning community to professional meetings contributes to the scope and depth of the knowledge they share.

Professional materials. Allocating funds to the purchase of professional materials allows the members of the learning community to continually grow as life-long learners.

PROVIDE VARIED OPPORTUNITIES FOR LEARNING COMMUNITIES TO DEVELOP

Although there are many different ways to organize learning communities, they are all focused on professional growth. A discussion of some popular formats for learning communities follows.

Organize study teams. Study teams provide the opportunity for teachers with similar interests and concerns to form a learning community. They work together to improve instruction that results in student achievement. See Section 21 for an in-depth discussion of study teams.

Establish open sharing groups. The professional activities of reflecting on practice and personal inquiry about needs, discussed above, become the topics of discussion of open sharing groups. This opportunity to collaborate with colleagues provides a means for teachers to resolve problems and gain new ideas and perspectives on issues as they listen and share in the group.

Develop book talks. Reading an article in a professional journal or a book on a professional topic is informative but rarely influences classroom practice. Book talks provide teachers with the opportunity to talk about the ideas expressed with others who will understand. Spouses, unless they are in the profession, usually are not interested. The support and enthusiasm of colleagues, who agree to try some of the ideas and share the results, may well lead to changes in classroom practice.

Grant professional-growth option days.   Treating teachers as professionals can reap large rewards. Provide each teacher with one day each year as a professional-growth option. Rather than taking a sick day for renewal, participating in a professional activity may provide the needed change of pace. The professional-growth option is the teacher's choice, or it may be an area of interest that the learning community is exploring. Options include any appropriate professional activity such as visiting another program, searching for resources, developing curriculum, or exploring sites of interest for class visits.

Teachers who wish to use their professional-growth option day should complete an application. (See Figure 14-1.) The process of completing the application helps the teacher to clarify both the purpose of the activity and how it will be used. The application provides you with the information about how the professional day will be used. Although you should question any application that is unclear or appears inappropriate, make it easy and pleasant to use the professional-growth option. At times when you are unsure about the professional nature of the activity, focus on how it will be used by the teacher and the learning community.

Create project-development communities.   Nothing is more motivating to teachers than respecting their commitment and creativity by giving them the opportunity to work on a project that is their felt need. The project should make an important contribution to the instructional effectiveness of the grade or the department. Here are some examples:

• Writing a curriculum to implement a new course of study.

• Infusing instructional strategies into an existing curriculum that teach students skills they will need on state examinations, such as how to respond to data-based questions or how to develop listening skills.

When a group of teachers express this kind of need, work with them to create a project-development community.

The project-development community should develop a detailed outline of the work they are undertaking. They may wish to circulate the outline to other teachers for their input and feedback. Be sure to review the detailed outline and the completed work of the community before it is shared with other teachers.

When released time for project-development work is not available, the project-development community generally meets outside of the school day to complete the project. They should be compensated. If funds are available, provide a stipend, or give the project-development community inservice credit.

See Figure 14-2 for a summary of the varied opportunities for the development of learning communities.

Figure 14-1

PROFESSIONAL-GROWTH OPTION DAY:
Application

*Please complete this application and give it to the principal
at least two weeks before the planned option day.*

Teacher _____ Assignment _____ Date _____

What professional activity will you conduct on your option day?

Why are you interested in this activity?

Where will you conduct the activity?

How, when, and with whom will you share the information you gather?

What date have you selected for the option day? *(Please notify the Assistant Principal.)*

Activity approved _____ Date _____

Please see me _____ Date _____

Figure 14-2

OPPORTUNITIES FOR THE DEVELOPMENT OF LEARNING COMMUNITIES

STUDY TEAMS

Teachers with similar interests and concerns work together to improve instruction that results in student achievement.

OPEN SHARING GROUPS

The professional activities of reflecting on practice and personal inquiry about needs become the topics of discussion as teachers collaborate in open sharing groups.

BOOK TALKS

Teachers talk with colleagues about the ideas expressed in books or articles that they have read as a means of improving classroom practice.

PROFESSIONAL-GROWTH OPTION DAYS

Teachers are provided with the opportunity to spend a day exploring a professional activity of their choice. Teachers who wish to use their professional-growth option day should complete an application that helps them to clarify both the purpose of the activity and how it will be used.

PROJECT-DEVELOPMENT COMMUNITIES

Teachers are given the opportunity to work on a project that is their felt need. The project should make an important contribution to the instructional effectiveness of the grade or the department. The project-development community should develop a detailed outline of the work they are undertaking. They should be compensated with a stipend or inservice credit.

Checking the Pulse of the Learning Community

In order for learning communities to be effective, teachers must feel safe, conduct themselves professionally, and be respected. That means teachers are free to express themselves and their ideas in a safe and confidential environment. It also means that teachers respect the professional community, the students, and the school community. Negative comments and put-downs are not tolerated.

When learning communities are respected, they are trusted to do professional work in a professional manner. In other words, the teachers in the community are talking about teaching and learning—*not* football scores, recipes, the latest gossip, or their children.

The work of the learning community, as a professional activity, is open to administrators. There are three reasons to attend or drop in on a meeting. First, to actively participate on equal terms as a professional educator. You may have read the book that the book talk group is discussing and be interested in hearing their opinions. Second, to take the pulse of the community to confirm that it is a safe and respectful environment. Third, to demonstrate your support of their efforts and interest in their work.

Understanding Your Role in Student Success

Change is almost always difficult, but change without explanation and clarification is traumatic. Before you attempt to implement a program of individualized growth plans that match data-determined needs, take the time to introduce and discuss the overall program with the staff. Explain what a growth plan program is, how it will work, and how it will be of value to them. Involve the teachers by providing the opportunity for them to express their feelings and explore their concerns. Then motivate and encourage teacher efforts throughout the growth plan process by being generous with your time, resources, and instructional support.

How to Introduce Individualized Growth Plans to the Faculty

Growth plans are most successfully implemented when they are both understood and accepted by the staff. Teachers must clearly understand how the growth plans will impact on them. They must believe that working on their growth will help rather than harm them. Their trust and confidence in you, based on past experience, will contribute to their acceptance of your program for instructional improvement. Their final acceptance, however, will come only after they have actually experienced the growth plan process and discovered that not only were they not harmed, but, rather, they were supported and assisted.

WHERE AND WHEN TO PRESENT THE PLANS

Gaining staff understanding and acceptance of a growth plan program based on individual needs begins with a full faculty introduction. The meeting used to present the rationale and concepts behind such plans should be carefully thought out. If possible, present your ideas at a time when no other matter of urgent need must be discussed. Growth plans, based on individualized needs, should be the major agenda item.

Faculty conferences may be used for this purpose. Since all members of the faculty will be present, this conference provides the opportunity to address all the factors at the same time. This gives you the advantage of a uniform presentation. In addition, the entire faculty will benefit from hearing the ideas, concerns, and questions expressed by their colleagues at the meeting.

Too often, however, large-group presentations can discourage open discussion. This disadvantage may be overcome by two strategies.

1. Plan a general introduction, followed by small discussion groups that then reassemble to share what was discussed in the small groups. Summarize the statements of the small groups with appropriate responses. Provide a closure that emphasizes the objective of the meeting.

2. Present the topic a second time during grade or department meetings.

The security of speaking in smaller groups will encourage some teachers to express their feelings, fears, and questions. In addition, a second presentation at a grade or department meeting provides another opportunity for teachers to hear the information and become familiar with the growth plans.

When teacher concerns and acceptance are a problem, the topic may be addressed at workshop sessions before or after school hours, during the lunch hour, or during staff-development programs. These additional sessions may be important to clarify the process and its implications for individual teachers.

WHAT TO EXPLAIN

Target your explanation at promoting the understanding that rather than lump all teachers into the same general category, in which they are all treated the same, being considered as an individual recognizes the skill level of each teacher. The following clarifications may prove helpful at presentation sessions:

1. **The growth plans are unique to each individual teacher.** The degree of help needed by each teacher is different. Those who need more assistance, such as new teachers, will be provided personalized help. Other teachers who require little or no help will have the opportunity to design and direct their efforts in areas in which they are interested.

2. **The growth objectives seek to be meaningful and effective.** Each teacher is involved in working on objectives that represent skill interests or needs expressed by the individual teacher and/or the administrator.

3. **The growth plans respect the professional skills of teachers.** The plans are designed to recognize the successful accomplishment levels of experienced teachers. Various data are gathered to confirm teaching skills that have been mastered and to identify areas of need.

4. **The growth plans provide for involvement of teachers in the selection of objectives.** The growth plans provide for a wide range of involvement by the professional staff. These range from total control of the objective and the plan (as in teacher-directed plans for the individual or peers), to involvement in the selection of the objective (as in collaborative plans), to assisted selection of objective (as in directed plans). This variety results in a plan appropriate for the needs and interests of each teacher.

How Growth Plans Contribute to Student Achievement

The use of personalized growth plans based on the data-determined needs of each teacher focuses your time and effort on the improvement of instruction for student achievement. As the needs of the individual teacher are clarified and the plan is selected and implemented, your level and degree of involvement becomes clear. You then know how much of your time and effort will be required to make each improvement effort effective and you can, therefore, allocate your time efficiently and effectively.

MAKE TIME YOUR ALLY

Using differentiated growth plans enables you to maximize the use of your time as you plan when to involve teachers in appropriate growth plans. You can economize time by controlling the number of directed growth plans you are involved with at the same time. This will give you the time to be involved with collaborative growth plans. You will also be able to initiate teacher-directed growth plans for individuals or peers who operate mostly on their own.

MOTIVATE TEACHERS

The use of diversified growth plans is a professional involvement that motivates teachers. Their accomplishments are recognized and they learn how to resolve their problems, which builds self-respect and confidence. Nothing is a greater motivator than success. It inspires teachers to seek continued growth.

Consider keeping the momentum going through praise and recognition. Each teacher's efforts should be recognized. A letter and/or a public announcement of efforts and accomplishments can result in tangible rewards of further accomplishments. The greatest result of your recognition efforts will be the motivation of the teachers to continue to grow.

Working Colleague to Colleague

You are the instructional leader and the principal teacher in the school. Your background and experience provide valuable direction for teachers' efforts.

GIVING IN-CLASS INSTRUCTIONAL SUPPORT

You provide the teacher with a valuable model to copy when you actually teach a lesson. One demonstration is worth ten thousand words. Do not hesitate to go into the classroom to show the teacher exactly what you are talking about by doing it.

You will gain tremendous respect by teaching a lesson even though you are admittedly putting yourself on the spot. Yes, you are at a disadvantage. You do not necessarily know every student and you may not be familiar with the topic. However, you can select a different topic, one suited to your area of expertise, for a demonstration of an instructional strategy. Your position as administrator will easily overcome any difficulties that might be anticipated by your lack of knowledge of the students. If you prefer to call on students by name, ask the teacher to have each student prepare a visible name card before you enter the classroom.

In-class coaching is another way to provide in-class support. The one model lesson may not be sufficient to help the teacher master the instructional strategy. Spending time in the classroom as a coach, helping the teacher thoroughly understand the technique or strategy, is usually very effective. If you cannot spend the time needed, or if you do not feel comfortable with the specific skills, arrange to provide a coach who does have the time and the skills. Coaches may be found among other teachers on the staff who can be released or among district office personnel. (See Section 21 for a discussion of coaching.)

Study teams provide a third effective in-class support system. Peer teachers in the school may work together to demonstrate specific areas of expertise for each other. This colleague-to-colleague assistance is a most effective way to help teachers learn instructional strategies. This system may be incorporated into the growth plan. (See Section 21 for a discussion of study teams.)

GIVING OUT-OF-CLASS INSTRUCTIONAL SUPPORT

Inservice or staff-development programs are out-of-class instructional support efforts that usually suffer from the "too much, too fast" effect. Although many of these efforts are well intended and even well designed, they often fail. Teachers cannot be expected to understand, digest, and implement new ideas or strategies after one or even two large-group presentations. These efforts provide only for teacher exposure to the idea, skill, or strategy. Exposure is very different from effective application, which requires practice and feedback to the teacher. (See sections 20 and 21 for a discussion of professional development.)

University coursework is usually a good means of providing out-of-class instructional support when the material presented is practical and if the professor also provides a means for the teachers to try the practices discussed and present their experiences. Actual in-class application is necessary to ensure the teacher's appropriate use of the strategy or technique.

Professional publications are an excellent source of out-of-class instructional support. Professionals should continually strive to be current by seeking information about their practice. Every teacher should have access to professional publications either because they subscribe to them, or because they are available in the professional library of their school. (See Section 14 for a discussion of learning communities.)

Obtaining Evaluation of Your Administrative Effectiveness

Everybody needs feedback to truly evaluate his or her effectiveness. Administrators are no exception. Do you want to know how the instructional staff views you and your involvement with them? Are you interested in the responses of the noninstructional members of the staff? Then ask them to assess your effectiveness. Are you very brave? Then ask members of the Parent Association and/or the School Leadership Team to also complete the assessment. If you are serious about your efforts and how you are perceived, these ratings will provide valuable information.

ASSESSMENT CRITERIA

Your position is more than a job, a role, a profession—it is a total involvement in the lives, feelings, actions, and efforts of the school population and community. Being an administrator today requires a delicate balance between leadership and collaboration.

A school administrator is a:

- Visionary of what could be, should be, and will be
- Constant supporter of the vision in words and actions
- Resource and a source for resources
- Guide who leads with the counsel and support of others
- Comrade who shares success, failure, joy, and despair

That is why it is so very difficult to reduce the role of the school administrator to a list of items. However, Figure 15-1 on pages 193–194 presents a suggested list of categorized items by which your leadership may be assessed. It is an attempt to capture most of the areas that are considered important and used in many district evaluations. The items are grouped into seven categories of responsibility: instructional leadership, organizational leadership, staff development, student support services, communication, community relations, and personal character.

Instructional leadership.   This category concerns itself with all your plans and actions in leading the instructional program. It includes how you plan, implement, monitor and evaluate the instructional program, and ensure that it is aligned with the vision. How the curriculum and instructional programs focus on meeting established standards, use technology, and consider emerging trends are also considered. A culture of high expectations and eliminating barriers to student learning are other aspects of instructional leadership that are assessed. The creation of a supportive learning environment in which all individuals are treated with fairness and dignity, with consideration of their diversified needs, and use of conflict-resolution and problem-solving skills are the last elements in this category.

Organizational leadership.   This second category deals with the management role. It asks if you manage human resources by utilizing staff effectively, and employ an effective administrative monitoring system. Your management of the daily operation of the school in a manner that maximizes learning and uses time effectively, as well as your management of finances and resources both within the budget and those secured from outside sources, are also considered. Interpersonal relations are concerned with the timely and appropriate manner in which problems are addressed and resolved and the inclusion of all stakeholders in the decision-making process.

Staff development.   This third category is concerned with how you provide for the effective growth of the staff. The staff-development program is assessed for how it promotes a focus on student learning consistent with the vision. Also considered is how the supervisory program meets the needs and directs the growth of the staff.

Student support services.   The fourth category deals with how you manage pupil personnel services. Opportunities for curricular, cocurricular, and extracurricular programs are considered. The area of pupil personnel programs and how you ensure confidentiality and meet the needs of students and their families are assessed.

Communication.   The fifth category is directed at communication with staff, parents, family, and students. Constant and effective communication with the entire school community, parents, students, and the community are considered.

Community relations.   The sixth category is concerned with the maintenance of district and community relations. Your visibility, active involvement, and communication with the larger community are considered. What you have done to develop relationships with community leaders and your program of community relations are assessed.

Personal character.   This seventh category relates to the ethical manner, integrity, and fairness with which your actions are taken. Your use of a personal and professional code of ethics that employs influence for educational rather than personal gain is considered. Consideration is also given to how legal and contractual obligations are fulfilled; if laws, procedures, and decisions are fairly, wisely, and considerately applied; and if you accept responsibility for all school operations.

Figure 15-1

THE ADMINISTRATOR'S ASSESSMENT CRITERIA

Please rate your administrator on each item below. Place an X under the selected number using the following scale.

The Adminstrator does this:
4 = ALWAYS   3 = MOST OF THE TIME   2 = SOME OF THE TIME   1 = RARELY   0 = NEVER

	4	3	2	1	0
One INSTRUCTIONAL LEADERSHIP					
Conducts Annual Planning and Evaluation					
The educational program is aligned with the vision, plans, and actions.					
Implementation plans are monitored.					
All programs are assessed using multiple criteria.					
Develops Curriculum and Instructional Programs					
Meeting standards is the focus of curriculum and program development.					
Technology is incorporated into teaching and learning.					
Emerging trends are used to determine their benefit, advisability, and appropriateness.					
Values High Standards for Student Performance					
There is a culture of high expectations for self, students, and staff.					
Barriers to student learning are identified, clarified, and addressed.					
Creates a Supportive Learning Environment for Students					
All individuals are treated with fairness, dignity, and respect.					
Learning experiences are consistent with the diversity of students' needs.					
Conflict-resolution and problem-solving skills are used by staff and students.					
Category score					
Two ORGANIZATIONAL LEADERSHIP					
Manages Human Resources					
Administrative monitoring system is used.					
Staff is utilized in effective ways.					
Manages the Daily Operation of the School					
Management decisions and operational procedures maximize learning.					
Time is used and managed effectively.					

Figure 15-1 continued

	4	3	2	1	0
Manages Finances/Resources					
Constraints, needs, and available resources are considered before decisions are made.					
Financial, human, and material resources from the community and outside sources are sought.					
Maintains Positive Interpersonal Relations					
Problems are addressed and resolved in a timely and appropriate manner.					
All stakeholders are involved in the decision-making process.					
Category score					
Three **STAFF DEVELOPMENT: Provides for the Effective Growth of Staff**					
Staff development promotes a focus on student learning consistent with the vision.					
The supervisiory program meets the needs and directs the growth of the staff.					
Category score					
Four **STUDENT SUPPORT SERVICES: Manages Pupil Personnel Services**					
Opportunities for curricular, cocurricular, and extracurricular programs are sought.					
Pupil personnel programs ensure confidentiality and meet the needs of students and families.					
Category score					
Five **COMMUNICATION: Communicates with Staff, Parents, Family, and Students**					
Effective communication is constant with the entire school community.					
Communication is consistent with parents, students, and the community.					
Category score					
Six **COMMUNITY RELATIONS: Maintains District/Community Relations**					
Visibility, active involvement, and communication with the larger community are maintained.					
Relationships are developed with community leaders.					
A program of community relations is followed.					
Category score					
Seven **PERSONAL CHARACTER: Acts in an Ethical Manner with Integrity and Fairness**					
A personal and professional code of ethics is used.					
Influence is used for educational rather than personal gain.					
Legal and contractual obligations are fulfilled.					
Laws, procedures, and decisions are fairly, wisely, and considerately applied.					
Responsibility for all school operations is accepted.					
Category score					
TOTAL SCORE					

194

USING THE ADMINISTRATOR'S ASSESSMENT

Introduce the assessment of your skills and abilities with a sincere request for honest and open feedback. Clarify that you really want to know what they think and believe about your effectiveness. If you want respondents to be honest and open, ask them not to identify themselves. Remaining anonymous prevents distortion of responses because of fear of reprisal or desire to curry favor. Responses that are not honest are of no value.

If you do conduct the assessment with various groups in addition to the instructional staff, code the assessment so that you know if the responses come from members of the instructional staff, noninstructional staff, or parents. You may wish to tally the responses from each group separately.

Respondents are asked to consider the evidence they have to rate you on each item in the seven categories using a scale from 4 to 0. You may wish to take a few moments to explain the scale:

- 4—Always (evidence is apparent *at all times*)

- 3—Most of the time (evidence is *usually* apparent)

- 2—Some of the time (evidence is apparent *once in a while*)

- 1—Rarely (evidence is *usually not* apparent)

- 0—Never (evidence is *never* apparent)

ANALYZING THE RESULTS

Hopefully, everyone who was asked to complete the assessment will return the form to the place you have designated. Post a reminder notice if you do not receive all the completed assessments within a week.

There are several ways to analyze the results. Figure 15-2 lists the total number of items by category, the highest possible score for each category, and the highest possible total score.

1. **Calculate your total scores.** Compare each form's total score with the highest possible score. Find your average score by adding all the scores and dividing by the number of forms that were returned. Determine the range of your scores by identifying your highest and lowest scores.

2. **Calculate your category scores.** Compare your scores with the highest possible scores for each category. Find your average category score by adding all the scores for each category and dividing by the total number of responses. Determine the range of your scores by identifying your lowest and highest scores in each category.

3. **Do a score comparison.** This information helps to give you a summary view of the respondents' assessment of you.

Figure 15-2
ANALYZING THE RESULTS

Category	Number of Items	Highest Possible Score
Instructional Leadership		
Planning and Evaluation	3	12
Curriculum and Instructional Programs	3	12
Standards for Student Performance	2	8
Learning Environment for Students	3	12
Category Total	11	44
Organizational Leadership		
Human Resources Management	2	8
Daily Operation of the School	2	8
Finances/Resource Management	2	8
Interpersonal Relations	2	8
Category Total	8	32
Staff Development	2	8
Student Support Services	2	8
Communication	2	8
Community Relations	3	12
Personal Character	5	20
Category Totals	14	56
Cumulative Total	33	132

HOW TO DO A SCORE COMPARISON FOR TOTAL SCORES

List the numbers 0 to 132 in a column. Count and record the number of responses that totaled each score; for example, the number of forms that totaled 132, 92, 64, and so forth. Now consider the score range. Figure 15-3 shows how to calculate and interpret the scores.

Think about the score range of 0 to 132 in four parts. Specifically:

- 0 to 32 = the lowest fourth
- 33 to 65 = the second fourth
- 66 to 98 = the third fourth
- 99 to 132 = the highest fourth

Group the number of scores in each fourth. Now, calculate the percentage of responses for each fourth by dividing the number of responses in each fourth by the total number of responses received. For example, 28 responses divided by a total of 40 respondents equals 70 percent. In Figure 15-3:

- 28 respondents or 70 percent rated this administrator 99 or above in the highest fourth.

- 6 respondents or 15 percent rated this administrator between 66 and 98 in the third fourth.

- 4 respondents or 10 percent rated this administrator between 33 and 65 in the second fourth.

- 2 respondents or 5 percent rated this administrator between 0 and 32 in the lowest fourth.

- Overall, 85 percent of the respondents rated this administrator above 66 out of a possible score of 132.

Using the Results of the Assessment

You may be surprised, delighted, disappointed, or in disagreement with the results. Remember, the scores represent the point of view of the respondents. Now you know the overall view as well as the categorized assessment of how you are perceived in the seven roles of an administrator. Using the results as a guide in the future will increase your effectiveness.

Reflect honestly on the category and items that have low assessments. Itemize specific examples of your actions or behavior that may have resulted in those scores. You may choose to add to these examples by consulting with selected staff members with whom you have an open relationship. Ask them to contribute their ideas to the list of examples you have itemized.

Figure 15-3
TOTAL SCORE COMPARISON

Score	Number of Responses	Range Group
132	4	
125	10	
116	6	28
108	4	
99	4	
96	2	
84	2	6
68	2	
64	2	4
52	2	
32	2	2
Total Responses	40	40

Now that you have a good source of data, use it to change your actions and behavior. Match each example of a low-rated item with several positive alternatives to that action.

For example, if you were rated low in the area of "manages the daily operation of the school," review the bell schedule, use of staircases, bus procedures, and dismissal procedures for lunch and at the end of the day. Identify areas that could be improved and form a group of staff members to develop a new plan.

As another example, if you were rated low in the area of "communication," examine how you communicate with the staff and the school community. Consider the frequency of communications, the form they take, and the subjects that are included. Invite members of the staff to review the materials you have gathered for examination and make the changes that are suggested.

As a last example, if you were rated low in the area of "creates a supportive learning environment for students," walk the school halls and classrooms to look for trouble spots. Pay careful attention to those areas that staff members have identified as problematic. Consider implementing a program in social–emotional learning, conflict resolution, or character building.

As you lead your school, remember that the most successful administrator is one who is viewed by the school community as an effective leader.

Working by Yourself or as a Member of a Team

There are several different ways in which you can and should assign responsibility to other administrators in the school. These, and the rationale for each, include:

1. **Each administrator will assume responsibility for some of the new teachers.** *Rationale:* There are a large number of new teachers in the school, each of whom would benefit from a directed growth plan. Since this growth plan is the most time-consuming, the load should logically be shared. You may wish to consider the area of expertise of the administrative staff to make maximum use of the available personnel. For example, those with early childhood experience should work with new teachers in grades pre-K to 2. Those with a math or science background or certification should work with new teachers in those departments.

2. **One administrator will work with all the new teachers.** *Rationale:* There are only a few new teachers on the staff who will benefit from a directed growth plan. One administrator may become an expert in this form of assistance.

3. **Each administrator will assume responsibilities for some marginal teachers.** *Rational:* There are a number of marginal teachers on the staff, each of whom would profit from a directed growth plan. This type of assignment can be frustrating and should be shared.

4. **One administrator will assume responsibility for all the marginal teachers.** *Rationale:* There are few marginal teachers on the staff who require directed growth plans. One of the administrators may know these teachers well enough to develop a relationship with them and help them to make changes in their instructional program. For other administrators, it may be a challenge they wish to take on.

5. **Each administrator will be assigned responsibilities for specific grades and/or departments.** *Rationale:* The school staff is equally represented with new, marginal, and experienced teachers among all grades and departments. An individual administrator may be more experienced and comfortable with a particular grade level or content area.

Meeting with the Administrative Team

The administrative team should meet on a scheduled basis to discuss the teacher growth plans. Three benefits result from the team's sharing of its work with teachers.

1. The specific growth plan for each teacher is explained and discussed, providing an instructional overview for the school.

2. Effective strategies and techniques are shared, expanding their use to other team members.

3. The administrative team may serve as a resource to brainstorm solutions to trouble spots that some administrators may be experiencing.

In this way, the administrative team may be maximally effective, both individually and collectively, as contributors to the collective effort to help teachers grow.

Part IV

How to Communicate for Student Success

Establishing a Secure Climate

Your primary goal is the achievement of a maximally functioning school in which students achieve and teachers work in a professionally rewarding and personally satisfying environment. Addressing standards for teaching that target students' achievement (discussed in Part I), knowing teacher needs (discussed in Part II), and matching growth plans to teachers' needs (discussed in Part III) are important elements in developing a professionally rewarding environment for teachers. But what are the elements of a personally satisfying environment?

Achieving personal satisfaction is a function of attitude and perception; the more positive the attitude and perception, the more personally satisfying the experience and, generally, the more successful the performance. This section explains how to establish a secure climate in which teachers have positive attitudes and perceptions that result in outstanding teaching performances.

The Impact of Basic Human Needs on Teacher Effectiveness

The development of teachers can be seen in relation to basic human needs. These needs are usually classified in a hierarchy that ranges from the uncomplicated physical to the complex psychological. Each need impacts on how teachers function, act, react, and, therefore, perform their role as instructors of students.

PHYSICAL NEEDS

The physical needs are the most powerful of all because they are essential for survival. They include the need for food, water, air, shelter, and sleep. The lack of satisfaction of any one of these physical needs will seriously hamper the individual from functioning. Have you ever worked with someone on a serious diet, or someone who is trying to find a place to live? Although other concerns may be attended to, they do not get the benefit of a full focus or a maximum effort until these needs are met. Yet, the abuse of these needs may become the means by which people express unmet higher order needs—we all know people who overeat or suffer from insomnia.

It is wise to be alert to these indicators of unmet needs among your staff. Although needs involved with the personal life of staff members are beyond your control, your understanding, sensitivity, and sympathy will help the individual function better. On the other hand, those unmet needs may relate to school problems over which you *do* have control. Each basic need is discussed in terms of its relationship to school life.

THE NEED TO BE SAFE

When physical needs are satisfied at an adequate level, the next need—safety— demands satisfaction. Feeling safe involves the need to live in a world that has security and stability, is predictable and consistent to some degree. That is why predictability and consistency are elements of gaining trust. (See Section 1 for a discussion of the behaviors that build trust.) This provides the individual with a realistic expectation of what to do, how to do it, and what the outcomes will be. Although it is true that change is inevitable and crisis must be faced, they do not have to be a part of daily life.

People with unmet safety needs appear anxious and insecure. Not only do they stop taking risks, but they also become defensive, even neurotic. This behavior is easily recognized in children who have been removed from their homes and families.

Teachers with an unmet need to be safe exhibit the following behaviors. They avoid any change. This may include a *refusal* to:

- Use new materials.
- Implement a new program.
- Rearrange the classroom furniture.
- Change their program or duty.
- Change their seat in the faculty lunchroom.

In addition, these teachers may become negative, critical, and defensive. This is shown by their need to:

- Justify their actions.
- Criticize other staff members, students, and materials.
- Find fault with everything around them.
- Act suspicious about the intent of decisions that involve them.

Teachers new to the school may feel unsafe in an unknown situation. They are nervous and fearful. They may appear to be distant and aloof, preferring isolation to interaction.

You can help teachers satisfy the need to feel safe:

1. **Establish rules that are observed consistently by everyone.** For example, teachers do not drink coffee while conducting class.

2. **Specify a realistic expectation for teacher performance of administrative and instructional tasks.** For example, all teachers plan for and conduct an extended literacy period each morning.

3. **Maintain consistent procedures for dealing with routine matters.** For example, books are ordered by completing a specific form that is then given to a specific person.

4. **Meet teacher expectation for commendation and delinquent action.** For example, commend teacher efforts by writing a letter, or deal with a delinquent action by holding a meeting to achieve problem resolution.

THE NEED TO BELONG

After safety needs are satisfied and individuals feel at home in the school environment, they begin to seek involvement with others. There is a strong desire to be accepted as a member of the group—as someone who is liked and invited into the circle of friends.

When the need to belong is thwarted and unsatisfied, the individual will restrict or abort efforts, energy, and commitment. Teachers whose needs to belong are unmet by the school organization and its staff will withdraw from the school community by:

- Isolating themselves from others
- Eating alone
- Not attending group social functions
- Not contributing to group work sessions
- Avoiding the faculty lounge

Since everyone strives to achieve a sense of belonging, that energy, effort, and commitment may be inappropriately directed to students. These teachers may:

- Select pet students.
- Buy student affection with favors or gifts.
- Apply class rules inconsistently to favor particular youngsters.
- Attempt to make students dependent upon them.

Of course, other students not targeted for satisfaction of the need to belong may become angry at what they see as unfair or unjust treatment. They may begin to mistrust and dislike the teacher and express this verbally to their parents and other members of the staff.

Teachers can be supported in their need to belong, to be liked, and accepted in the following ways:

1. **Encourage the display of warmth and friendliness by active modeling.** For example, a morning smile, an afternoon wish for a pleasant evening, a question about the health and well-being of the person and his or her family can become contagious.

2. **Foster the development of collegial work groups.** Encourage teachers to form learning communities. (See Section 14.)

3. **Promote social gatherings by assisting efforts to plan such events.**

4. **Actively participate in social efforts and give special attention to new and isolated staff members.**

5. **Resolve interpersonal conflicts** by holding a meeting, and practicing the skills of conflict resolution, mediation, and negotiation.

6. **Give attention to the need to provide comfortable and attractive meeting places** by assisting and supporting staff efforts to paint and decorate them.

THE NEED FOR ESTEEM

Once the need to belong and be accepted has been satisfied, individuals move from wanting to be accepted into the group to becoming contributing and outstanding members of the group. Being a member of the group is not enough, however; individuals now wish to be admired and respected by the group. When this need is met, teachers feel confident about their ability, secure about their actions and decisions, and proud of their performance.

The need for esteem can be inhibited when school organizations do not provide the means to recognize, acknowledge, and prize staff achievements. This could result in teachers:

- Feeling threatened
- Feeling insecure about their efforts
- Mistrusting the administrators and the school organization
- Being discouraged
- Not taking initiative and responsibility

Teachers can be helped to fulfill the need for esteem:

1. **Publicly recognize their efforts.** For example, place a letter of commendation in the teacher's file and the school news bulletin, if appropriate.

2. **Value their achievement.** For example, ask them to speak at grade or department meetings, faculty conferences, or sessions during professional-development activities.

3. **Respect their status.** For example, ask the teacher's permission before removing a student from the class.

The Power of Listening

More than 75 percent of the day is spent in verbal communication. The problem is that most of us have concentrated our educational learning on how to write and read, and spent very little time on how to speak and even less on how to listen. Yet, confusion, misinterpretation of events, and lack of clarity about intent generally occurs because of a failure to listen clearly and accurately.

The act of listening contributes significantly to building a secure climate, and a helpful and caring relationship that promote professional interactions which are perceived as supportive and result in teacher growth. Those who seek to speak with us want our undivided attention, understanding, and considered responses to their messages. Only by sincerely listening can we truly understand the full range and impact of what someone else is saying.

Being a good listener requires putting ourselves on hold. That means suspending the quick response, the suggestion, and the judgment. Most of us would much rather talk than listen. Even when we are silent while someone else is speaking, we often concentrate on forming a response rather than waiting until we have a clear understanding about the message being expressed.

Effective listening is a powerful skill that impacts every aspect of your role as administrator. It is especially powerful in influencing teacher's actions that result in student achievement. The three components of effective listening require using the skills of attending, seeking to understand, and deferring evaluation while avoiding natural inhibitors (Figure 16-1).

ATTEND

Attending to the speaker communicates that you are interested in the person and his or her message and that you are willing to spend time listening. The first rule of attending is to focus on the speaker and the message. Focusing on the speaker is an action that the speaker can see by observing your body language. Resist distractions that you may cause by talking or fidgeting with papers, or those caused by others such as a telephone call, the fax machine, or a note. Other elements of attending that the speaker cannot see are within the listener's power of control. Even though they are not visible, they will be communicated by a lack of information about the message delivered. Do not allow your mind to wander. Sustain attention even if the message is not of immediate interest. Avoid allowing filters to communication, caused by immediate problems needing solution or a personal issue, to distract you. Taking notes may be helpful. Most of all, be patient.

SEEK TO UNDERSTAND

The mind of the listener is actively involved in mental processing while listening to the message. The two aspects of this metacognitive process with which the brain is involved are selecting and organizing the information, and viewing the data through

Figure 16-1

THE POWER OF LISTENING

Attend

Focus on the speaker and the message.

Resist distractions.

Stop your mind from wandering, even if you are not interested.

Put other professional and personal issues issues aside.

Take notes.

Be patient.

Seek to Understand

The brain seeks to select and organize.

Try to understand, even if the message is complex or vague.

Record questions.

Defer Evaluation

Weigh the message against:

• internal beliefs/past experiences

• emotions and attitudes

• opinion of the speaker

• visual image of the speaker

Keep emotions in check.

the listener's perception. Continue to listen and seek to understand even when the information becomes difficult, confused, or complex. Sometimes the message the speaker sends is deliberately unclear. It is coded with feelings of fear and insecurity in an attempt to try out the message to see if it is accepted. The listener must decode the message to understand. When the message is not clear, record questions that may need to be asked for clarification.

DEFER EVALUATION

It is impossible to separate ourselves from who we are. Each of us has an internal belief system formed very early in life by our family and a set of past experiences that confirm or modify those beliefs. These emotions and attitudes act like filters in the listening process and block, distort, create suspicion, or enhance the message. For example, listeners may react emotionally when semantics leads to interpretation that may be correct or incorrect. Some words or expressions such as, "Those kids are dumb" or "Those parents don't care" are loaded because they carry special meaning. Remember to keep your emotions in check because you may not clearly understand the message.

How the message is evaluated is also related to the listener's opinion about the intelligence and importance of the speaker. For example, could your evaluation of messages delivered by parents, teachers, kitchen staff, vendors, or state auditors be different?

The visual image the speaker projects in attractiveness and appropriateness of dress also influences evaluation. For example, does a teacher in jeans and a tee shirt, or one wearing a shirt and tie make you more likely to agree to a request? Is the sincerity or importance of a person's request diminished by the person's use of jewelry or makeup?

The Language of Communication that Impacts Student Success

Direct interactions with people are the major form of administrative communication. It is the quality of those interactions that determine the potential for teacher growth. That is why the language of communication is critical to the goal of student achievement. It is not only what is said, but also how it is said and how the speaker looks while saying it.

Support, challenge, and opportunity are the requirements for teacher growth. These are accomplished through the language of communication. Active listening focuses on teacher support through communications that express caring, interest, understanding, empathy, validation, and encouragement. Reflection focuses on providing challenge and opportunity through communications that seek to empower teachers by requiring them to extend their thinking.

Active Listening Establishes a Climate for Growth

Active listening is directed at making teachers feel comfortable, accepted, and understood. This climate sets a framework in which the teacher is validated and encouraged to reflect deeply about the teaching and learning process without fear of criticism and judgment. There are three aspects to active listening: nonverbal active listening, active listening, and interactive listening.

NONVERBAL ACTIVE LISTENING

All of us communicate without speech or print. Our nonverbal language sends powerful messages. Consider the following incident: A smiling teacher enters the administrator's office for a conference. She stops smiling as soon as she sees the administrator. Although the administrator has not said or written anything, a message has been sent and received.

Nonverbal language is a powerful tool that should not be used unconsciously. When it is used without thought and purpose, opportunities to make teachers feel comfortable and accepted are lost. Or, resulting negative reactions may prevent you from reaching your goals.

Positive nonverbal communication. The visible actions of positive nonverbal communication send the following messages:

- I care about you.
- You're important.
- I'm interested in you.

You are practicing positive nonverbal communication with your body, arms, hands, face, and voice when you do the following:

1. **Body.** Sit next to or across from the other person. Relax your body and turn to face the other person. Lean forward toward the other person. Move slowly and infrequently during the meeting,
2. **Arms.** Keep your arms relaxed and open, resting on the table, the arm of the chair, or in your lap.
3. **Hands.** Keep your hands open with the palms facing up. Use your hands to gesture or to lightly touch the other person.
4. **Face.** Show expression on your face. Smile and nod frequently. Look directly at the other person and maintain eye contact.
5. **Voice.** Maintain silence except for an occasional "uh huh."

Negative nonverbal communication. The visible actions of negative nonverbal communication send these messages. You or the other person is:

- Distracted or disinterested
- Suspicious and on guard
- Nervous and fearful
- Angry and hostile

You or others are sending negative nonverbal communication with the body, arms, hands, face, and voice when you or they do the following:

1. **Body.** Sit at a desk with the other person at the side of the desk or in front of the desk, placing an authoritarian barrier between the persons. Tense the body and turn away from the other person. Lean back, away from the other person. Move quickly and frequently during the meeting by shifting position in the chair or getting up and down from the seat.

2. **Arms.** Keep the arms tense and crossed or out of sight.

3. **Hands.** Close or clench the hands or intertwine the fingers tightly. Hands are used to finger point.

4. **Face.** Present a "frozen" facial expression, showing only a frown or a "deadpan" look. Focus the eyes elsewhere, not directly on the other person, and blink frequently. Raise eyes and look at the ceiling.

5. **Voice.** Grunts or makes other low-level sounds.

Figure 17-1 presents a comparative summary of positive and negative nonverbal communication.

Positive nonverbal communication places the other person at ease. He or she feels safe, cared about, and comfortable. This is the climate in which honest and open communication can take place.

Negative nonverbal communication is counterproductive to your goals. When you recognize this behavior in the person with whom you are communicating, concentrate on positive behaviors, especially leaning in and smiling. It is very difficult to maintain a frown when looking at a smile. Just getting that first smile will help to break the barriers of fear and suspicion that are preventing productive communication towards growth and change.

ACTIVE LISTENING

Active listening communicates by sending the following messages:

- I seek to understand what you are saying.
- I am sensitive to your feelings.

Two actions communicate the messages of active listening.

Paraphrase.   Paraphrasing restates or summarizes what the speaker has said. This tells the speaker that I have heard what you said. It also communicates that I am seeking to understand what you are saying and so I am reflecting it back to you for clarification.

Figure 17-1

NONVERBAL COMMUNICATION

	POSITIVE	NEGATIVE
Body	sit next to the person	sit behind a desk
	body relaxed	body tense
	body turned to face	body turned away
	lean toward	lean away
	move slowly	move quickly
	move infrequently	move frequently
Arms	relaxed	tense
	open	crossed
Hands	palms up	hands clenched
	use to gesture	do not use
	touch other person lightly	point with finger
Face	expressive	frozen
	smiling	frowning/deadpan
	look at person	look elsewhere
	eye contact	no eye contact
	eyes open	eyes blink often
Voice	silent	high-pitched
	sounds of agreement	grunts

Express recognition of emotions.   Statements that express the emotions of the speaker communicate that I can recognize how you feel. I am able to hear the hurt in your voice or the anger in your words and tone.

Some sample language of active listening follows.

- "So, you are saying that there are some students who do not do homework no matter what you have tried."
- "Say more about your plans for using writing as a part of social studies."
- "I hear you saying that you are excited about taking the course on cooperative learning."
- "You are feeling very frustrated."
- "I can feel how hurt you were by the remarks of that parent."
- "You are working very hard to reach every student."

INTERACTIVE LISTENING

Interactive listening communicates the following messages:

- Your ideas are valid.
- You have the power to use those ideas.

Two actions communicate the messages of interactive listening.

Validate proposals.   Statements that validate the actions proposed express confidence in the teacher as a professional. They show support for the ideas that are proposed.

Encourage actions.   Statements that encourage the teacher to take action on the ideas proposed express the belief that the teacher has the ability to be successful.

Here is some sample language of interactive listening.

- "You have some good experiences with getting the support of the parents."
- "That is an exciting idea."
- "You know how to set up the groups."
- "That strategy should work well with the English language learners in the class."

See Figure 17-2 for a summary of active listening and Figure 17-3 for samples of the language of active listening.

Figure 17-2

COMMUNICATION SKILLS: ACTIVE LISTENING

Nonverbal Active Listening

Purpose ▶ Caring & Interest

Message: I care about you.
You're important.
I'm interested in you.

Actions: • Positive body language
• Silence

Active Listening

Purpose ▶ Understanding

Message: I seek to understand.
I am sensitive to
your needs.

Actions: • Paraphrase to restate or
summarize the speaker's words

• Statement of recognition of the
speaker's feelings

Interactive Listening

Purpose ▶ Problem Solving

Message: Your ideas are valid.
You have the power.
You have the ability.

Actions: • Statements that validate
actions proposed

• Statements that encourage
actions proposed

Figure 17-3
SAMPLE ACTIVE LISTENING LANGUAGE

Nonverbal Active Listening

- *Eye contact*
- *Nod your head*
- *Lean in*
- *Smile*
- *"Uh huh"*

Active Listening

- *"So you are saying that . . ."*
- *"Do you mean . . . ?"*
- *"I hear you saying . . ."*
- *"You are feeling . . ."*
- *"I can feel your hurt about . . ."*
- *"You are working very hard."*

Interactive Listening

- *"You have had this . . ."*
- *"That is an exciting . . ."*
- *"You know how to . . ."*
- *"That should work with . . ."*

Reflection Fosters Teacher Growth

Active listening establishes a climate of trust and acceptance that sets the stage for change and growth. Reflection moves beyond building confidence and validating effort. It focuses on teacher growth.

PURPOSES OF REFLECTION

The process of reflection is essential to the development of empowered teachers who are self-directed professionals. Reflection helps teachers to extract meaning from their experiences as they engage in metacognition—that is, thinking about their thinking as they planned and implemented instruction. In this process, they monitor their teaching and ask for feedback. These are the actions of professionals who are continuing learners about the art and science of teaching and about themselves as teachers.

MAKING IT HAPPEN

The administrator's goal is to help teachers make reflection a habit of the mind in which they engage as a natural outcome of every teaching experience. The vehicle for reaching this goal is communicating through asking questions. Rule number 1 for conferencing with teachers is ASK, DON'T TELL. (See Section 9.) Authentic and sustained growth involves commitment and responsibility, and is therefore in the hands and the minds of teachers. They must own it! However, you are the agent of the change process. By asking questions, the teacher is guided to examine instructional practices, reflect on his or her effectiveness, and seek ways to help every student to achieve. The total involvement of the teacher in thinking, creating, and designing instructional improvement is therefore critical.

Using the tools of active listening helps teachers to feel comfortable and encourages them to speak openly and professionally about instructional practices. This sets the stage for reflection through questions that focus on particular aspects of instruction, probe for information, and seek clarification.

Focus on instruction. Questions that focus on instruction ask the teacher to analyze and reflect on specific aspects of instruction. Teachers are asked to discuss their impressions and assessments of the lesson. They are also asked to recall data that supports these impressions and assessments. Teachers are encouraged to infer relationships between student achievement and their actions.

Some sample questions that focus on instruction are:

- "What went very well in the lesson?"
- "What did not meet your expectations?"
- "What surprised you?"

- "Why do you think that happened?"
- "What did you see students do to demonstrate that they understood?"
- "How did the instructional strategy you selected produce the outcomes you achieved?"

Probe for information.   Questions that probe for information ask the teacher to fill in the gaps in statements that were made. Teachers are asked to extend what they have said or did to provide more information on the subject. Teachers are encouraged to explore the reasons for their decisions and actions and the resulting outcomes.

Here are sample questions that probe for information.

- "Say more about why you selected that instructional strategy."
- "Can you explain why you grouped students in this way?"
- "What do you mean when you say it takes time?"
- "Have you considered other ways to deal with off-task behaviors?"
- "What is the next topic in this unit?"
- "Are there other ways to arrange the students into groups?"
- "Why do you prefer to have students copy notes from the board?"
- "Do you see large uses of cooperative learning?"

Seek clarification.   Questions that seek clarification ask the teacher to explain statements or actions that are not clearly understood. Teachers are asked to clarify generalizations or vague statements by using more precise words and terms. Teachers are encouraged to think deeply beneath the surface statement that they have made to clarify their real meaning.

The following sample questions seek clarification:

- "Are you saying that nothing was learned in this lesson?"
- "Why do you believe your fifth-period class is hard to teach?"
- "How about the students in your other classes?"
- "Do you mean you have exhausted all possible ways of involving parents?"
- "When you say they don't care, who you mean?"

See Figure 17-4 for a summary of reflection and Figure 17-5 for samples of the language of reflection.

Figure 17-4

REFLECTION: FOSTERING GROWTH

REFLECTION

Moves beyond confidence
to growth

PURPOSES

- Develop reflection as a
  habit of the mind

- Empower the teacher

- Develop self-directed teachers

**MAKING IT
HAPPEN**

QUESTIONS THAT:

- Focus on instruction

- Probe for information

- Seek clarification

Figure 17-5

SAMPLE LANGUAGE FOR REFLECTION

FOCUS ON ASPECTS OF INSTRUCTION

    What went very well?

    What did not meet your expectations?

    What surprised you?

    What student actions demonstrated those results?

    How did the strategy you select produce the outcomes?

PROBE FOR INFORMATION

    Say more about . . .

    Can you explain . . . ?

    What do you mean . . . ?

    Have you considered . . . ?

    What is the next . . . ?

    Are there other ways . . . ?

    Why do you prefer to . . . ?

    Do you see larger uses of . . . ?

SEEK CLARIFICATION

    Are you saying . . . ?

    Why do you believe . . . ?

    How about . . . ?

    Do you mean . . . ?

    Why do you think . . . ?

    When you say . . . ?

When to Use Which Communication Language

Active listening and reflection are used interactively throughout communication. The skillful communicator uses nonverbal active listening throughout the meeting to send the message that the teacher is important, cared about, and the focus of attention.

The skillful communicator knows when active listening is needed to convey the messages that "I seek to understand and I empathize with you." To help a teacher who is feeling defeated, confused, or hurt, for example, the skillful communicator knows when interactive listening is needed to validate the teacher and build his or her confidence. To support and build the confidence of the teacher who may be off balance when involved in learning something new, the teacher must give up or modify what is known and believed to be open to new knowledge and strategies.

The skillful communicator also knows that questions that stimulate reflection should be used in every meeting to help teachers focus on aspects of instruction, explain decisions and actions taken, clarify and articulate the problem and then propose viable solutions. However, the administrator as a skillful communicator is aware of the level of experience and degree of knowledge of the teacher, and keeps these in mind when selecting the growth plan and the communication language that can be used. Refer to Figures 11-3, 12-2, 13-3, and 13-4 to note the differences in the language of communication used at the planning conferences for teachers in directed, collaborative, or teacher-directed growth plans.

Writing Effective Communications

Have you ever felt as if you were drowning in a sea of paper? Indeed, written messages have become a daily and essential part of how we communicate about everything we do. Yet the written word is a demon that can trip you up!

Since your written message depends on its reader for interpretation, be aware of the three problems that can arise here:

1. Subtle clues, hidden in the words we assume are neutral, can cause emotional reactions.

2. Outside influences, at the time of the reading, can cause misinterpretations.

3. A lack of clarity can confuse the reader.

This section will help you deal with these three problems by presenting strategies for writing effective and humane communications.

The Strengths and Weaknesses of Written Communication

Written communication is in constant use because it serves several purposes:

- The written words permanently record the message. Words are indisputable once they are set on paper.

- A written message may clarify, explain, direct, or guide a complicated process. When a series of actions is required, the best way to transfer that information is in writing.

- Written messages may be kept and reread for recall and clarification.

There are, however, several weaknesses to consider about written communication:

- Written messages are thoughts frozen on paper. Once recorded, they cannot be retracted.

- The written message offers no clarification or modification beyond the specific words stated.

- Written communications do not provide the benefits of verbal and nonverbal information and explanation.

Written Communications that Achieve Their Purpose

Three factors guide written communications that achieve their purpose:

1. **The format that is chosen** because the appearance of the communication sends the first important message even before it is read

2. **The clarity of the communication** so that it is correctly understood

3. **Selecting the right words** to ensure that the intended message is delivered

SELECT THE MOST APPROPRIATE FORMAT

Even before a written communication is read, the reader sees how it looks. The appearance of the communication sends the first signal about the nature of the message. Of the several formats available, the writer's first task is to select the one most appropriate to achieving the intended purpose of the communication.

Memo.   A memo is used more often than other written formats because it is a quick and efficient means of communicating information. The memo can be addressed to an individual, for example, to schedule the date and time for a meeting with you. A memo can be sent to a group to inform the sixth grade that its request for a trip to Washington, D.C. has been sent to the superintendent for approval. A memo can also be sent to a general audience to inform the staff of the date of the next districtwide staff-development day. The messages communicated by memos are usually not of a personal nature, but rather ones that give information.

One advantage of using a memo is that it is more likely to be read sooner than a letter. Picture the amount of paper in a staff member's letterbox every morning. When sorting the pile of paper with little time before classes begin, which would you read first, a memo or a letter? Did the memo win? It usually does. That makes the memo effective for communicating dated information that you would like to be sure is read immediately, such as informing a group of teachers about a meeting that is scheduled or canceled. This may be particularly important when a security issue—such as construction workers in the building—or a health issue—such as nonfunctioning toilets on the fourth floor—must be communicated. Although the memo has the best chance of being read, there is no guarantee. How to be sure that memos containing important information, stuffed into students' knapsacks, will reach parents is a problem that defies solution.

Letter.   Although writing a letter takes time, it provides the opportunity to express specific and detailed information. A letter is a formal means of communicating messages of an informational or personal nature that carry weight and importance. For example, would you prefer a commendation for your file be in the form of a letter or a memo? I am sure you would prefer the more formal and official format of a letter. Which format would you use to inform the superintendent about a security problem in your school? You probably selected the letter for three reasons. First, you want the problem to be given serious consideration. Second, the letter serves to document your notification about the problem. Third, the superintendent is your supervisor and sending a letter demonstrates respect.

Letters are usually addressed to individuals, such as a staff member who is consistently late. Letters can also be addressed to a group or a general audience; for example, a letter of commendation for an outstanding science fair might be addressed to the science department, or a letter announcing an award received by the school might be addressed to "Dear Parents."

Flyer.   The flyer is the best format when an event is announced or promoted. Because a flyer has no form to be followed, it provides the opportunity for creativity and uniqueness in design that will make it appealing to the eye, interesting to read, and hopefully successful in sending its message.

MAKE THE MESSAGE CLEAR

Clarity is always of prime importance in any written communication. Set the stage at the start of any communication by establishing your role and the purpose of the communication.

The format of the memo—*from, to, subject, date*—provides all of this information. However, this is not true for a letter. When writing to a member of your staff, it may not always be necessary to establish your role. It is understood, and your signature at the bottom of the letter is followed by your title. When you are writing to someone outside of your immediate staff, however, it may be very important to state who you are at the outset; for example, "As principal of the school."

The purpose of the communication should become obvious in the first few sentences of a letter. For example, "My purpose in writing to you is to respond to the request you made of your son's teacher." These definitive statements cannot be misinterpreted.

The next important clarity factor deals with the reader's familiarity with the subject. At times, this is not necessary because the person with whom you are communicating brought the problem to you. At other times, however, it may be important to consider the reader's lack of background and experience with the subject. An extensive explanation may be required for the reader to understand the intent of the letter. Whenever possible, it may be advisable to attach that background information to the letter and make reference to it rather than include it in the body of the letter; for example, "A five-year history of correspondence about this matter is attached for your information."

USE WORDS EFFECTIVELY

The use of precise words sends the intended message both clearly and succinctly. Examine the following pairs of sentences that show effective and ineffective use of words on the same topic:

WORDS USED EFFECTIVELY	WORDS USED INEFFECTIVELY
1. **Clear** The standards for your grade include instruction in literary response and expression.	1. **Vague** The grade's curriculum provides for variety and balance.
2. **Cordial** I am delighted that our conference gave us an opportunity to chat about several matters.	2. **Impersonal** Several of your concerns were discussed during our conference.
3. **Thoughtful** I have given consideration to your proposal and have reached a decision.	3. **Arbitrary** Your proposal is not accepted.
4. **Specific** The problem may be resolved by assigning teams of students to complete specific tasks.	4. **General** The problem is concerned with classroom management.
5. **Important** Students should be sent out of the room with a pass or a written note.	5. **Trivial** Use the correct form when sending an ill child to the office.
6. **Logical** Before using the new material, preview it and discuss it with other teachers.	6. **Illogical** Use the new material within one week.
7. **Concrete** Positive behavior-modification techniques have proven to be very effective discipline strategies.	7. **Abstract** Youngsters require security and acceptance to be able to function in a group.

8. **Pleasant**

Your difficulty in using the overhead projector was probably due to a lack of experience with this instructional device.

8. **Insulting**

Using a machine you know nothing about was a stupid move that resulted in disaster.

9. **Focused**

This action is harmful and is not to be continued.

9. **Wordy**

Although this has not happened before, even though it is always more likely to occur again once such a pattern has developed, it is important to both know and understand that this action, without exception, cannot continue.

10. **Focused**

This action is harmful and is not to be continued.

10. **Curt**

Stop this action immediately.

Using the Communication Formats

Figure 18-1 provides a summary of the communication formats.

COMMUNICATING WITH A MEMO

Always use the proper form when composing a memo. Stating who is sending the memo, to whom, on what subject, and the date provide essential information in a quick form that might hasten the reading of that memo. Make the subject line informative so that it communicates the nature of the message in just a few words. By their nature, memos should be brief and clearly worded, providing all the necessary information. Using space effectively will also contribute to the readability of the memo. See Figure 18-2.

LETTERS OF REPRIMAND THAT ENCOURAGE CHANGE

Letters of reprimand are never easy to write, but they accomplish two purposes. First, they provide documentation of the behavior or actions exhibited by the individual. Second, formally informing the individual by writing a letter that will be placed in the file may effectively stop the behavior or actions.

Begin the letter with a statement of purpose. Include the specific history of the behavior or actions. Present the cause-and-effect relationship of the actions or behavior or what the results have been or could be. State actions that will be or could be taken. See Figure 18-3.

Figure 18-1

Written Communication

Memo

Use proper form.

| To: |
| From: |
| Subject: |

Make it brief.
Provide all necessary information.
Use space effectively.

Letter of Reprimand

State purpose of the letter.
Specify history.
Present cause/effect relationship—what results.
Action to be taken.

Letter of Commendation

State what was done, when, and where.
Explain why this is to be commended.
Comment on the effect on the school/organization, etc.

Flyer

Make it attractive.
Use few words.
Provide all information.
Use space creatively.

Figure 18-2

MEMO

To: The Staff of George Washington High School

From: Leslie Brown, Principal

Date: April 9, 2002

Subject: Construction Alert

Beginning Tuesday, April 10, exit 8 on the east side of the building is closed for construction until further notice. This exit cannot be used while the outside doors are being repaired. Please keep students away from the construction area since it presents problems with both security and safety.

Construction workers have been instructed to wear identification badges labeled Done Right Construction Company. The involvement of the workers in the activities of the school will be limited to their use of the nearest restroom.

Thank you for your continuing assistance in making our schools safe.

Figure 18-3
LETTER OF REPRIMAND

The Cedar Grove School

November 28, 2002

Dear Ms. Gilmore,

My purpose in writing this letter is to discuss your repeated lateness. An examination of the sign-in sheet documents that you have been late, from 3 to 15 minutes, twelve times in the last seventeen days. The time sheets for the previous two months show a similar pattern. In September, you were late ten out of fourteen days. In October, you were late seventeen out of twenty-two days.

On October 10, we met to discuss this situation. You explained a number of reasons for your lateness, which included traffic conditions, car problems, health issues, family concerns, and household responsibilities. At that time, we discussed the problems that result when you are late. The primary concern is that your class is unattended. Other staff members, who attempt to assist with the supervision of your class, must leave their students unattended. Being late contributes to the anxious state of mind with which you enter your classroom. Your lateness also prevents you from being prepared for the day's instruction and limits your ability to be effective.

This is a very serious matter that must be resolved immediately. Continued lateness will result in two actions. First, your pay will be reduced for the amount of time you are late. Second, an official letter will be sent to the district personnel office for action.

I hope you have found a means to resolve this problem and that from this time forward, you will arrive on time. If I can be of any assistance, please call on me.

Sincerely,

Matthew Hunt, Principal

LETTERS OF COMMENDATION THAT ARE APPRECIATED

Letters of commendation serve multiple purposes. They contribute to building a secure climate by addressing the need for esteem. In addition, they serve to communicate your appreciation for the efforts that have been extended and therefore contribute to building and sustaining the trust of the staff.

Write a detailed letter that the teacher can include in his or her personal file for later use as a reference or recommendation. State specifically what the commendable action or activity was, when it was done, and where it took place. Explain why this action or activity is to be commended. Comment on the effect this action or activity had on the school, organization, or population. See Figure 18-4.

SUCCESSFUL FLYERS

At times, the flyer sent home makes the difference between a successful and unsuccessful event. There are four considerations when composing a flyer. First, make it attractive. There is a much better chance that people will stop to read a flyer that catches their eye. Second, use as few words as possible, but be sure all the important information is included. Less is more in communication, so use space creatively. See Figure 18-5.

Figure 18-4
LETTER OF COMMENDATION

Arthur Ashe Middle School

December 5, 2001

Mr. Lawrence Hudson
Science Department Chairperson
Arthur Ashe Middle School
Logansville, Connecticut

Dear Mr. Hudson,

I wish to congratulate you for presenting the most successful Science Fair that the Arthur Ashe Middle School has ever had. Over 85 percent of the students in the sixth, seventh, and eighth grades participated in the fair during the last week of November. Not only was the participation large, but the quality of the projects was outstanding. The judges—composed of teachers from the high school, members of the Board of Education, and the community—had a very difficult time selecting this year's prize winners.

During the month of November, you worked tirelessly to involve every member of the science department in the preparation of their students for the district science fair. You prepared a report outline as a guide for the teachers to use with their students. You provided presentation samples that teachers could use as demonstrations for their students. You made yourself available to every teacher and student for assistance. Your efforts were rewarded in several ways.

Every teacher in the middle school science department participated in the Science Fair. Second, a very large number of students actually completed projects that were on display. Third, the projects were of very high quality. You have sent the significant message to the entire community that science is considered an essential part of the educational program in our school. You have also communicated the commitment of the staff and their respect for your leadership.

Thank you for a job that was very well done with tremendous effort and sincere commitment.

Sincerely,

Rosa Cruz
Principal

Figure 18-5

SAMPLE FLYER

CHERRY LANE ELEMENTARY SCHOOL
announces the annual

BOOK FAIR

Help your child to love books and reading.

Support our school and its programs.

Dates: Wednesday, March 14
and
Thursday, March 15

Place: Front Hall Lobby
Cherry Lane Elementary School

Times: 9 A.M. to 11:30 A.M.
and
1:30 P.M. to 2:30 P.M.

Over 500 titles will be on display!

Reasonable prices!

Proceeds will be used for Arts in Education Activities!

Sponsored by the Parents Association of the Cherry Lane Elementary School

Communicating with Yourself: Keeping Track of What You Are Doing to Help Students Achieve

Most administrators state their intent is to focus on student achievement. But when their activities and records are examined, student achievement does not occupy the major use of their time. Paperwork, phone calls, meeting with parents, and student discipline keep them trapped in their offices. The discrepancy between intent and actual activities can be changed by taking a hard look at two factors.

1. How time is used
2. How records of teaching and learning are kept

Making the Most Use of Time

The need to set priorities becomes obvious when your role as administrator is compared to the amount of available time.

PRIORITIZING THE USE OF TIME

Here is the hard question: What are the most effective uses of your time? Of course, everything that is done in the course of the day has a purpose. But are these purposes of equal value? If student achievement is the first priority, then it must be considered the most valuable use of your time. The following list of activities lead directly to learning and achievement and should be considered the *first priority* for your time:

- Observing instruction
- Making informal visits

- Conferencing with teachers about instruction
- Working with teachers on growth plans
- Reviewing teacher and student artifacts
- Joining the discussions of a learning community
- Being visible at study team meetings
- Attending professional-development workshops
- Attending department- or grade-level meetings
- Researching and reflecting on effective instructional practices

Other activities are necessary to keep the school running but have little direct impact on learning and achievement. The following list of activities may be considered a *second priority:*

- Disciplinary meetings with individual students
- Meetings with parents
- Meetings with auxiliary staff
- Central office meetings
- Parent group meetings
- Faculty meetings
- Visits to school halls and grounds
- Answering phone calls
- Paperwork and reports
- Ordering
- Supervising bus and lunch activities

The last category of activities has no direct impact on learning and achievement and does not contribute to running the school. The following activities should be given the *lowest priority:*

- Correcting errors
- Dealing with complaints
- Resolving minor issues

ALLOCATING TIME EFFICIENTLY

The first step in organizing the use of your time according to priorities related to teaching and learning is to assess your current use of time. Keeping an accurate daily log of your activities for at least five school days is the best way to do this. Those administrators who keep a detailed schedule may need only to review it at noon and the end of the day to record notations of what actually happened. Those who do not keep such planned schedules can create a daily log of their activities that can be recorded on an ongoing basis. Keep the log simple so that you can carry it with you. Figure 19-1 offers a sample of how it might look.

When logs or schedules are available for at least five days, you can begin an analysis of how your time is actually used. This can be done by assigning each activity in the log or the schedule to one of the three priority categories discussed earlier: priority 1—learning and achievement, priority 2—running the school, and priority 3—no direct impact on learning and achievement. Your knowledge and information about each activity will determine the priority assigned. Figure 19-2 provides a sample.

Considering one day at a time, add up the time spent in activities in each priority and record it on a summary sheet. Then consider the percentage of time spent that day with each priority. Figure 19-3 shows a sample for one day.

It is up to you to reflect on the results of your analysis. Having the information about how you use your time may help you to confirm your commitment to student achievement as your first priority. On the other hand, the analysis may help you to make changes that bring your intent to prioritize student achievement closer to the reality of how you actually use your time. Here are some possibilities.

- Find ways to delegate clerical work to secretaries or assistants.

- Schedule paperwork at times when students and staff are not in the building.

- Reduce the number of student referrals by helping teachers use more effective behavior-modification approaches.

- Act on referrals only after other means have been tried.

It is unrealistic to think that a total focus on the first priority of student learning and achievement can happen all the time. Some activities, such as district meetings or official visits from state agencies, are not usually under the administrator's control. There are, however, other factors that can be controlled, such as when to meet with parents, return or accept phone calls, listen to complaints, write reports or letters, and respond to a request for a student referral. The key to effective use of time is to recognize that which you cannot control and work on those factors that you can control.

Here are some guidelines to consider:

- If it has to do with student learning and achievement, do it first.

- Devote the maximum time possible to student achievement when students and staff are in the building.

- Select the best times for observations and conferences and schedule those appointments at least one week in advance. It is harder to cancel an appointment and reschedule it than it is to stick to a schedule.

- Plan to do reports, answer phone calls, and read materials after school hours.

- Be prepared to take work home with you as a part of your responsibilities.

Figure 19-1

SAMPLE LOG

Monday   February 25, 2002

Time	Activity
8:00–8:45	Walked through the halls and chatted with teachers and lunch workers
8:45–8:55	Monitored student use of the staircases
9:00–9:10	Spoke with a book company about an order
9:10–9:40	Met with Ms. Fearson about her directed growth plan
9:40–10:00	Met with Mrs. Holmes, parent of Allison Gaines
10:00–10:40	Overview observation of Mr. Frank
10:45–11:00	Reflected on the observation and planned the conference
11:00–12:00	Worked on comprehensive plan for the district Responded to 3 phone calls
12:00–12:15	Monitored student lunchroom
12:15–12:45	Ate with teachers in the faculty lunchroom
12:45–1:00	Visited the lower school study team
1:00–1:40	Conference with Mr. Frank about the observation
1:40–1:50	Met with 3rd-grade teacher Mrs. Seldom about a custodial complaint
1:50–2:30	Reviewed student artifacts—-grade 6 mathematics tests
2:30–2:45	Monitored bus dismissal
2:50–3:05	Prepared for the School Leadership Team meeting
3:05–3:15	Spoke with teachers informally
3:15–5:00	School Leadership Team meeting
5:00–5:30	Answered mail and returned phone calls

Figure 19-2

ASSIGNING PRIORITIES TO THE LOG SAMPLE

Monday   February 25, 2002

Priority	Time	Activity
2	8:00–8:45	Walked through the halls and chatted with teachers and lunch workers
2	8:45–9:00	Monitored student use of the staircases
1	9:00–9:10	Spoke with a book company about an order
1	9:10–9:40	Met with Ms. Fearson about her directed growth plan
3	9:40–10:00	Met with Mrs. Holmes, parent of Allison Gaines
1	10:00–10:40	Overview observation of Mr. Frank
1	10:40–11:00	Reflected on the observation and planned the conference
2	11:00–12:00	Worked on comprehensive plan for the district Responded to 3 phone calls
2	12:00–12:15	Monitored student lunchroom
2	12:15–12:45	Ate with teachers in the faculty lunchroom
1	12:45–1:00	Visited the lower school study team
1	1:00–1:40	Conference with Mr. Frank
3	1:40–1:50	Met with 3rd grade teacher Mrs. Seldom about a custodial complaint
1	1:50–2:30	Reviewed student artifacts—grade 6 mathematics tests
2	2:30–2:45	Monitored bus dismissal
2	2:45–3:05	Prepared for the School Leadership Team meeting
2	3:05–3:15	Spoke with teachers informally
2	3:15–5:00	School Leadership Team meeting
3	5:00–5:30	Answered mail and returned phone calls

Figure 19-3
SAMPLE SUMMARY SHEET

Week of February 25 to March 1, 2002

	Monday 2/25	Tuesday	Wednesday	Thursday	Friday
Total Time	*9 hrs. 30 min.*				
Priority 1	3:15 (34%)				
Priority 2	5:15 (55%)				
Priority 3	1:00 (10.5%)				

Keeping Track of Teaching and Learning

Focusing on learning and achievement as the first priority includes keeping accurate records about the *what, when, why,* and *with whom* of your activities. Keeping a calendar, log, or schedule of activities is essential for maintaining effective records. These records serve to guide you in setting goals, making suggestions, and monitoring progress. There are various ways to record the activities related to learning and student achievement.

FORMAL RECORDS

Formal records are written records that require the teacher's signature and are placed in the teacher's file. They become a part of a growing body of information about the teacher.

The teacher's file, as an official collection of data, is subject to specific requirements:

1. The teacher must sign everything in the file.

2. The teacher must have a copy of everything in the file.

3. The file is open to the teacher's inspection.

Data appropriate for formal records include appropriately signed forms discussed in previous sections. A list of these forms follows:

- Overview Conference Summary
- Classroom Environment Observation Form
- Time-on-Task Review
- Observation Plan
  Observation Write-up
- Directed Growth Plan
  Plan Specification
  Plan Review
- Collaborative Growth Plan
  Plan Specification
  Plan Review
- Teacher-Directed Growth Plan for the Individual
  Plan Specification
  Plan Review
- Teacher-Directed Growth Plan for Peers
  Plan Specification
  Plan Review

This formal accumulation of data, however, provides no opportunity to record and maintain records about material not kept in the teacher's official file. That is the purpose of informal records.

INFORMAL RECORDS

There are three types of data appropriate for informal records. These include:

1. Your private notes, reactions, thoughts, and projections about both formal and informal efforts

2. Reminders, due dates, requests made, suggestions given, books loaned, and reported data

3. Ongoing data that is gathered that may not be signed by the teacher, such as notes or memos from informal visits (see Section 5), plan review memos (see Section 8), and the top sheet for student artifacts review (see Section 8)

MAINTAINING INFORMAL RECORDS

There is no one best way to keep informal records. Some administrators keep electronic records. Others prefer to keep hard copies with handwritten notes. You must decide what works best for you. Some suggestions to help you get started follow.

What to record.   The individual data log serves as a summary and reminder of information about each teacher. (See Figure 19-4.) An entry should be made about each piece of data that has been gathered and significant teacher interactions. The entries include the date and form of the data. The comments and personal notes you make are guides to future actions. Keeping a schedule or log of your activities will help you to remember what to record.

Use a looseleaf binder.   The binder should contain the individual data logs for each teacher. It may be helpful to keep a copy of notes sent to the teacher about informal visits, artifacts, and plans that were reviewed in the looseleaf. These may then be used as the specifics for follow-up.

Use separate teacher files.   A separate and individual file may be used as an alternative means of collecting informal data and recording notes. The file would include the same information suggested for the looseleaf binder.

Organizing the data.   You may prefer to keep topic-specific records together rather than place informal data behind the individual teacher's log page. For example, you might keep one looseleaf binder for all plan review memos sent, arranging them

Figure 19-4
INDIVIDUAL DATA LOG

Teacher's Name ___Kerry Roberts___ Assignment ___4-201___ Year ___2001-2002___

DATE	FORM OF THE DATA	COMMENT	NOTES
9/20	Overview Conference	Difficulty in maintaining discipline with three disruptive students	Ask the study team to assist the teacher in planning a behavior-modification program.
9/27	Informal Visit	Behavior-modification chart is posted All students are on task	Continue informal visits to monitor.
10/11	Overview Observation	Directed growth plan was begun	Meetings scheduled for work on level of questions.
10/21	Informal Visit	Two students are having difficulty with addition with exchange	Memo to the teacher to order squared material. Schedule a visitation to Mr. James's classroom to observe how squared materials are used.
11/4	Plan Review Memo	Only two mathematics concepts are planned for the week	Plan review memo sent. Check mathematics plan for wk of 11/10.
11/14	Observation Topic-questioning	Marked improvement in the level of questions asked Teacher states that the behavior-modification plan is going well	Note questions asked during informal visits.

alphabetically. A second binder or file folder might contain all top sheets for student artifact reviews.

The advantage of maintaining topic-specific records is to allow you to easily compare progress and quality of instruction between and among teachers with similar assignments. For example, you could review grade or department objectives for student writing activities, or you could compare plans for the seventh-grade science teachers.

Topic-specific records are a disadvantage when you want to review the progress of individual teachers by monitoring ongoing data. You would need to pull several sets of data to conduct this review.

No matter how you keep records, the key to communicating effectively with yourself about what you are doing and how you are keeping track of those activities is to keep a daily calendar, schedule, or log.

Part V

Professional Development that Impacts Student Achievement

Professional Development that Leads to Student Achievement

Rigorous student achievement standards measured by high-stake assessments have been established across the nation. Schools today do not only provide education; they are expected to ensure learning. Teachers are expected to not only teach the curriculum; they are expected to build a bridge between the learning standards and the needs of each learner. At the same time, there is a growing knowledge base and increasing consensus about what teachers should know and be able to do to help all students successfully reach the standards. These expectations demand that teachers have a deep knowledge of subject matter, a good understanding of how students learn, the ability to make complex decisions, and a commitment to working closely with colleagues. This cannot happen without effective and ongoing professional development that creates and sustains a highly prepared teaching force for all, not just some, of our children.

Adult Learners

Understanding teachers as adult learners supports efforts directed at increasing teachers' knowledge, skills, and abilities to make students successful. A discussion of factors to incorporate into your work with teachers follows.

CONTROL THE SITUATION

Adults need to be self-directed. They should never believe they are being treated as children. Their participation in learning is always voluntary even when required. This is because they can be required to attend, but they cannot be forced to listen, accept, and apply what was discussed. Therefore, provide teachers with the broadest number of choices possible. Involve them in designing choices whenever possible. Emphasize the benefits of participating and present meaningful incentives, when appropriate. For example, offer a new set of materials, an additional preparation period to experiment with the strategy, and assistance in their classroom.

USE PRIOR KNOWLEDGE

Adults have a wealth of knowledge and experience. Use this knowledge and capitalize on these experiences to provide a link between what they know and are comfortable with and the objectives to be learned. For example, teachers may have successfully used a strategy that is similar. They may have previously heard about the strategy or seen it used in another setting.

MOTIVATE BY NEED

Adults are motivated by the need to solve real problems. Relate proposed learning experiences to concerns that teachers express and problems with which they want help. Ask them to state these problems and address them in the workshop whenever possible.

PERFORMANCE CENTERED

Adults are performance centered in their orientation to learning. Provide ways in which new learning can be immediately applied to their situations. Rather than asking teachers to wait before trying out new ideas, because the materials have not come or the strategy has not been presented in its entirety, encourage them to try out pieces and parts with which they are comfortable. For example, learning how to implement cooperative learning is a complex process that cannot be accomplished in one session. Teachers, however, can begin to plan how to group their students, or actually try a small group activity as the first steps in applying the practices.

SWITCH PERSPECTIVE

Adults may need to change their perspective to accept something new. Sometimes, new strategies may differ dramatically from what teachers have been doing over a long period of time. For example, for teachers who believe that students should take their own notes as a means of concentrating attention and focus on the lesson, using advance/graphic organizers requires a new perspective on the teaching and learning process. Encourage teachers to ask questions, reflect critically, and engage in dialogue with their colleagues.

The workshop plans presented in this section have woven the adult learning factors into the discussion.

Selecting Topics for Professional Development

There are four areas to consider when selecting topics for professional development: strategies verified by research to improve student achievement; diagnosed needs of staff members; building and district initiates; and staff involvement in the selection, plan, and design.

STRATEGIES VERIFIED BY RESEARCH TO IMPROVE STUDENT ACHIEVEMENT

Research has uncovered strong links between certain teaching practices and positive student achievement. Programs that districts invest in often provide student-achievement data as a part of their information materials. Look for research verification as you consider the topic for professional development. Review the Standards for Teaching that Target Students' Achievement, discussed in Section 2, and the examples that follow.

- Classroom management practices that help to maintain an orderly environment
- Reinforcing effort and providing recognition
- Effective use of instructional time
- Keeping students actively involved in their learning
- Monitoring student learning throughout the instructional period
- Setting objectives and providing feedback
- Teaching to varied modalities
- Use of graphic and advance organizers
- Questions and cues to access prior knowledge
- Group or team learning approaches
- Cooperative learning

DIAGNOSED NEEDS OF STAFF MEMBERS

Selecting topics for professional development that relate to the diagnosed needs of staff members is an effective means of raising the level of instruction. Refer to Part II for a detailed discussion of the full range of diagnostic data that can be collected and six different collection tools. Group teachers with similar needs and, whenever possible, ask them to select which of the areas of need they wish to work on at this time. The professional-development activities in which they engage should be included in their individual growth plans.

BUILDING AND DISTRICT INITIATIVES

Professional development must be conducted before any new program, instructional strategy, or instructional schedules are adopted by the school and/or the district if they are to be successful. For example, teachers will not be successful with a mathematics program that relies on manipulatives, or a literature-based approach to reading, or moving from 45-minute to 90-minute class periods without being involved in professional-development activities that provide the information, clarification, and commitment required for their success.

STAFF INVOLVEMENT IN THE SELECTION, PLAN, AND DESIGN

When participants in professional development are not involved in its planning, they frequently end up feeling alienated and distrustful, and they sit through sessions with no intention of using the ideas in their classrooms. This negative attitude may be magnified when the design of the workshops fails to include factors that influence teaching and learning, such as the nature of the school and the community, and the differences in the levels of experience of teachers in the group.

It is important that those who will be expected to implement the focus of the professional development be a part of its planning. Since not every professional can be part of the planning group, staff members should select their representatives. Their peers should hold those who represent the staff in high esteem so that their judgment will be respected and accepted. The planning group plays a vital role in several ways. It selects the topic or approves the topic suggested by the school or the district with a full understanding of the rationale for its selection and the need it is intended to serve. The planning group provides vital information about the specific characteristics of the school community, its attitude, and the levels of experience of the staff that can then be used to design an effective plan for professional development. The planning group can also provide suggestions about the time and place for the professional development activity to be conducted. The planning group can become cheerleaders for the professional development when its participation is real and its involvement is meaningful. That positive attitude will influence others.

Determining the Time, Place, and Frequency for Professional Development

Adult learners require learning environments that are physically and psychologically comfortable. These factors can make or, in some instances, break even the best professional-development efforts.

MAKE THE TIME FRAME ATTRACTIVE TO TEACHERS

Without question, the single most desirable time frames for professional development are those days in the school calendar when school is closed for students because the days have been set aside for professional development. Schools districts are beginning to recognize the benefits of professional development and building those days into the school calendar. Although this is a great start, two, three, or even four days over the course of a school year are just not enough. When school districts have not created these opportunities, or the opportunities for professional development are limited, there are several time frames that can be used for professional development. Each of them has benefits and limitations so they must be carefully considered. Include the planning group in discussing these alternatives, suggesting others, and making the decision.

- Conduct professional development during the school day and release teachers from their instructional responsibilities.

  Benefits:

  Teachers are asked to participate as a part of their regular working day.

  Teachers feel they are treated as professionals.

  Limitations:

  There is a shortage of substitutes to cover the teachers' assignments.

  The cost of substitutes must be included in the professional-development budget.

  Substitutes are not always of high caliber and students lose valuable instructional time.

- Conduct professional development after the school day and pay teachers for their participation.

  Benefits:

  No instructional time with students is lost.

  Substitutes are not needed.

  Limitations:

  The cost of paying the teachers must be included in the professional development budget.

  Teachers may be tired after a day of teaching.

  Teachers may have family responsibilities after school that divide their attention.

- Conduct professional development on a weekend or days when school is not in session and pay teachers for their participation.

  Benefits:

  No instructional time with students is lost.

  Substitutes are not needed.

  Teachers are not fatigued.

  Limitations:

  The cost of paying the teachers must be included in the professional-development budget.

  Teachers may have family responsibilities that make their attendance difficult and contribute to dividing their attention.

  Teachers may feel resentful about participating during a time frame that they believe belongs to them.

  Religious observers may be prevented from attending.

PAY ATTENTION TO THE NEED FOR CREATURE COMFORTS

A clean, attractive, and spacious setting away from a school and the district office is ideal for professional development. That is the kind of atmosphere in which teachers feel respected, professional, and ready to learn about enlarging and enhancing their professional practice. If you plan to conduct the professional-development sessions in a rented space, include those costs in your budget. That decision may well bring you large returns on the expense in the form of teacher willingness to accept and transfer the ideas presented.

When an alternative to a school or the district office is not an option, check on the following factors:

1. The availability and proximity of restrooms

2. When, where, and by whom the food will be served

3. Adequate space for planned activities

4. Comfortable chairs and tables

Wherever the professional-development session is held, provide:

- **Morning coffee and food.** The availability of coffee often contributes to an earlier arrival of participants.

- **Adequate parking facilities.** You do not want to start a professional-development day with angry participants.

- **Breaks every one-and-a-half to two hours.** Adults need to get up and stretch.

- **Supplies and equipment in good order** that contribute to the professional-development plan. Nothing is worse than planning to show a video that demonstrates a key activity with a defective VCR, tape, or monitor.

- **Sufficient quantity of clear and attractive handouts.** Be prepared for coffee spills and other unanticipated events, such as additional participants or guests.

ONE SHOT IS NOT ENOUGH

Professional development that impacts teaching and learning does not happen in one session. Like many other worthwhile learning experiences, professional development is a process that requires sufficient time; supportive, nonthreatening feedback; and opportunities for discussion, networking, and observing what others are doing. This process enables teachers to first understand, then master, and finally effectively integrate the strategies or techniques into their practice. Be sure you plan follow-up sessions that are two or three weeks apart. Section 21 presents specific strategies for linking the workshop objectives to classroom practice and student achievement between workshop sessions and after the sessions have ended.

Plan Effective Workshops
that Include All Components

Effective professional-development sessions proceed through three training components that are necessary for most teachers to acquire facility with the workshop objectives. The factors related to adult learners have been integrated into the training components. The components are: presentation of theory and research, demonstration/reflection/discussion, and practice with feedback. But first, get their attention!

ICEBREAKERS/HOT STARTS/JUMP-STARTS

Although for many participants, learning is its own reward and coming to a workshop is both exciting and interesting, for others, just the opposite is true. It therefore may be beneficial to first get their attention. Break down the walls of inhibition, lethargy, overload, or just plain disinterest. The following quick activities will set the tone of the workshop, wake up participants, and get them immediately involved.

- Throw a ball made of a soft material, such as wool, into the group. Tell the participants: "If you catch the ball, you must introduce yourself, your role in the school, and what you are interested in learning. Then throw the ball to someone else."

- Ask participants to get up out of their seats, walk around the room, and find someone they do not know. They then introduce themselves to this person and share a personal goal for this year.

- Ask participants to reflect by themselves and then write down their personal goal for the workshop. They then share that goal with the person on their right or left. Ask some of the participants to share their goals with the large group.

- Distribute candy wrapped in papers of assorted colors. Ask participants to find someone else who has the same color wrapper and introduce themselves and their personal goals.

PRESENTATION OF THEORY AND RESEARCH

This first stage of professional development provides teachers with the theory, research, and information that support the objectives of the professional-development session. It helps to answer questions in teachers' minds about why they are here and why they are doing this. Teachers must believe that the strategies and techniques presented are not just another fad, but rather a substantive way to increase student achievement. There is a delicate balance to maintain in this first stage between giving too much technical information that overwhelms participants, and not enough to be believed. Three strategies may help to maintain this balance.

1. Draw a comparison between the theory and research and a learning experience that adults may have had so that they can use something familiar, from their prior

knowledge, to build a bridge to the new information. For example, most adults have experienced learning to drive a car, ride a bike, play golf, and/or swim.

2. Present the statistical information in easy-to-read graphs, charts, and/or diagrams that clearly display the information.

3. Use familiar symbols that contribute to understanding the information, such as arrows, mountain climbing, and sunbursts.

DEMONSTRATION/REFLECTION/DISCUSSION

This component begins with clear *demonstrations* of the recommended practice. It may include live modeling, videotapes, detailed narrative descriptions, and even vividly described and labeled examples. In short, when trying to learn a new skill or concept, it helps to see it or visualize it in action.

Participants are then asked to *reflect* individually or with a peer by thinking aloud about the demonstrations. They now have the opportunity to construct their own understanding of what they saw and make it meaningful to them and their situations.

These thoughts are *discussed,* explored, shared, and further clarified with a small group of no more than eight peers. It is important to keep the discussion groups small because this increases the involvement of all participants. Shy people are more likely to feel confident to speak up and those who tend to dominate are usually more considerate of their group members' desire to contribute their ideas. The discussion phase is most productive when the group maintains its focus on the topic rather than getting sidetracked. Assigning the peer groups a specific task may be helpful in keeping them focused. The task directs them to explain what they saw, and discuss application alternatives and possible application concerns with their suggested solutions. Section 21 provides additional suggestions for continuing these small-group discussions between workshop sessions and after all the sessions have been completed.

PRACTICE WITH FEEDBACK

Having opportunities to *practice* a new skill and receive immediate *feedback* in a safe environment contributes tremendously to learning. When learning a new skill or technique, it helps to try it out with the support of others. Small-group activities, designed to allow teachers to practice using the strategies in simulations, are the next workshop component. Each participant has an opportunity to role-play the strategy. The group provides feedback and encouragement to the participant about the performance with the trainer's input as he or she monitors the practice session.

Figure 20-1 presents a planning guide for professional-development activities that may be used as a checklist.

Figure 20-1

PROFESSIONAL-DEVELOPMENT PLANNING GUIDE

GUIDELINES	PLAN
Topic Selection Verified by research Diagnosed staff needs Building/school initiative	
Staff Involvement Selection Plan Design	
Time Frame	
Location	
Creature Comforts Setting Parking Breaks Supplies/equipment Handouts	
Number of Sessions	
Follow-up	
Workshop Components Theory and research Demonstration Reflection Discussion Practice with feedback	

Linking the Workshop to Student Achievement

Effectively planned and conducted workshops contribute to teachers' understanding and the development of an initial level of skill about new strategies and techniques. But linking the workshop objectives to student achievement requires teachers to have more extensive skill development and consistent practice with feedback than can be accomplished in the workshop sessions alone.

How to Make Professional Development Work in the Classroom

Three powerful strategies will contribute to making professional development work in classrooms and result in increased student achievement. Help teachers to risk the stages of doubt and fear that surround the learning of new practices by guiding and promoting the process of learning, having teachers watch each other teach, and discuss what was observed.

GUIDING AND PROMOTING THE PROCESS OF LEARNING

Administrative support, encouragement, and acknowledgment are key elements in the learning process that need to be expressed frequently both verbally and in short communications. Teachers will then begin to shift their concerns from how the strategies will affect them personally to how the strategies will contribute to student achievement. This shift in concerns is supported by the teachers' belief that they are in control of their learning because they are given a safe and risk-free environment in which to practice the strategies. This means their efforts during the learning process will not be evaluated. When teachers are given the time and assistance they need to be successful, they will feel capable and ultimately be successful in doing what is asked of them.

TEACHERS WATCH EACH OTHER TEACH

Professional-development strategies and techniques are learned successfully and transmitted more effectively into classroom practice when teachers have the opportunity to watch each other practice the new strategies in their classrooms. As peer observers collect information for the teacher by recording the teacher's actions and the student behaviors that result, they achieve three benefits.

First, they give feedback to the teacher being observed about what they saw. This feedback provides the observed teachers with the opportunity to see themselves through another pair of eyes.

Second, the peer observers become more aware of their own teaching efforts as they compare what they are observing with their own practices. This awareness may influence their actions and lead to useful changes.

Third, the peer observers are helped to better understand how to implement the strategy or technique by seeing good ideas that they can incorporate into their own teaching.

Being observed by a peer may seem threatening at first, but as teachers realize their peers are helping them, not judging them, the threat is replaced by powerful and constructive collegial interactions. When teachers watch each other teach in a collegial atmosphere, the walls between classrooms break down, and the isolation and need for self-protection sometimes experienced by teachers are eliminated.

TEACHERS DISCUSS WHAT WAS OBSERVED

The greatest benefits of the peer-observation process are achieved when teachers think about and discuss what they observed and how student learning was impacted. As teachers continue to practice new techniques in their classrooms, observe each other, and give and receive feedback, they begin to identify strategies that have the greatest influences on student learning. Peer discussions provide the opportunity for teachers to share their successful ideas and future plans with other teachers, along with their concerns and those strategies that were less successful.

Organizing Study Teams

Study teams formalize the collegial interactions discussed above by ensuring their consistency. There is a special kind of strength that develops among a small group of teachers who meet regularly to improve their professional practice. When teachers hear about the instructional problems of their colleagues and collaboratively engage in suggesting solutions to solve the problems, they grow as professionals in competence and confidence about their ability.

WHAT STUDY TEAMS CAN DO

Teachers eliminate the isolation of teaching when they consistently participate on a study team. Teachers learn they are not alone with their questions and problems. They can work with other teachers who have similar situations and interests to seek solutions.

Members of the study team coach each other about how to improve instruction that results in student achievement. They build a learning community of teachers that continuously supports each other. They encourage each other to examine student data, and then provide assistance in the analysis of that data to determine which students are on target, those who have some areas that require reinforcement, and what is preventing some students from achieving. Having that information, the study team thinks together to identify the strategies that should be tried. The study team watches each other implement the selected strategies, and provides feedback to support, encourage, and improve their colleagues' efforts. Teachers in this process deepen their knowledge of instruction and subject matter.

Teachers who are engaged in study teams become more confident about their instructional practice. They feel valued as professionals because they are meaningfully engaged with substantive work that results in student success. The respect and acknowledgment they receive inspire them to continuously seek ways to grow professionally.

Figure 21-1 provides ten reasons for the effectiveness of study teams.

HOW STUDY TEAMS WORK

Identify team members. Study teams usually bring together teachers with similar assignments and responsibilities. These may be teachers on a grade level, for example, or members of an instructional unit such as primary educators. Team members may be members of a particular department, such as English teachers, or members of interdisciplinary teams. Study teams are most effective when their members are knowledgeable about, interested in, and committed to the same areas of concern.

Establish ground rules. Each study team establishes its own ground rules. These are the ways in which the study team will operate. These ground rules are tailored to the needs of the individuals in the study team. For example, if the team includes an individual who is usually late, one selected ground rule might be: "Be on time all the time." If individuals on the team are usually negative about most things, a selected ground rule might be: "Only positive comments, please." Ground rules may also specify the process the study team will use, such as making decisions by consensus or limiting discussion to agenda items. The number of ground rules should be kept to a minimum by selecting only four or five and be visible as a reminder to all members of the team.

Figure 21-1

WHAT STUDY TEAMS CAN DO

THE TOP TEN REASONS FOR USING STUDY TEAMS

1. Eliminate the isolation of teaching.

2. Encourage teachers to work together to solve problems.

3. Enable teachers to coach each other about strategies that result in student achievement.

4. Build a learning community of teachers who continuously support each other as they engage in teaching and learning.

5. Encourage teachers to use data they have gathered as evidence of student learning and needs in their planning.

6. Deepen teachers' knowledge of instruction and subject matter.

7. Help teachers to become more confident about their instructional practice.

8. Value teachers by providing meaningful engagement with substantive work.

9. Inspire teachers through respect, acknowledgment, and achievement of student success.

10. Directly influence teacher effectiveness, which leads to student achievement.

Determine the roles of team members.   Each member of the study team assumes a role and responsibility that the team has identified as important to its work. Here is a sample list of roles and responsibilities.

- *Organizer:* Prepares the agenda for the team meeting by requesting input from team members and reviewing the minutes of previous meetings.

- *Recorder:* Prepares and distributes the minutes of the meeting within a given time frame.

- *Resource seeker:* Finds, secures, and distributes resources for the team to use.

- *Overseer:* Reminds team members about the ground rules and helps to keep the team's attention on the task.

- *Mediator:* Resolves conflict by seeking consensus.

- *Process observer:* Observes team meetings to ensure that everyone has and uses the opportunity to participate and be heard.

Some of these roles may be assumed by the team leader, while others are usually rotated among study team members.

Agree on meeting logistics.   Meeting consistently and frequently are the hallmarks of effective teams. Ideally, teams meet at least once per week. The effectiveness of the team's work diminishes when too much time passes between team meetings. The opportunity to discuss and analyze the results of solution strategies that were agreed upon and acted upon by team members may be lost. Reaching agreement on when and where to meet sometimes becomes difficult. When this happens, the study team can build consensus by negotiation and compromise. The team must find a way to reach agreement among those who do not want to come early to meet before classes begin, stay late after classes have ended, work during the lunch break, or give time during their preparation periods. These problems disappear when the school or district provides time for study team meetings. Several suggestions for low-cost meeting strategies are presented later in this section.

Select what to work on.   Study team members collect data about how their students are doing. These data come from many sources. Teachers observe their students individually and as a group during and after instruction. They evaluate what their students produce, and how their students perform when they answer questions, complete assignments, and take teacher-made and standardized tests. Team members bring the diagnostic data to team meetings to analyze and discuss with their team to find the trouble spots and the gaps that are holding back students. The team becomes a powerful force for students' success when the shared data is used to identify what the team will work on.

Identify solution strategies to be undertaken. The team proposes solution strategies to eliminate the problems that have been identified. Team members agree on the specific strategies that will be undertaken. Each member of the team agrees to try a proposed strategy and bring information about the results of those efforts to the team meeting. A specific time frame should be established. Strategies that can be completed in a short time frame, such as using a graphic organizer to help students understand the sequence of events, or refining directions given to students, may be reported to the team at the next meeting. Other strategies that may take more time, such as reorganizing how students are grouped for instruction, or integrating reading and writing with social studies, or creating rubrics to assess students' projects, might be scheduled for discussion in two or three weeks.

Team members coach each other to provide assistance and support with implementing the strategies agreed upon. They may work together to develop materials and/or observe each other using the strategies or materials. Team members provide objective feedback to each other about what they observed and then discuss and analyze how well it worked.

Specify how to evaluate the team's work. The team establishes criteria to evaluate how well the solution strategies worked usually by collecting new data. These data are discussed at team meetings and used to direct the team's future actions. Since the study team evaluates the effectiveness of its work and the next steps in the process in a confidential environment, team members are open and honest about the results and what next must be done to achieve continued student success.

Figure 21-2 presents a framework for organizing the study teams.

STUDY TEAM LEADERSHIP

Designating a peer leader for the study team usually helps the study team be more productive and effective. Peer leaders provide guidance for team members as they analyze data to identify what to work on, and effectively apply the strategies and techniques that will have an impact on student achievement. They oversee the organizational aspects of the team and provide reminders about the ground rules. They also help the team to work collaboratively in a positive and professional climate. The team leader may assume some, but not all of the roles that team members share or rotate. Preparing the agenda and overseeing the work of the team are appropriate responsibilities for a study team leader.

The following guidelines may be of help to study team leaders, as well as to the members of their study team as they gain experience and confidence.

- **Practice good communication skills.** Use nonverbal, active, and interactive listening skills discussed in Section 17 and learn when to use which one. Become proficient at positive body language because how you look when you say something is often more important than what you say. Watch your voice rate and pitch as you communicate, especially if you are excited.

Figure 21-2
ORGANIZING STUDY TEAMS

WHO is on the team? What are their roles?

WHAT are the ground rules?

WHEN/WHERE will the team meet?

HOW do we know what to work on?

WHAT solution strategies will be undertaken? By whom?

HOW will the work of the team be evaluated?

- **Be open.** Be sure all relevant information is shared. Speak specifically using examples. Challenge assumptions, inferences, and stereotypes and invite questions and comments.

- **Establish and maintain trust.** Remind team members about being consistent and dependable. Establish and maintain a safe climate in which difficult issues can be discussed and reflection is encouraged. Do not allow cheap shots and putdowns by anyone.

- **Manage conflict.** Focus on what the individual needs, not his or her position about what is wanted when looking for solutions. Agree to end disagreements by finding solutions. Make decisions by consensus so that everyone agrees.

- **Be productive.** Be sure an agenda is prepared in advance of the meeting and all team members are asked for items. Encourage all team members to participate and remain focused on the topic under discussion.

These guidelines are summarized in Figure 21-3.

LOW-COST MEETING STRATEGIES

When schools and districts provide time for study teams to meet and for study team members to work with each other, the work of the team is more effective. Some suggestions for finding time follow.

1. Administrative personnel cover one teacher's class each day to allow the released teacher the opportunity to observe a study team member.

2. Schedule large-group instruction by combining several classes to attend a musical performance or an art exhibit, view a video on a subject-related topic, listen to a speaker, or observe a presentation. The study team can meet during this period.

3. Combine classes that have independent assignments to complete. Study team members can meet during this time frame.

4. Begin classes 30 minutes late once a week. Ask study team members to arrive 30 minutes early, giving the study team one hour for its meeting.

5. Dismiss classes 30 minutes early once a week. Ask study team members to remain 30 minutes beyond the usual closing time, giving the study team one hour to meet.

6. Pair teachers from two different study teams so that each teacher on the same team is released by a teacher from another team who will work with two classes while the released teachers meet with their study team. The pairs switch on another day, releasing the teachers from the other study team for their meeting.

Figure 21-3
GUIDELINES FOR EFFECTIVE TEAMS

❏ **Practice Good Communication Skills**

Listening patterns

Nonverbal clues

Voice influences

Paraphrasing

❏ **Be Open**

All relevant information is shared.

Assumptions, inferences, and stereotypes are challenged.

Speak specifically and use examples.

The intent of important words is discussed.

Reasons behind statements are explained.

Questions and comments are invited.

❏ **Establish Trust**

Team members are consistent and dependable.

A "safe" climate is established and maintained.

Difficult issues are discussed.

Cheap shots and putdowns do not exist.

Self-reflection is practiced.

❏ **Manage Conflict**

Needs, not positions, are the focus.

Disagreements are resolved by finding solutions.

Decisions are made by consensus.

❏ **Be Productive**

An agenda is prepared in advance.

Discussions are focused.

All members of the team fully participate.

7. Hire a team of four or five substitutes for one day every other week. Each hour of the day, the substitutes release the members of one study team for a team meeting.

8. Study team members are released from faculty, grade, or department meetings on a rotating basis, at least once per month, to provide compensatory time for study team meetings.

Coaching for Transfer to Practice
that Impacts Student Achievement

Coaching offers a personalized peer-assistance process that is more focused than the collegial interactions and study teams discussed above. It provides intensive, one-on-one, in-classroom assistance to help teachers with the transfer to their instructional plans of complex skills and strategies presented in the workshops. Coaching is also effective when working with directed growth plans for teachers who are new to teaching and those who have many critical skill needs. Section 11 provides a description of the coach in a directed growth plan.

WHEN TO INSTITUTE COACHING

Coaching requires a commitment of time and money, so it should be considered carefully before any action is taken. There are four factors that may influence the decision to institute coaching.

1. **The gap between current practice and professional-development objectives.** Coaching may be desirable when the nature of the skills and strategies to be implemented into classroom practice are very different from current practice. For example, instituting a constructionist approach to teaching and learning for teachers who normally use a textbook or workbook approach to instruction, or a cooperative learning approach to teaching for teachers who normally use whole-group instruction, represent dramatic departures from current practice. Coaching may give these teachers the help they need with making applications to their individual teaching situations.

2. **The complexity of the skills and strategies teachers are to master.** The more complex the skills and strategies, the more in-classroom assistance will be needed before teachers can effectively incorporate them into their classroom instructional applications. For example, project-based learning requires the extensive preparation of learning targets, available resources, diversified activities, and multievaluation criteria, including the use of portfolios. Coaching may prevent teachers from becoming overwhelmed and giving up or implementing the strategy in a less than adequate manner.

3. **Link to school-improvement plans.** Professional-development strategies that are tied to school-improvement plans and increases in student test scores are critical. For example, if a balanced literacy program is expected to achieve stated gains in students' scores, it may be wise to employ coaching as a way to ensure that teachers are using the program effectively. Similarly, when an interdisciplinary social studies and literature program is expected to reduce student conflict, coaching could make a big difference in actual results by helping teachers be successful with their instructional applications.

4. **Teachers' level of experience and commitment.** Classrooms are the real world of teaching. Finding ways to implement professional-development targets takes time, effort, and knowledge that is often difficult for those who are new to teaching and resisted by others. Consider both the level of experience and the commitment of staff members to determine those teachers who may need the assistance, encouragement, and close follow-up that coaching can provide to ensure quality and consistency with the application of professional-development objectives to instruction.

COACHING REQUIREMENTS

The expert who is designated as coach may be an administrator, staff developer, the workshop trainer, university personnel, or a peer teacher. Coaching requires a great deal of time in the classroom and in discussion with the teacher. Since time, availability, and the job description that follows are important factors, a peer teacher usually makes the most effective coach. Coaches are usually compensated with a stipend or bonus in addition to receiving released time to coach and recognition as an expert. At times, coaches are given stipend or bonus but no released time. These coaches are expected to conduct a coaching program before and/or after school, or during lunch or a preparation period. There are severe limitations to this arrangement both in the availability of the individuals and their desire to be involved. The quality and success of this type of coaching plan is limited.

When a peer teacher is selected as the coach, provision must be made for released time for the coach to work with the teacher. It is usually easier and advantageous to release teachers to be coaches in secondary schools by reducing the coach's teaching assignments. Larger numbers of teachers could be involved as coaches presenting expertise in different disciplines. Releasing teachers from classroom responsibilities is generally more difficult at the elementary level. Designating a full-time peer coach is advisable. There are several advantages to this. First, there is no issue about removing the teacher from his or her classroom. Second, the coach is continuously available, not only during released periods. Third, the coach can effectively work, one-on-one, with a number of different teachers in the same building, or in schools in close proximity, over a period of time.

COACHING GUIDELINES

Coaching is a professional and collaborative activity between a coach who has knowledge and skill, and a teacher who needs more help than can be provided through the staff-development process. Here are some guidelines for the job of coach.

- **Coaches are consistent and dependable.** Coaches remain with the same teachers for the length of the coaching relationship unless asked to stop the activity. Being able to count on the coach for help over time lowers anxiety and builds confidence that can result in the teacher's success.

- **Coaches are collegial.** Coaches behave in a professional manner and treat teachers with respect and dignity. Although coaches may not develop a close and lasting friendship with the teacher, they should be cordial, cheerful, empathetic, and accepting. When a coach does develop a close and personal relationship with the teacher, care should be taken to avoid a protective or defensive attitude.

- **Coaching relationships are confidential.** Coaches provide a safe environment in which all information discussed remains between the coach and the teacher. Coaches do not provide evaluative information to administrators, and they do not write evaluation reports for the teacher's file. You, as administrator, are expected to make independent assessments about the teacher being coached. You should also provide information and direction to the coach about the teacher's skill needs you have observed in the classroom and determined from analysis of collected student data.

- **Coaches give truthful and objective feedback on teaching performance.** The feedback is nonevaluative and nonjudgmental. The coach uses objective data about the teacher's performance that has been gathered from observing the teacher and the students.

- **Coaches involve the teachers in reflection.** Coaches encourage their teachers to think for themselves. Teachers are asked to reflect, analyze, and discuss the objective data their coach has collected. Teachers are asked to consider the results they have achieved and the reasons for these outcomes, and make suggestions about how to solve problems.

- **Coaches offer suggestions for improvement.** The coach enlarges, reinforces, and builds on ideas that the teacher expresses by offering suggestions or alternatives. These suggestions often come from the coach's personal experiences. The coach also models the strategies and techniques that are suggested.

THE COACH AS COMMUNICATOR

Most of the work of coaching is conducted through discussion. Since what is said and how it is said are the powerful vehicles to teacher growth and development, the coach requires good communication skills. Section 17 provides a discussion of the language of communication including the three forms of active listening.

The following hints will help coaches communicate successfully:

- **The coach thinks before answering.** Hidden messages and individual agendas are identified.

- **The coach understands him- or herself and issues being addressed.** That information is used to control off-track messages, focus on true goals, and reach closure.

- **The coach asks productive questions and makes honest and simple statements.** Alternatives are stated and concepts are clarified by selecting and organizing information.

- **The coach acknowledges feelings expressed.** The emotional tones in discussions are recognized and understood. The information is used to acknowledge and support the teacher.

Figure 21-4 provides coaches with the opportunity to conduct a self-appraisal of their communication effectiveness. Coaches may check their self-perceptions by asking the teachers they coach to also complete the appraisal about them.

Figure 21-4

COMMUNICATION EFFECTIVENESS: A SELF-APPRAISAL

	1 Never	2 Generally	3	4	5 Always
1. I understand and attempt to harmonize my own assumptions, feelings, and attitudes and the assumptions, viewpoints, feelings, and attitudes of others.					
2. I try honestly to see things from the other person's point of view and I consider the import of my decisions on these people.					
3. I establish a climate of trust by listening carefully to the actual and emotional content of what others have to say before offering comment, information, and advice.					
4. I speak pleasantly and courteously with due regard for the feelings of others.					
5. I keep faith with my colleague, report facts honestly, and listen sincerely.					
6. I maintain a delicate balance between talking and listening, using both to good advantage.					
7. I use available information about the personal make-up of those with whom I communicate.					
8. I do not write or speak above the comprehension level of people with whom I communicate.					
9. I recognize that powerful communication unites what I say with how I behave.					
10. I recognize communication as the essential link for everything that is done.					

Subtotals

Total / 50

Ensuring that Professional Development Impacts Student Achievement

Your role in supporting and enhancing a well-planned and implemented professional-development program is to ensure that what was presented is understood, accepted, and integrated into the teachers' instructional choices, and then used in instruction to help all students to be successful. There are two ways you can fulfill this role: (1) by focusing teacher growth plans on professional-development topics and (2) by monitoring study teams to help them function at high levels of effectiveness.

Incorporate Professional-Development Objectives into Growth Plans

The objectives of the professional development program can be supported and enhanced by incorporating them into the objectives for growth plans. It may be important to select growth plan objectives for teachers new to the school on professional development topics that were presented before they came. This is especially important for those topics that are integrated into the instructional nature of the school. For example, if students are placed heterogeneously in mixed-ability groups, new teachers may need to learn the instructional strategies previously presented in professional-development sessions to successfully teach these mixed groups.

Some teachers may need one-on-one assistance to incorporate the objectives targeted in professional development into their instructional plans. Learning communities, even study teams, may not provide enough help. In these instances, make the topic of the professional development the growth plan objective.

Other excellent teachers may wish to extend or enlarge the strategies presented in the professional development sessions, so they select those objectives for their growth plans.

The type of growth plan selected to implement the professional development growth objective depends on the level of readiness of the teacher. Teachers who express fear or frustration with their attempts to implement the strategies, or even the prospect of using them, should be placed in a directed growth plan and guided to understand and integrate the new strategies. Those teachers with some background and understanding may only need your support in a collaborative growth plan to be successful. Other master teachers may elect to work independently or with a peer on a teacher directed growth plan to extend and enhance their use of the strategy.

As with all growth plans, you monitor the progress made by the teacher toward meeting the growth plan objectives. The teacher is involved in setting evaluation criteria and evaluating the success of the plan. Refer to Part III for a discussion of growth plans.

Drop in on Study Team Meetings

Study teams contribute enormously to the growth and development of teachers. Although the teams are usually professional and task oriented, they should not be neglected.

All individuals and groups within the school deserve to be important enough to warrant a visit from the administrator. When the interactions are positive, teachers appreciate these visits as a means of drawing attention to their work and efforts.

These visits serve two important purposes. First, it is an opportunity for you to demonstrate your interest in the team, express positive comments about the importance of the team's work, and even contribute in some way to the team's discussion. Second, the visit allows you to monitor the work of the study team.

MONITOR STUDY TEAM PROGRESS

Members of the study team select the area of focus for their work. Helping their members to implement professional development strategies is certainly of prime importance and may be suggested for the consideration of the team following a professional development session. There are two nonnegotiable considerations when a topic for the study team is selected:

1. The topic must deal with improving student achievement.
2. The topic must serve the needs of the members of the group.

There are two aspects of the study team that you should monitor:

1. The way in which each study team functions
2. The progress of the study team toward meeting the goals it has established

Here are some guidelines you can use when observing a study team. You should be able to assess if the guidelines are met fully, partially, or not at all.

Determine the climate of the group.   First, determine if all of the members of the group are there. Attendance at group meetings is of primary importance because it is an indication of how important the group is to its members. Listen to the conversation for expressions of respect and dignity that group members give each other; for example, positive body language is visible, members of the group listen to each other, and everyone is encouraged to express an opinion. Watch how the group interacts to see if members are following the ground rules they established and note if all of the members participate in the discussion.

Look at procedures the group follows.   Determine if the meetings are regularly scheduled by listening to the conversation for such comments as "At our meeting last week . . . ," or "Having one week to gather the data for our next meeting was not realistic," or "It has been such a long time since our last meeting that I do not remember what we planned to do." Try to answer the following questions. Are meeting agendas visible and are participants referring to them? Is someone taking notes of the points made? Are minutes of a previous meeting visible? If you are present at the end of the meeting, listen for a summary or closure.

Define the topic of conversation.   Hopefully, the participants are not discussing football scores, recipes, their children, or new cars. Here is what they should be discussing.

- **Data.** They might be talking about: gathering data by testing or observing the students for a particular set of skills; analyzing the data to determine student mastery, needs, or gaps in their knowledge; using the data to plan instruction that will result in student progress.

- **Instruction.** They could be talking about lessons they have planned and asking for the group's feedback. Materials may be suggested to enhance the lesson. Strategies for teaching the skills or concepts may be offered.

- **Concerns/problems.** Individuals may be asking the other members of the group for their ideas about a problem they have with a new student or a disruptive student. The group may be discussing a concern shared by all the members related to student teasing.

Note the plans established.   The discussion should focus on a plan to improve student progress and eliminate the problem by addressing what the data show. The group may decide on a number of actions to be taken. For example, they may plan to watch each other teach a particular lesson to improve the strategies used, design new lessons, or try new materials or strategies. Each member of the group should plan to report the results of the planned activities to the group at the next meeting.

Assess the coach's leadership.   Watch the actions and behavior of the coach to look for leadership skills. Look at how the coach guides, facilitates, and encourages the discussion in a supportive manner. Consider the questions that the coach uses to promote reflection on the topic under discussion. Note how the coach directs the discussion to help the group make decisions and confirm their plans.

Figure 22-1 presents a guide for monitoring study teams.

MAKE STUDY TEAMS BETTER

Remember that study teams should serve the needs of their members. Be flexible about their organizational style so long as they meet regularly to discuss and plan for student achievement.

There are instances when you may have to take some action. These include study teams that:

- **Do not function.**

  The study team may meet so infrequently that the members are unable to follow through on their plans. They make no progress on improving instruction. Or, they may not meet at all, which serves no purpose.

- **Exhibit a lack of respect for their members.**

  You may have observed the study team or heard about their inappropriate actions and language. Members of the team may shout at each other or attack other members with an accusing tone or language. Teams that cannot treat each other with respect will not be able to achieve their goals. Their focus of concentration is on insult not inquiry for the benefits of their students.

- **Have no plans to improve student achievement.**

  The team may meet frequently and treat each other with respect but little or nothing is achieved at those meetings. The team may be unable to set a team direction for the improvement of instruction and student learning and create a plan for team members to follow.

In these instances, consider taking any of the following actions:

- Meet with the study team members to discuss the problems that are preventing the team from being effective and help them to learn how to make their work meaningful.

- Meet with the coach to determine the causes for the team's ineffectiveness and help him or her to plan for improvement.

- Become a member of the team and participate in the meetings to model team effectiveness.

- Assume leadership of the team to provide structure for the team's development into a functioning team.

- Disband the study team and move the members into other teams. Some personalities are just bad matches and the members of a nonfunctioning team may be productive and effective on other teams.

Figure 22-1

MONITORING STUDY TEAMS

	Fully	Partially	Not at all
Climate			
All of the members are present			
Feeling of respect and dignity			
Follow established ground rules			
All participate			
Procedures			
Meetings are regularly scheduled			
Follow an agenda			
Notes are taken			
Minutes of former meetings kept			
Closure/Summary			
Topic of Conversation			
Data			
Gathering data—testing/observing			
Analyzing data			
Using data—Alternate ranking			
Grouping by need			
Creating mixed groups			
Instruction			
Lesson design			
Materials to be used			
Strategies to try			
Concerns/Problems			
Academic needs			
Social and emotional needs			
Behavior management			
Plans to Improve			
Watch each other teach			
Bring new lessons to discuss			
Try new materials and report			
Try new strategies and report			
Coach's Leadership			
Guides/facilitates/encourages			
Questions			
Directs			
Other			

Copyright © 2002 by John Wiley & Sons, Inc.

272

Part VI

Enhancements for Student Success

How Student Success Can Be Enhanced

There are additional areas to consider when student achievement is at stake. These include standards, motivation, how classes are organized, social–emotional learning, and technology. Each plays a critical role in ensuring that students are successful by enhancing how they are taught.

Standards and Student Success

Standards are embedded in the curriculum, which can be defined as what is intentionally taught to students. There are five elements to consider when we consider standards, each with its own questions to be answered.

- **Content—What students should learn.** What is important about this subject or discipline? Which facts should students be able to recall? Should students be able to identify relationships among these facts or ideas? Should students be able to apply their knowledge to a real-world situation? Should students be able to analyze and evaluate the information?

- **Sequence—The order in which the content is taught.** What comes first? How is the information organized? Is it timeline based, problem based, concept based, or relationship based?

- **Duration—The length of student involvement with the content.** How much instructional time should be spent on the content, concepts, and the skills to be learned?

- **Scope—The range and depth of the learning experiences.** How much should be taught about each aspect of the content? How extensive and comprehensive should the content be?

- **Assessment—The ways in which learning will be evaluated.** What types of assessments will be conducted? Will standardized tests be used? Are there state-mandated examinations? Will teacher-made tests be developed? Will performance assessments be used? What is the form of the assessment? Will students need to respond to short-answer, essay, data-based, or application questions? When will the assessments be conducted?

Almost every state has defined standards for pre-K through grade 12 in all disciplines. The purpose of establishing these standards is to ensure that every student is taught the knowledge, skills, and understandings deemed essential by the state legislature as presented by the state educational agency. The bad news is that this takes decisions about the content of the curriculum out of the hands of educators. The good news, however, is that in most cases, the standards have been constructed with wide participation and are reasonable for students to achieve. They also provide a means of addressing issues of class, race, and gender discrimination as well as inequalities in expectations, remediation, and resources provided. In addition, the standards created are usually in line with those endorsed by national associations in each discipline. In these instances, teachers do not have any involvement in developing the content of the curriculum. They do, however, have control over *how, what,* and *when* they teach those standards.

TEACHERS' CONTROL OF STUDENT ACHIEVEMENT

Teachers deliver the curriculum to their students surrounded by the four walls of their classrooms. No matter how conscientious the administrator, classrooms are visited infrequently and for short periods of time. No one can possibly stand by each teacher every hour of the day for every day of the year. The plain and simple truth is that teachers teach what and how they want to teach.

Curriculum standards must be taught if students are to be successful. In most states, the use of high-stakes tests is one means of exercising control over the curriculum standards and measuring student achievement, as well as teacher and administrator accountability. Student achievement is dependent upon both what is taught and how it is taught—and these are in the hands of the teacher.

Teachers must be involved in analyzing the standards and high-stakes assessments to ensure they teach the concepts, understandings, and skills that will be measured if students are to be successful. That is not to say that the curriculum is the scope of the test. It is, however, essential that students be prepared to respond to both the content and format of the assessments. For example, if the assessment requires students to respond to data-based questions, teachers must design instruction that gives students experience with examining and responding to authentic data about the content. If students are required to write essays as a part of the assessment, they must be taught how to compose essays that express their ideas about the content.

GIVING TEACHERS OWNERSHIP

Laying it out for the teachers is not sufficient. Teachers need to be involved with their colleagues in discussions that allow them to express their ideas and exercise ownership over the curriculum standards. These collaborations usually result in the development of a better plan for delivery of instruction than an individual teacher could achieve without the input of his or her peers. This is one way in which adults can feel in control of their activities.

These professional discussions should result in well-defined plans for:

- teaching the curriculum standards

- the order in which the standards will be taught

- the length of student involvement with each aspect of the content

- the range and depth of the learning experiences presented

- the ways in which the learning experiences will prepare students for the format of the assessments

REFINING TEACHERS' PLANS

Providing the opportunity for teachers to work together on how the standards will be delivered has several additional benefits.

Collaboration.   The value of collaboration is reinforced and builds teachers' confidence in their work and expected outcomes. Teachers who are involved in reaching collaborative decisions are more likely to follow the plan. There is a feeling that "we are all in this together." They also know there is somewhere to go to talk about concerns and success and they continue to seek the input of the group. Learning communities and study teams focus ongoing discussions on how well the plans are achieving the desired results. See sections 14 and 21.

Monitoring.   Administrators can use the plan outline to monitor the implementation of the plan. The lesson plans of teachers of grade 9 English or grade 4 Language Arts, for example, can be compared. In addition, the periodic collection of student artifacts will reveal if students are being provided with opportunities to learn the required content and skills and how well they are mastering them.

Motivation and Student Success

Motivation and achievement are not the same. Motivation certainly contributes to achievement, but it is also important as an outcome on its own. Educators want their students to be interested in learning and maintain a long-term involvement in learning. We want students not only to achieve, but also to value learning and put forth the effort necessary to gain knowledge and skills. Such a student, for example, selects to continue her study of a second language beyond the three required years because she loves the language.

Three factors influence students' motivation and ultimately their success. They are self-confidence, praise, and rewards.

SELF-CONFIDENCE AND STUDENT SUCCESS

The key to success in school and in life is our image of ourselves. Self-confidence is the belief that "I have the ability and capacity to perform what is asked of me." For most students, confidence in their ability is generally related to a specific task. Young children have a positive view of themselves and their abilities with high expectations for their success. They relate effort with ability. To them, working hard is being smart.

As children get older and progress through the grades, their beliefs in their abilities are exchanged for the teacher's evaluation of their ability. In essence, it is not what the student thinks of himself or herself, or what the teacher really thinks of the student, but rather what the student *thinks* the teacher *thinks* about him or her that really matters.

Older children also change their view about the relationship between effort and ability. They believe effort can help you to be successful but only to the limits of your ability to be successful. When you ask a student in a typical school in the United States why he or she was successful on a test, you get responses such as "It was easy," or "I was lucky." Students rarely respond, "I studied hard," or "I was really prepared." Effort, therefore, may threaten self-confidence because "if I try hard and fail, I demonstrate my limited ability."

The problems teachers face with students who have low self-confidence is that these students try to avoid failure by not trying or being very slow to start. In their minds, "If I didn't expend the effort to try, my failure cannot be related to my ability." Telling these students that they can do well, or even guaranteeing it, usually does not work. However, these students invest greater effort when they believe the goal is attainable. Here are two strategies to try.

1. Give low-confidence students short-term goals.
2. Provide specific strategies to reach each goal.

Once students are clear about how to reach a goal and can focus on the strategies that will help them, they are more likely to move toward the larger outcomes.

PRAISE THAT RESULTS IN STUDENT SUCCESS OR FAILURE

Most teachers try to say something positive about every student's work. The problem is that the positive statement is often something unimportant, not related to the task, or untrue. For example, praising a student for handing in incomplete and messy homework by telling him "At least you tried" will not be accepted as praise by the student. What he did (the handing in) was unimportant to the task, which was the completion of the assignment, and in truth he did not try at all.

Other ways in which teachers attempt to praise students may have a negative effect, such as praising a student for having her notebook open and ready to take notes. Praise for an easy task or praise for actions that are below the student's ability send the message that the student lacks the ability to do more or better work and you have low expectations for her success. Here are some guidelines for praise that is accepted, believed, and serves to encourage students.

- **Praise actions that are important and related to the task.** "You created a good outline for your team to use in completing the task."

- **Praise something specific rather than making a general statement.** "You asked an important question about the reasons for those actions."

- **Use praise sparingly.** Repeated comments such as "good" or "good job" satisfy no one but the teacher and are not believed by the students. Using praise when it is deserved is believed and desired. Students may strive to get these infrequent expressions of true commendation. See Figure 23-1.

Figure 23-1

GUIDELINES FOR GIVING PRAISE

- Praise actions that are important and related to the task.

- Praise something specific rather than making a general statement.

- Use praise sparingly.

REWARDS AND STUDENT SUCCESS

It seems that most adults believe children will maintain their interest and work harder if they are given rewards and incentives. Rewards are generally selected over any other means of increasing on-task behavior including reasoning, punishment, or even ignoring. Many programs in our schools use rewards as a normal part of instruction by giving stickers, stars, or smiley faces for correct responses, participation, or task completion. As students progress through school, they become more and more controlled by rewards.

Rewards, incentives, or recognition for work may have positive effects on some students. It may increase their feeling of confidence and self-worth, and influence motivation and interest in learning. However, rewards and incentives may not be necessary or even beneficial for all students. Some students are motivated to complete their work and stay on task simply because they enjoy being challenged. These students are responding to intrinsic motivation that comes from within and have no need or may even be insulted by extrinsic rewards.

Students who are intrinsically motivated appreciate incentives that recognize their consistent efforts. These students should be given appropriate and challenging choices whenever possible that recognize their efforts and abilities and identify their interest in achievement. The choices they are given should be at the same level of difficulty as those given to other students. If the choices make the assignments easier, they are being rewarded with work that is of less value. If the work is considerably more difficult, they are being penalized for their motivation. Here are some examples.

- **A choice of which task to complete from among several of equal difficulty.** Because other students are told which task to complete, intrinsically motivated students are being rewarded by being able to select which task has the greatest appeal for them.

- **A choice of which activity they will perform to meet the task.** Being able to select how they will complete the task by selecting the activity that is of greatest interest to them rewards their motivation.

- **The selection of the time frame in which the work will be done.** While other less-motivated students may have a strict time frame for completion of a task, intrinsically motivated students may have the option to use time more flexibly.

- **The sequence in which they will complete the work.** Less-motivated students may be required to follow a pattern for completion of the work. Being able to select the order in which they will complete the assignment may reward motivated students.

- **The place where they will do the work.** Most students would be required to complete the work in the classroom, while more motivated students may be able to select the library, computer room, or another location.

The giving of choice fosters the student's belief in his or her ability to exercise personal control over learning, and increases both motivation and interest. See Figure 23-2.

Figure 23-2

INTRINSIC MOTIVATION

Sample incentives that recognize and reward consistent effort:

- A choice of which task to complete from among several of equal difficulty

- A choice of which activity to perform to meet the task

- The selection of the time frame in which the work will be done

- A choice about the sequence in which the work will be completed

- A choice of places where the work will be completed

Class Organization and Student Success

How classes are organized has a tremendous impact on student achievement. Students are usually grouped for class placement in heterogeneously mixed-ability groups, or tracked homogeneously in single-ability groups. Schools have been tracking students by assigning them to separate ability groups designated as bright, average, and slow since 1920. Each track has its own goals, curriculum, and outcomes. Once a student is tracked into a particular group, he or she is rarely moved.

Even though tracking remains a popular means of organizing students, the reasons that supported tracking are gone. Tracking was supported by the idea that students were being provided with an education that best suited their abilities and prepared them for different roles in society. Low-level, nonskilled jobs for which low-track students were being prepared no longer exist. The few that do exist will most probably be gone in the next ten years, as robots are able to perform the work. In a recent survey, employers listed knowing how to think and be responsible as vital job skills for employment. We are living in an age that requires all workers in our society to be able to work together to solve problems and produce positive outcomes.

The establishment of standards for what all students should learn, and their related assessments, which all students must pass, bring the practice of tracking into question. Social promotion is a thing of the past, replaced by the conviction that all students can learn. This is supported by graduation requirements in most states that are connected to exit examinations. The lower level diplomas of former years have been eliminated. There is only one route to a high school diploma in most states and it is on the same track for all students.

TRACKING AND STUDENT FAILURE

The widely held belief that low-track and remedial classes help these students, since they allow teachers to individualize instruction and focus on particular learning deficiencies, is just not true. Considerable research on the subject documents the following results:

- **Students in general do not profit from enrollment in low-track classes.** Teachers of low-track classes generally expect their students to learn less at a lower level of achievement and so that is what usually happens.

- **Students in low-track classes do not learn so much as students with similar abilities and skills who are placed in heterogeneous classes.** Teachers of low-track classes generally teach less or a simplified version of the curriculum. Students in these classes have less access than other students to challenging content, engaging learning experiences, and resources.

- **Minority children are more frequently placed in low-track classes than other students of similar ability levels.**

DETRACKING AND STUDENT ACHIEVEMENT

All students have access to the opportunity to succeed when tracking by ability grouping is removed. Many benefits result when students of varied ability levels are placed heterogeneously into class groups.

- **Less able students have positive role models from whom to learn.** Students share their learning strengths and styles. Students have the opportunity to watch the way in which their peers organize work, think through a problem, select resources, and use the resources to complete a task.

- **Students of different ability levels are able to work together and learn about each other.** Myths and misconceptions about students from ethnic or racial groups that are different from their own are eliminated. New cultural and racial knowledge and understandings enrich each student.

- **Racial and ethnic segregation are eliminated.** Since minority students are generally placed in low-track classes, these racial and ethnic divisions are eliminated.

- **Instruction for all students improves.** Heterogeneously grouped classes require that teachers do more instruction of small groups and less instruction of the whole class. Student-to-student interaction is increased, with the opportunities for students to think about the concepts being taught and construct their own understanding of them.

ALTERNATIVES TO TRACKING

School districts that have eliminated tracking and provide equal opportunities for achievement for all of their students have developed some strategies that work. Figure 23-3 provides a summary of these alternatives.

- **Small-group instruction.** Students within classes are grouped by ability for instruction some of the time. In this way, the individual learning needs of each student can be addressed.

- **Extended time.** Students who experience difficulty with complex or difficult information may be given time extensions for projects and tasks. They may also be allowed to progress through a unit of study at a slower pace.

- **Alternative testing.** Some students may be offered alternative ways of demonstrating their knowledge of the content. Some students may be more successful when required to demonstrate their knowledge and skills by performing a task rather than answering questions or writing essays.

- **Tutoring.** After-school or Saturday tutoring may be provided to any student who lacks particular skills or experiences difficulty with subject content.

- **Peer-mediated strategies.** Students work together in cooperative groups to complete extended tasks. Students help each other master concepts and skills required to complete the task.

• **Buddies.** Students select a buddy to support them with the work they are expected to complete. Buddies provide information and homework assignments that were missed when one of the students was absent. Buddies help each other learn material and study for tests.

Figure 23-3

ALTERNATIVES TO TRACKING

• **Small-group instruction**

Students are grouped by ability for instruction some of the time.

• **Extended time**

Students who experience difficulty are given time extensions for projects and/or progress through a unit of study at a slower pace.

• **Alternative testing**

Alternative ways of demonstrating knowledge of the content, by performing a task rather than answering questions or writing essays, are offered.

• **Tutoring**

After-school or Saturday tutoring is provided to students who lack particular skills or experience difficulty with subject content.

• **Peer-mediated strategies**

Student groups work together to help each other master concepts and skills.

• **Buddies**

Student buddies help each other learn material, catch up on missed material, and study for tests.

Social–Emotional Learning and Student Achievement

Social–emotional intelligence is the ability to be aware of and manage your emotions so that you make responsible decisions and establish positive relationships. This is the intelligence that can lead you to success in school and a happy and productive life. Daniel Goleman, author of *Emotional Intelligence,* is the founding member of the Collaborative to Advance Social Emotional Learning (CASEL). Its central mission is to establish social and emotional learning as an essential part of the education process that makes students more successful in school and life.

CASEL has targeted two strategic areas for its work. First, the professional development of teachers to enable them to teach the skills of social–emotional learning to their students to enhance their emotional, cognitive, and behavioral skills. Second, work with administrators to develop their social–emotional intelligence to enable them to lead highly successful schools. Becoming socially and emotionally intelligent is important for everyone in the learning community—students, teachers, administrators, and parents—if we are to create safe, caring, and responsive schools and classrooms in which children can be successful.

DEFINING SOCIAL–EMOTIONAL LITERACY

Social and emotional literacy has four primary attributes with related competencies. All of them are important life skills that lead to students' success in school. The attributes are awareness of self and others, positive attitudes and values, responsible decision making, and social-interaction skills. The following discussion presents the attributes and explains the competencies. See Figure 23-4 for a summary of the attributes and competencies.

Awareness of self.   Competencies are:

- *Awareness of feelings:* You are aware of your own feelings to the degree that you can identify them and understand their causes. For example: "No, I don't feel frustrated, I feel angry because this is not the first time this has happened."

- *Management of feelings:* Once aware of your feeling, you have the capacity to remain calm by managing those feelings in any way that works for you.

- *Understanding yourself:* You know and accept your own strengths and weaknesses, which allows you to be confident and optimistic about the ways in which you deal with daily challenges.

Awareness of others.   Competencies are:

- *Taking perspective:* You accurately understand and present the perspectives of others. This is best accomplished by really listening and seeking to understand by being sensitive to social and situational clues.

Positive attitudes and values.   Competencies are:

- *Personal responsibility:* You engage in behaviors that are safe and healthy. This includes avoiding addictive and harmful substances. You are honest and fair in your dealing with others.

- *Respect for others:* You appreciate and accept individual and group differences and the rights of all people.

- *Social responsibility:* You contribute to the community and protect the environment.

Figure 23-4

ATTRIBUTES OF SOCIAL–EMOTIONAL LEARNING

Attributes	Competencies
Awareness of Self	Awareness of feelings
	Management of feelings
	Understanding yourself
Awareness of Others	Taking perspective
Positive Attitudes and Values	Personal responsibility
	Respect for others
	Social responsibility
Responsible Decision Making	Problem identification
	Problem solution
	Goal setting
	Social norm analysis
Social-Interaction skills	Active listening
	Express communication
	Cooperation
	Negotiation
	Refusal
	Seeking help

Responsible decision making.   Competencies are:

- *Problem identification:* You identify situations that are problems and assess the related risks, barriers, and resources.
- *Problem solution:* You develop a reflected solution to a problem, implement it, and then evaluate the outcomes.
- *Goal setting:* You set positive and realistic goals for yourself.
- *Social norm analysis:* You analyze and critically evaluate social, cultural, and media messages that relate to the norms accepted by the peer group and personal behavior. You learn to challenge the acceptance of high-risk behaviors such as fighting, carrying a gun, drinking, and smoking.

Social-interaction skills.   Competencies are:

- *Active listening:* You attend to a speaker both verbally and nonverbally, so that you receive a message as it was intended by that speaker and demonstrate that the speaker was understood.
- *Expressive communication:* You initiate and maintain conversations that express your thoughts and feelings clearly. You communicate different content to different audiences both verbally and nonverbally.
- *Cooperation:* You take turns and share with both pairs and groups.
- *Negotiation:* You use the skills of conflict resolution by considering all the perspectives of those involved in a conflict and helping them to peacefully find a solution acceptable to all.
- *Refusal:* You say "no" in a clear statement and mean it as a way to avoid or delay taking action in situations in which you may be pressured.
- *Seeking help:* You identify the need for support and assistance, and then access available and appropriate resources.

SOCIAL–EMOTIONAL LEARNING AND STUDENT SUCCESS

Disruptive classrooms often result because students do not know how to respond to their emotions or interact with others. Many teachers leave education because they do not know how to deal with the unsafe, unhappy, and unproductive learning environments that result from the acting-out behavior of students with social and emotional needs. These teachers cannot manage the level of stress they experience over these difficulties.

Although many schools and districts initially became involved with teaching the attributes of social–emotional learning through their competencies to reduce and eliminate disruption and violence, they quickly realized the gains in student achievement that can result when classrooms are safe, caring, and respectful. The following is an exploration of how classrooms can become safer, more caring, and more respectful environments in which students can be successful.

Awareness of yourself and others.   Students who are aware of their feelings and can manage them are less likely to act out in class when they feel hurt or unhappy. These students begin to consider how a situation may look from another student's point of view instead of overreacting to a situation. These competencies reduce the personal attacks that characterize some classrooms. In addition, students are given skills that help them handle the academic challenges of everyday life in the classroom.

Positive attitudes.   By understanding and appreciating the differences among students in their classes, students learn to value the rights of all people. Name-calling and blame-placing are reduced as students accept the responsibility for being honest and fair in their dealings with all individuals and groups. Classrooms and schools become safer because students stop pushing, punching, and playing tricks on each other because they are different. Instead, they demonstrate constructive and healthy behaviors, which contribute to everyone's safety.

Responsible decision making.   Students who have learned how to identify and solve problems are less likely to resort to extreme behaviors when they are faced with obstacles. Setting both positive and realistic goals for themselves reduces the possibilities of disappointment and anger over failure. These students are not so susceptible to peer pressure and the potentially harmful messages of the media because they have learned how to critically evaluate the possible outcomes of acting on those messages. They are, therefore, less likely to participate with gangs that steal and vandalize. They are also more likely to have second thoughts about smoking, drinking, and engaging in unprotected sexual relations.

Social-interaction skills.   Students who have learned how to express themselves both verbally and nonverbally are better communicators of their thoughts and feelings both in the classroom when responding to the teacher, and outside the classroom when speaking with their peers. Active listening helps to reduce conflicts caused by miscommunications because the listener is focused on receiving and understanding the message of the speaker. Learning how to take turns and share materials increases the opportunity to learn from and with classmates. Students who learn how to negotiate are able to settle disputes among themselves without adult intervention or violence. Shouting and disruptive behavior that could result from being pressured are avoided by learning to say no as a means of avoiding pressure or delaying actions. Students who learn that it is not only desirable, but intelligent to know when you need to reach out for support and assistance are more likely to avoid placing themselves at risk.

IMPLEMENTING SOCIAL–EMOTIONAL LEARNING THROUGH INSTRUCTIONAL STRATEGIES

The competencies of social and emotional learning can be taught through instructional strategies. Some of these include:

JOURNAL WRITING:

- Write about your feelings and how you handle them.
- State what you do when you are angry, frustrated, scared, unhappy.
- Write about your personal strengths and weaknesses.
- See a situation from someone else's point of view.

COOPERATIVE LEARNING:

- Learn about the cultures of the students in the class.
- Study environmental concerns of the neighborhood and suggest solutions.
- Evaluate media advertisements.
- Take on the solution of a problem.

GROUP DISCUSSIONS AND DEBATES:

- Debate proposed solutions to problems.
- Present a situation from different perspectives.
- Discuss the cause and effect of particular decisions.
- Discuss how to know you need help.

SCRIPT WRITING AND ROLE-PLAYING:

- Create a script that presents a situation that occurred in the classroom. Ask students to role-play the script.
- Create a script about a situation in which you felt pressured. Ask students to role-play the script.

IMPLEMENTING SOCIAL–EMOTIONAL LEARNING THROUGH SUBJECT CONTENT

The competencies of social and emotional learning can be taught through curriculum content. Here are some examples.

LANGUAGE ARTS:

- Present a book study about a culture represented in the classroom.
- Write an essay that presents the problem of the main character and discuss how it was resolved.
- Write a letter to the proper agency to explain a neighborhood concern.

SOCIAL STUDIES:

- Explore decisions that were made in historical controversies.
- Negotiate a compromise between two different points of view.
- Discuss the cultural diversity of the United States.
- Study incidents of prejudice and discrimination in history.

PHYSICAL EDUCATION:

- Communicate for team success.
- Win games with team work.
- Do your personal best.

SCIENCE:

- Solve a problem using scientific data.
- Make a decision based on collected data.
- Experiment using the scientific method to document results.
- Gather data to support your conclusions and results.

CHARACTERISTICS OF A SOCIAL–EMOTIONAL SCHOOL IN WHICH STUDENTS ACHIEVE

Schools in which social–emotional learning is taught and practiced and students achieve have the following visible characteristics:

RESPECT IS DEMONSTRATED:

- Students speak respectfully to adults.
- Students speak respectfully to each other.
- Teachers treat each other in a respectful manner.
- Teachers treat students respectfully.

- Administrators are respectful in their behavior and language with all members of the learning community.
- Parents are treated in a respectful manner.

INTERACTIONS ARE POSITIVE:

- Decisions about all aspects of the school are made collaboratively.
- The leadership team is widely representative of all school populations.
- Parents are welcomed, greeted, and invited to participate in the life of the school.
- Communications with staff, parents, and community are frequent.
- Students positively interact with each other in classrooms as a part of the teaching and learning process.
- Students positively interact with each other in areas outside of the classroom, such as hallways, staircases, restrooms, lockers, the cafeteria, and school yard.
- Teachers collaborate with their colleagues in learning communities and student teams.
- Members of the school community meet frequently.

CONFLICTS ARE RESOLVED:

- Conflict-resolution strategies are taught to all students, practiced in all environments, and used by all the members of the school community.
- Peer mediators are trained and peer mediation is used as the first means of resolving conflicts for all school populations.
- Negotiation is requested and used when conflicts cannot be resolved through the conflict-resolution or mediation process.
- Problems are addressed and resolved in a timely manner.

SOCIAL–EMOTIONAL LEARNING COMPETENCIES FOR ADMINISTRATORS

Administrators who demonstrate social–emotional intelligence model the competencies for the school community. Their commitment is to the development and maintenance of a safe, caring, and responsive school community and environment characterized by classrooms in which students are successful. Marcia Knoll, and Janet Patti of Hunter College, City University of New York (CUNY), developed the following social–emotional competencies for administrators. Figure 23-5 gives you the opportunity to conduct a self-evaluation of which competencies you have down pat and those you need to develop to some degree.

Figure 23-5

SOCIAL–EMOTIONAL COMPETENCIES FOR ADMINISTRATORS: A SELF-EVALUATION*

Rate yourself on each competency for your command of this skill.				
Perfect	Good	Fair	Weak	None
5	4	3	2	1

Practice self-reflection to heighten your awareness of self and encourage this self-reflective process in others as a part of daily events and supervisory activities.

Model the communication skills of active listening, I messages, diffusing anger, paraphrasing, and positive body language.

Resolve issues by using problem-solving strategies, such as conflict resolution, consensus building, mediation, and negotiation.

Establish a safe, nurturing environment in the school by practicing equity, respecting individuals, and having a caring attitude that serves as a model for students, staff, parents, and the community.

Explore your own cultural competence, prejudices, and biases and seek to understand how these impact interactions with others. Use these understandings to influence others to value and establish diverse cultural understandings in educational settings.

Develop a school culture that establishes social–emotional learning as an integral part of the school's core values, organization, instruction, curriculum, student interactions, and socialization.

Promote a democratic school community that works together by using team-building strategies and shared decision making to establish trust.

*Marcia Kalb Knoll and Janet Patti, Hunter College, City University of New York (CUNY).

- Practice self-reflection to heighten your awareness of self and encourage this self-reflective process in others as a part of daily events and supervisory activities.

- Model the communication skills of active listening, I messages, diffusing anger, paraphrasing, and positive body language.

- Resolve issues by using problem-solving strategies, such as conflict resolution, consensus building, mediation, and negotiation.

- Establish a safe, nurturing environment in the school by practicing equity, respecting individuals, and having a caring attitude that serves as a model for students, staff, parents, and the community.

- Explore your own cultural competence, prejudices, and biases and seek to understand how these impact interactions with others. Use these understandings to influence others to value and establish diverse cultural understandings in educational settings.

- Develop a school culture that establishes social–emotional learning as an integral part of the school's core values, organization, instruction, curriculum, student interactions, and socialization.

- Promote a democratic school community that works together by using team-building strategies and shared decision making to establish trust.

DEMONSTRATING SOCIAL–EMOTIONAL INTELLIGENCE

What you *do* to demonstrate your social–emotional intelligence is more important than what you say. When you have these competencies, you demonstrate them by your behavior, actions, and the manner in which the school is organized and functions. Social–emotional intelligence becomes a way of life for everyone in the school community.

How do you demonstrate that you value reflection for yourself and others?
Teachers are given time to reflect on their work individually and in groups. Staff meetings are characterized by the interactive nature of and active participation of those in attendance—whether you are present or not. Members of the staff keep journals as a means of recording thoughts and events for future reference and comparison.

How do you model communication skills?   Nonverbal, active, and interactive listening skills are used when communicating with adults and young people to express caring, interest, support, and a belief in the individual. Paraphrasing is employed to express both sensitivity to the speaker's needs and a desire to understand the issue or the problem. Listening skills are used to focus sustained attention on the speaker. Reflective conferencing is used to extend thinking by probing for information, seeking clarification, and asking the speaker to find solutions. See Section 17 for a full discussion of these skills.

How do you resolve issues?   The skills of conflict resolution are taught and used by administrators, teachers, students, and other adults in the school community. Decisions are reached by consensus rather than by voting. This means that everybody talks through and modifies the suggestions made until there is total agreement to support one solution. Situations in which conflict exists are mediated or negotiated to find a solution that is acceptable by all.

How is a safe and nurturing environment established?   Trained teachers teach social–emotional learning tools to the student body. School programs, both of a curricular and cocurricular nature, are designed to meet the needs of the community as a whole. Students' work is highly valued and on display throughout the building. Themes that reflect the nature and interests of the community are used in instruction and school programs. For example, books selected for the literature series may reflect the culture of the students in the school. The caring attitudes of administrators are reflected in the way in which all members of the community communicate. Barrier-free access to entrances and exits and security measures that are employed recognize the safety and well being of everybody in the school community. Pride in the environment is demonstrated by a clean, well-maintained, and visually appealing facility.

How are personal cultural competence, prejudices, and biases explored? Books, pictures, and regalia about the cultures of the students are visible in your office and public areas. Groups, committees, and teams are representative of the diverse cultural groups within the school. Classrooms are organized to reflect all of the cultures in the school. Efforts are in effect to ethnically balance the staff. Most classrooms use a rich multicultural curriculum. A school code has been written and is used to prohibit racial bias, language, and action. The code is equally enforced among all students. Issues of personal bias have been explored by the staff and by students within their classrooms. Prejudice and discrimination are topics that are studied in the context of the curriculum.

How is social–emotional learning made an integral part of the school's core values?   Staff-development efforts focus on the skills and competencies of social–emotional learning. Teachers teach the strategies to their students and everyone uses them in daily interactions. Peer mediation is used by adults and students to resolve conflicts. The school community verbalizes social–emotional learning as a core value of its vision statement.

How is a democratic school community promoted?   Shared leadership is central to the organization of the school. Each member of committees, groups, and teams assumes the responsibilities of leadership at some time. Collaborative decision-making using consensus building is used to reach decisions. All members practice trust-building strategies.

See Figure 23-6 for a summary of observable actions matched to the competencies.

Figure 23-6

OBSERVABLE ACTIONS MATCHED TO COMPETENCIES*

Social–Emotional Competencies for Administrators	Observable Actions
Practice self-reflection to heighten your awareness of self and encourage this self-reflective process in others as a part of daily events and supervisory activities.	Teachers self-reflect about outcomes. Interactive meetings are conducted with staff. Time set aside for teachers to reflect individually or as a part of a group or team. Staff members keep reflective journals.
Model the communication skills of active listening, I messages, diffusing anger, paraphrasing, and positive body language.	Active listening language used in all communications with adults and young people. Paraphrasing is used in communication. Listening skills are used in communication. Reflective conferencing is used in supervision.
Resolve issues by using problem-solving strategies, such as conflict resolution, consensus building, mediation, and negotiation.	Conflict resolution is employed as needed in all situations. Consensus building is used with staff and students. Conflict situations are negotiated or mediated.
Establish a safe, nurturing environment in the school by practicing equity, respecting individuals, and having a caring attitude that serves as a model for students, staff, parents, and the community.	Assignments and schedules are equal for all. Social–emotional learning is encouraged as a part of the school program. Curricular and cocurricular programs meet the social–emotional, physical, and intellectual needs of the community. Children's work is displayed. School and classroom themes reflect the community. Caring communications are visible between teachers, between teachers and students, and between students. Facilities are barrier and hazard free. Security measures are in place. Facilities are clean, well maintained, and visually appealing.

Figure 23-6 continued

Social–Emotional Competencies for Administrators

Explore your own cultural competence, prejudices, and biases and seek to understand how these impact interactions with others. Use these understandings to influence others to value and establish diverse cultural understandings in educational settings.

Develop a school culture that establishes social–emotional learning as an integral part of the school's core values, organization, instruction, curriculum, student interactions, and socialization.

Promote a democratic school community that works together by using team-building strategies and shared decision making to establish trust.

Observable Actions

Evidence of information about cultures of the students.
Celebrations of diversity are held.
All cultural groups of the school are represented on school leadership teams, committees, and groups.
Students in each classroom reflect the cultural diversity of the school.
Efforts are in place to ethnically balance the staff.
A multicultural curriculum is used in most classrooms.
A school code that prohibits racial bias, language, and action is in effect and followed.
Issues of personal bias have been explored as individuals or groups.
Prejudice and discrimination are discussed in the context of the curriculum.

Staff development focuses on social–emotional learning topics.
Teachers use social–emotional strategies in their work with students and adults.
Peer mediation is used in conflict situations.
Committees use social–emotional learning strategies to resolve issues.
Social–emotional learning is central to core values, vision, and mission.

A shared leadership team is in place with a rotating leadership.
Collaborative decision making is used.
Trust-building strategies are used by all school people.
Teams act in a collaborative manner.

295

*Marcia Kalb Knoll and Janet Patti, Hunter College, City University of New York (CUNY)

Technology and Student Success in the Twenty-First Century

To be successful in the twenty-first century, students must learn how to function in an increasingly complex and information-rich society. This means that knowing how to use technology will help students be more successful with every aspect of their lives. Technology can be used to enhance learning, increase the quality and productivity of work, and contribute to making every-day chores and responsibilities of living easier and more efficient. Technology can enable students to develop the capacity to be informed, responsible, and contributing citizens when it is integrated into an effective educational environment.

TECHNOLOGY AND STUDENT ACHIEVEMENT

Good learning environments, even excellent ones, can become outstanding when educational technology is used productively. This often involves rethinking and redesigning the teaching and learning processes. There are four advantages to this.

1. The classroom focus shifts from what and how the teacher is teaching to what and how the students are learning. This changes classrooms into learning environments that look and function in dramatically different ways from what we usually see today. These are environments in which students are engaged in using technology that they can direct and control to successfully complete learning objectives.

2. The teacher's role changes from instructor to facilitator and guide. The most important responsibility of the teacher is to create and supply a learning environment that provides students with learning opportunities, challenges to explore, and dilemmas to resolve. Students are able to construct their own understanding in such a learning environment.

3. As students are productively engaged with technology, the teacher is able to engage in one-on-one discussions with students. This personalized attention to each student provides meaningful interaction and desired results.

4. By its very nature, technology allows students to engage in learning activities using their style preferences and at their own pace.

Even without the dramatic change to technological learning environments, using technology productively in today's classrooms enhances student achievement. Rather than pouring knowledge into students' minds for them to memorize, technology provides opportunities for students to access, analyze, relate to prior knowledge, apply, and evaluate the information. This process creates learning that is long-standing because it is constructed by the student.

Technology-capable students are high achievers. Here is what they are able to do.

- Use technology to find information beyond their one textbook. They can search the web, access articles, even explore the great museums of the world on a virtual tour.

- Seek information on particular topics by reviewing original source materials, examining a subject from divergent points of view, and communicating with experts. They can then analyze, evaluate the information, and draw their own conclusions.

- Generate relevant information to solve real problems and make considered decisions.

- Use technology as a tool to creatively and effectively demonstrate learning outcomes by designing charts, graphs, spread sheets, and writing text.

- Communicate and collaborate with others in their classroom and around the world to produce information and publish their products.

FOUNDATION SKILLS OF TECHNOLOGICAL LITERACY

The six foundation skills of technological literacy are presented with their related knowledge and competencies. This framework can be used to plan opportunities for students to master these skills and achieve enhanced success in learning and communication.

FOUNDATION TOPIC	KNOWLEDGE, COMPETENCY SKILL
1. Basic Operations and Concepts	Understand how technology systems work.
	Know how to operate technology systems.
	Become proficient in the use of technology.
2. Social, Ethical, and Human Issues	Use technology ethically.
	Use technology systems, information, and software responsibly.
	Appreciate and support lifelong learning, collaboration, personal pursuits, and productivity that technology offers.
3. Technology Productivity Tools	Use technology to enhance learning, increase productivity, and promote creativity.
	Collaborate with others to prepare publications and produce creative works.
4. Technology Communication Tools	Use telecommunications to collaborate and interact with peers, experts, and other audiences.

	Use a variety of media and formats to communicate information and ideas to multiple audiences.
5. Technology Research Tools	Locate, collect, and evaluate information from a variety of sources.
	Process data and report results.
	Evaluate and select new information resources and innovations to enhance task production.
6. Technology Problem-Solving and Decision-Making Tools	Use resources for solving problems and making informed decisions.
	Employ technology in the development of strategies for solving problems in the real world.

TECHNOLOGY HALLMARKS FOR SCHOOL LEADERS

A collaborative team is developing technology standards that will guide school leaders. These standards will help you play a major role in supporting the efforts of your teachers and contributing to the development of effective technology plans for your districts.

The following are some of the constructs that serve as hallmarks for school leaders:

- Enhance the development of curriculum and the delivery of instruction by identifying, using, and evaluating appropriate technologies.
- Support the development of technology-enriched learning environments that encourage innovation in teaching and learning.
- Use technology in student-centered environments that meet the needs of individual students.
- Use technology to guide and support instruction that focuses on higher-level thinking, decision-making, and problem-solving skills.
- Ensure that professional-development opportunities fully prepare teachers to use technology for effective instruction.
- Improve instructional practice and student outcomes by employing technology in the collection, analysis, interpretation, and reporting of collected data.
- Conduct assessments of staff proficiency and effectiveness with the use of technology to plan professional-development opportunities.
- Ensure equity of access to technology resources.

Curriculum Design and Student Achievement

Learning activities that are created when teachers get together to write curriculum are not curriculum. They are usually interesting and useful ways for teachers to involve students in learning. Standards, learning objectives, and performance indicators are also not the curriculum. They form the substance of what is to be learned. Both of these, however, are important elements in designing the curriculum framework.

Curriculum Framework

There are five elements in the design of a curriculum framework. Each element contributes to providing a comprehensive approach to teaching and learning that results in student achievement.

MEANINGFUL CONTENT

The content of the curriculum is what is intentionally taught to students. State standards must certainly be included if students are to be prepared for state assessments. But the content of the curriculum can be far more comprehensive than what is included in the standards. Preferences of the district and school community can also be a part of the knowledge and information selected for the content. For example, some districts and schools may select to include a unit on the Holocaust when teaching World War II. Specific pieces of literature that explore heroes of India, South America, Africa, and Asia may be included in the Language Arts or Social Studies curriculum.

Learning tools, also called study skills, are the second, often-neglected aspects of the content of the curriculum. These are the skills that give students the strategies they need to be successful when gathering, organizing, and managing their learning of the content. These include, for example, outlining information, notetaking, using an organizer, finding information, test-taking skills, skimming and scanning, time management, writing a report, and writing an essay.

DESIGNING ESSENTIAL QUESTIONS

These are the large conceptual questions that students explore on their way to learning and understanding the content. They provide an answer to why we are studying this topic, aside from its inclusion in the standards. These questions have no one right answer and should be phrased so that they cannot be responded to by yes or no. Essential questions go to the heart of the topic and should be a major focus of the information being studied so that students can explore ideas to find insights about the subject, for example: Does being right mean doing the right thing? What is human nature? Do laws make people behave? Does power have to be absolute? What makes us Americans?

REFLECTION FOR UNDERSTANDING

A meaningful curriculum does not focus on students memorizing information that is quickly forgotten. It focuses on long-term learning that results when students are asked to reflect, consider, explore, and discover on their way to understanding the content. A well-designed curriculum provides numerous opportunities for students to think about what they are learning and construct their own understanding as individuals and in groups. Refer to Section 2 for a full discussion of this topic. Figure 2-6 presents processing strategies and Figure 2-7 explains how to form questions that raise the level of what students are asked about the content.

TEACHING AND LEARNING

Teaching and learning are the heart of the curriculum. These are the learning strategies and teaching activities that are designed to deliver the content of the curriculum to the students. When these strategies and activities actively involve students, students learn more at a higher level of understanding and with greater retention. The curriculum design specifies what students will do and what the teacher will do in the teaching and learning process. The types of activities with which students will be involved individually and in groups as well as the tasks they will be asked to complete are defined. Refer to Section 2 for a discussion of this topic. Figure 2-5 presents instructional strategies that actively involve students in learning. Figure 2-8 presents grouping strategies that enhance instruction.

ASSESSMENT

Students' understanding of the content should be assessed throughout the teaching process to determine if learning is taking place and to identify individual and group needs. Assessments take many forms.

Ongoing assessment is a part of every teaching episode. Assessments can be conducted in many ways. For example, the "do now" is a popular high school assignment at the beginning of the instructional period. It can be used to assess previous learning or call on information that should have been acquired through completion of the homework assignment. The "do now" can also serve as the "set" or motivation for the lesson that is to be taught by asking students to reflect on some part of the topic. The multiple ways of conducting these ongoing assessments are discussed in Section 2 and summarized in Figure 2-10.

Assessment can also serve to evaluate learning at the end of the unit. These assessments are more comprehensive. The format that these assessments take should mirror the format of required state evaluations to allow the students to become familiar with how they are expected to respond. Good assessments limit or eliminate short-answer, true–false, and multiple-choice questions. They focus instead on questions that require an extended response or essays to engage the students in learning that is beyond memorization.

PERFORMANCE ASSESSMENT AND SCORING RUBRICS

Performance assessments require students to complete a task to demonstrate their learning of the content. These tasks may be completed as individual or group learning experiences. The tasks may be short term—involving one or two instructional periods—or they may be long term—requiring an extended period of time. The tasks require students to use the information learned in the unit, gather more information, and then use their constructed knowledge to create a product. Some examples follow.

1. You are location specialist because of your knowledge about the climate, occupations, and living conditions of the regions of the United States. That means you will be able to advise people about where in the United States they should make their home.

   • You will need to consider the skills of the individuals, their particular life preferences, and their family needs.

   • You will need charts and graphs containing information about each region and comparing the regions.

   You will present a description of the individuals you would counsel to settle in two different regions of the United States.

2. We have studied several wars in which the United States was involved. You will use your knowledge about one war and the individuals involved to become a conflict-resolution specialist.

   • Consider the causes of the war you have selected.

   • Identify the characteristics and background of the individuals who played important roles in the government at that time.

   • Design a strategy to resolve the conflict and prevent the war.

   You will present your conflict-resolution strategies to a group of judges who will ask you questions and then assess the strength of your strategies.

Performance assessments are usually graded by using a rubric that is designed with the students. The mystery of assessment is reduced when students know what is expected of them and they have some benchmarks to use for self-assessment. The rubric specifies the criteria for the product that is to be prepared, and the indicators of effort and participation that will be considered. Students are able to identify what they must do to achieve a grade of "excellent" or "good" as well as what will be graded as "unsatisfactory." Students are then able to complete the task more successfully because they can use the rubric to guide their work and compare the finished product with the criteria.

Rubrics always contain criteria that set standards for student performance. But they may differ in important ways. Some rubrics are checklists for the teacher to indicate if the student did or did not complete each required aspect of the assignment. Other rubrics are more complex. They contain the various required components of the performance, each with its own criteria for achievement. Figure 24-1 presents a sample rubric that may be modified for any content area.

See Figure 24-2 for an overview of the curriculum framework.

Figure 24-1
RUBRIC TO ASSESS HOMEWORK

Excellent	Satisfactory	Unsatisfactory
Turned in on time	Turned in on time, but may need revision	Turned in after the due date
Complete	One part is missing	Two or more parts are missing
Detailed and full responses	One or two details and/or responses are missing	Three or more details or responses are missing
Neat and legible	Mostly neat and legible	Lacks neatness and legibility

Figure 24-2
CURRICULUM FRAMEWORK

STANDARDS, CONTENT, AND LEARNING TOOLS

Which standard(s) are being addressed? What are the essential knowledge, information (content), and skills (learning tools) students will be required to master?

ESSENTIAL QUESTIONS

What are the large conceptual questions students will explore on their way to learning and understanding the content?

REFLECTION FOR UNDERSTANDING

How will students be involved in thinking, reflecting, exploring, and discovering experiences that foster their understanding of the content?

TEACHING AND LEARNING

What are the teaching and learning experiences that will actively involve students as individuals and as part of a group or team? What will students be asked to do? What will the teacher do?

ASSESSMENTS AND SCORING RUBRICS

How will students' understanding be assessed? What quizzes and tests, activities and/or assignments, performance tasks or projects will be designed? Will a rubric be used to evaluate tasks and/or projects?

CURRICULUM SAMPLES

The following curriculum samples are presented in the curriculum framework format.

Sample Curriculum

English Language Arts   High School   Novel: *To Kill a Mockingbird*
Prepared by Gerard Palionis, New York City Public Schools

Standards, Content, and Learning Tools

Which standard(s) are being addressed?

Standard 3: Critical Analysis and Evaluation

- Students will analyze experiences, ideas, information, and issues.
- Students will use oral and written language that follows the accepted conventions of the English language.
- Students will present their opinions and judgments from a variety of perspectives.

What is the essential knowledge, information (content) students will be required to master?

Overarching understandings: Concepts of right and wrong

- Individuals as agents for good and evil
- Context (time and place) that influences events and attitudes
- Prejudice and its influence
- Family dynamics and its impact
- Society and its attitudes
- Integrity, courage, and kindness as human values

What are the skills (learning tools) students will be required to master?

- Essay writing
- Outlining
- Skimming and scanning for information
- Preparing and presenting a debate

Essential Questions

What are the large conceptual questions students will explore on their way to learning and understanding the content?

- Why are values essential to human existence?
- What is the difference between right and wrong?

Reflection for Understanding

How will students be involved in thinking, reflecting, exploring, and discovering experiences that foster their understanding of the content?

- The students will compare the context (time and place) of *To Kill a Mockingbird* with the context of *Mulatto* by Langston Hughes.

- The students will classify the different characters in the novel according to whether they are agents for good or agents for evil.

- The students will speculate about the family dynamics of and the influence of prejudice on these two important characters in the novel: Scout and Mayella Violet Ewell.

- The students will examine this problem: Society and its prejudicial attitudes. The students will define the problem, identify the obstacles to its solution, generate alternatives, select an alternative, and evaluate the solution.

- The students will decide which of these human values is the most worthy of emulating: integrity, courage, or kindness.

Teaching and Learning

What are the teaching and learning experiences that will actively involve students as individuals and as part of a group or team? What will students be asked to do? What will the teacher do?

- Imagining they are Atticus Finch, students will design and plan Tom Robinson's defense for his trial.

- Using a gallery walk, students will evaluate the novel's six major characters (students move in groups to each character posted and record their ideas).

- The students will debate the adequacy of Atticus Finch's defense of Tom Robinson using a web outline advance organizer.

- Using a think-pair-share, students will examine their own views, and explore the views of others with regard to racial prejudice.

- Using a brainstorming technique, the students will identify the themes that occur in the novel.

Assessments and Scoring Rubrics

How will students' understanding be assessed? What quizzes and tests, activities and/or assignments, performance tasks or projects will be designed?

- Students will work in cooperative groups to design Tom Robinson's defense for his trial. The work of the cooperative groups will be assessed for completeness, accuracy of details, creative solutions, and participation. The class will prepare a rubric.

- Students will write a series of short essays about the themes that occur in the novel, which were identified through the brainstorming activity. Some of the short essays will be assigned as homework.

- Final examination—the completion of an essay:
  a. Explore competing values in the novel. Evaluate their merits.
  b. What is the difference between right and wrong? Cite specific events from the novel to support your view.

Will a rubric be used to evaluate tasks and/or projects?

Rubric to evaluate the final essay:

Criteria	*Outstanding*	*Good*	*Minimally Acceptable*
Legibility	Clear and neatly presented	Clearly presented	Readable
Grammar	Sentence structure and punctuation are correct	One or two errors in sentence structure or punctuation	Three to five errors in sentence structure or punctuation
Spelling	One error	Two to five errors	More than five errors
Fluency of ideas	Clear, logically presented	Clear, reasonable presentation	Clear, some reason is employed
	Cites novel persuasively	Cites novel	Few citations from the novel
Complexity of thoughts	Creative, unique Thought provoking	Creative ideas	Few creative ideas

Sample Curriculum

Mathematics—The Stock Market   Grade 7

Barbara Kissane   New York City Public Schools

Standards, Content, and Learning Tools

Which standard(s) are being addressed?

Standard 1:   Students will use mathematical analysis to pose questions, seek answers, and develop solutions.

Standard 3:   Students will understand mathematics and become mathematically confident by:

- communicating and reasoning mathematically
- applying mathematics in real-world settings
- solving problems through the integrated study of number systems and data analysis

What are the essential knowledge, information (content) students will be required to master?

- The relationship between the role of consumers and companies that are traded on the stock market
- How stocks are issued and traded
- Who buys stocks
- What a share of stock is
- How news events and economic events affect the price of stocks
- What the New York Stock Exchange, AMEX, and NASDAQ are
- The differences between the two major markets
- What the Dow Jones Industrial average is
- Who the major brokers are
- Where and by whom stock information is published
- How to trade stocks
- How to read the stock columns
- What a stock chart is
- How to obtain an annual report

What are the skills (learning tools) students will be required to master?

- Fractional parts
- Percents
- Decimals
- Converting fractions to dollars and cents
- Adding and subtracting whole numbers and fractions
- Creating and reading graphs and charts
- Interest rates
- Money, savings, and banking
- Writing a business letter
- Using the Internet to locate sites of major companies and describe the information available

Essential Questions

What are the large conceptual questions students will explore on their way to learning and understanding the content?

- How is mathematics a part of daily life?
- How does the average person play a role in a large company?

Reflection for Understanding

How will students be involved in thinking, reflecting, exploring, and discovering experiences that foster their understanding of the content?

- To compare changes in the stock market with current national and international events
- What it means to be successful today
- How entrepreneurs differ between the United States and China

Teaching and Learning

What are the teaching and learning experiences that will actively involve students as individuals and as part of a group or team? What will students be asked to do? What will the teacher do?

- Complete an analysis report.
- Give an oral presentation.
- Design a poster.
- Build a portfolio.
- Create graphs.
- Keep a journal of current information about five different companies they have selected.
- Create a chart to track each company's daily stock closing price for two weeks (change to fraction, decimal, and percent).
- Write a letter to one of the companies asking for a copy of the annual report.
- Create a line graph for each company tracked showing the closing price of the stock for the two-week period of study.
- Use the graphs to identify the company with the greatest dollar profit, greatest percentage of change, worst dollar loss, and worst percentage of change.
- Presentation by a research analyst from Bear Stern. Following the presentation, students will analyze their company's stock using their charts and journals and prepare an analyst report.
- Go on a trip to the gallery of the New York Stock Exchange.

Assessments and Scoring Rubrics

How will students' understanding be assessed? What quizzes and tests, activities and/or assignments, performance tasks or projects will be designed?

- Demonstrate the ability to read the stock column by using a newspaper to locate a particular company and report the closing price of the stock in fractions, decimals, and percent.
- Vocabulary test requiring students to match terms with their meanings.
- Evaluation of accuracy of the analyst report of the performance of the stock for one of the companies they studied.
- Letter requesting their annual report will be evaluated for use of correct business letter form and language structure.
- Student journal will be reviewed for daily entries and notations.
- The line graph prepared for each company to track stock prices over a two-week period will be assessed.
- The graphs identifying the company with the greatest profit, percentage of change, worst loss, and worst percentage of change will be assessed.

Will a rubric be used to evaluate tasks and/or projects?

Rubric to evaluate the chart, line graph, and analyst report:

Criteria	3—Outstanding	2—On Target	1—Not There Yet
Method used	Uses exemplary methods and organization	Uses appropriate methods and organization	Uses inappropriate methods and organization
Correctness of data, language, usage, vocabulary	No errors	Few or minor errors	Makes significant errors or omissions
Originality	Shows creativity	Uses expected approaches	Uses faulty reasoning
Effort	Goes beyond requirements	Meets all requirements	Does not meet all requirements

Sample Curriculum

Social Studies—Immigration   English Language Arts   Grade 4
Ester Estevez, New York City Public Schools

Standards, Content, and Learning Tools

Which standard(s) are being addressed?

Standard 1: History of the United States and New York

- Students will use a variety of intellectual skills to demonstrate their understanding of major ideas, era, themes, and turning points in the history of the United States and New York.

Standard 1: Reading

- Students will read and understand informational materials.
- Students will read aloud fluently.

Standard 2: Writing

- Students will produce a report of information.
- Students will produce a response to literature.
- Students will produce a narrative account (biography).

Standard 3: Speaking, Listening, and Viewing

- Students will participate in a one-on-one conference with the teacher.
- Students will participate in group meetings.
- Students will prepare and deliver an individual presentation.

Standard 4: Conventions, Grammar, and Usage of the English Language

- Students will demonstrate a basic understanding of the rules of the English language in written and oral work.
- Students will analyze and subsequently revise work to improve its clarity and effectiveness.

What are the essential knowledge, information (content) students will be required to master?

- How economic and political events abroad contributed to immigration to the United States
- How nineteenth-century immigrant groups adjusted to life in New York City
- The history of a community is filled with contributions by males and females of varied cultural and socioeconomic backgrounds
- How Americans benefited from the contributions of immigrant groups and individuals

What are the skills (learning tools) students will be required to master?

- Research skills
- Narrative writing
- Interview techniques
- Notetaking
- Outlining
- Graphing
- Proper use of the English language orally and in writing

Essential Questions

What are the large conceptual questions students will explore on their way to learning and understanding the content?

- Is immigration the only answer?
- Where has immigration taken us as a nation?

Reflection for Understanding

How will students be involved in thinking, reflecting, exploring, and discovering experiences that foster their understanding of the content?

- Reflect on your personal experiences and describe the everyday life of immigrants in New York City.
- Compare and contrast the experiences of present-day immigrants with those of previous generations.
- Solve problems that are experienced by immigrants.
- Consider decisions that faced immigrants.

Teaching and Learning

What are the teaching and learning experiences that will actively involve students as individuals and as part of a group or team? What will students be asked to do? What will the teacher do?

- Research the immigrant groups that came to the United states over the past 100 years. Keep notes about the information gathered.

  Create a timeline to show immigrations trends.

  Create a graph to demonstrate the numbers of immigrants who came from different groups.

- Create the flags of at least four immigrant groups that came to the United States.

  Write a report about the symbols that those flags use.

  Compare the symbols with those represented in the flag of the United States.

- Interview a person you know who is an immigrant.

  Write a narrative account of that person's immigrant experience.

- Read six books related to immigration.

  Report on the thoughts and feelings of the main character in one of the books.

  Select a favorite passage from one book to read aloud.

Assessments and Scoring Rubrics

How will students' understanding be assessed? What quizzes and tests, activities and/or assignments, performance tasks or projects will be designed?

- Notes recorded about the research on immigrant groups checked for completeness
- Timeline to show immigration trends graded for accuracy and neatness and originality
- Graph to demonstrate the numbers of immigrants who came from different groups graded for accuracy, neatness, and creativity
- Report about the symbols of the flags of four immigrant groups and the reproduction of the flags of the four immigrant groups will be graded for their completeness, accuracy, artistic expression, and comparisons made with the symbols of the flag of the United States
- Questions used to interview an immigrant will be evaluated for depth of information requested
- Narrative account of that person's immigrant experience will be evaluated for completeness of the information, understanding of the account, and use of grammar and spelling
- Report on the thoughts and feelings of the main character in one of the books will be evaluated for insight into the character's feelings and thoughts, and use of grammar and spelling
- Oral reading of a favorite passage from one book will be evaluated for oral expression, fluency, and reading accuracy

Will a rubric be used to evaluate tasks and/or projects?

Rubric for the interview conducted and the narrative account:

Criteria	*Excellent*	*Satisfactory*	*Minimally Acceptable*
Interview questions are comprehensive	Important data collected All aspects are included (what, why, when)	Important data collected Most aspects are included	Some important data collected Few aspects are included
Reported information	Contains all the collected data	Contains most of the collected data	Contains some of the collected data
Understanding of the information: facts and emotions of the person	Demonstrates understanding of the facts and emotions of the person	Demonstrates some understanding of the facts and emotions of the person	Does not demonstrate an understanding of facts or the emotions of the person
Use of grammar and spelling	One or two errors in grammar and spelling	Three to five errors in grammar and spelling	More than five errors in grammar and spelling

Leadership for Student Achievement

The changing demands on schools in the twenty-first century require leaders who can challenge staff to mobilize their energies and adapt to changing requirements while controlling the stability and efficiency of the school organization as a whole. Leaders need to respond to the needs of diverse populations while maintaining high standards for instruction, which result in high levels of achievement. Today's leaders also need to know how to communicate, collaborate, engage in participatory decision making, use consensus building and mediation, and understand professional development. These multifaceted roles shift the way we look at all members of the school community. Students become clients and customers rather than the product that results from our efforts. Teachers become initiators of action and innovators of strategies rather than an element of staffing. Principals become conductors of the total learning environment rather than managers of a building.

Curriculum Leadership

You play a critical role in creating a school environment that ensures learning activities are relevant to students' needs. A textbook series and packaged materials do not adequately meet the needs of growing numbers of our students. Assisting teachers to learn the skills required to modify the curriculum for individuals and groups of students, therefore, becomes a pressing need. That is why it is so important for you to have a working knowledge of curriculum. You can then assist teachers to modify a curriculum so that it is better suited to the needs of their students. For example, you can help teachers develop instructional adaptations that address the learning needs of English language learners, inclusion students, and students with diverse learning styles.

ACTIONS OF CURRICULUM LEADERS

There are three curriculum leadership actions that help students to achieve.

1. **Model the curriculum process.** Engage teachers in dialogues about how their instructional plans are aligned with all aspects of the curriculum framework. (Refer to Figure 24-2.) Help them to design quality instruction that results in successful student outcomes.

2. **Assist teachers to modify the curriculum.** Help teachers to analyze instructional difficulties that may result when their instructional approaches do not match the needs of individuals or groups of students. Work with teachers to design curriculum modifications that meet the needs of their diverse student populations.

3. **Encourage teachers to develop a curriculum knowledge base.** Provide guidance and support for learning communities and/or study teams that select to take on a study of the principles of curriculum knowledge. Encourage these teachers to take increasing responsibilities for curriculum decisions for their department or grade.

Instructional Leadership

Instruction is "how" curriculum is delivered. It is the varied strategies and approaches that teachers use in classrooms to help their students achieve learning objectives. Recent studies have documented that student achievement is strongly influenced by principals. There is no doubt that school leaders require extensive knowledge about instruction.

Perhaps your most essential function as an administrator is to provide instructional leadership by overseeing teaching. Effective teaching can be promoted by encouraging teachers to learn how to use a variety of instructional strategies, which will expand their instructional choices. One effective way to encourage teachers to try new instructional strategies is for you to model them. Help teachers learn the strategies so that they are comfortable using them in the classroom.

Students increasingly bring a variety of learning needs, styles, and perspectives to the classroom. For learning to take place, teachers must present students with varied instructional opportunities. Carefully selecting from among a variety of instructional strategies those activities that will best match the diverse needs of the students will result in achievement. High-quality instructional leadership is needed to ensure that instruction is responsive to students' learning needs. You can foster student achievement by guiding teachers to master an array of instructional strategies from among which they select those that are most appropriate to the particular learning outcomes to be achieved. Refer to Figure 9-2 for areas of reflection when designing instruction.

You also play a key role in monitoring students' progress to determine the effectiveness of the classroom curriculum, student achievement, instructional practices, and the use of textbooks and materials. Collecting and reviewing a wide range of artifacts will provide invaluable information. See Section 8 and Figure 8-3 for a summary of student artifacts and Figure 8-5 for learning targets and questions to ask.

ACTIONS OF INSTRUCTIONAL LEADERS

Here is what effective instructional leaders do:

- **Model a wide range of instructional strategies.** Any opportunity that presents itself—planned or unplanned—can be used effectively. This includes faculty conferences, planned professional development sessions, or meetings of study teams and learning communities.

- **Provide opportunities for teachers to be involved in professional development.** Make maximum use of district opportunities for professional development. Plan professional development sessions built on topics of specific importance to the success of the student population. Encourage teachers to become involved in professional development sessions of interest to them outside of the school or the district. See Section 20.

- **Extend the impact of professional development by creating and encouraging teachers to participate in learning communities and study teams.** The staff refines knowledge and grows professionally by sharing instructional practices, problems, and successes. See sections 14 and 22.

- **Continually monitor student progress by collecting and reviewing artifacts, and conducting informal visits and observations.** Continuous involvement with teaching, learning, and student outcomes provides the information needed to achieve high student achievement. See sections 5, 8, and 9.

- **Promote the use of a variety of assessment strategies.** Using diverse assessment techniques throughout the learning process informs instruction and improves achievement. See Section 2.

- **Encourage the use of performance assessment.** Providing alternative ways in which students can demonstrate learning contributes to understanding, achievement, and promotes student interaction. See Section 24.

Further Readings

Alfonso, R. J., and Goldsberry, L. F. 1982. Colleagueship in supervising. In T. J. Sergiovanni (Ed.), *Supervision of teaching*. Alexandria, VA: Association for Supervision and Curriculum Development.

Anderson, R. H., Snyder, K. J. (Eds.). 1993. *Clinical Supervision: Coaching for higher performance*. Lancaster, PA: Technomic Publishing.

Barth, R. S. 1991. *Improving schools from within*. San Francisco: Jossey-Bass.

Brandt, R. (Ed.). 1992. *Educational Leadership 50*. Theme Issue on "Improving School Quality." Alexandria, VA: Association for Supervision and Curriculum Development.

Brophy, J. E., and Good, T. L. 1974. *Teacher-student relationships: Causes and consequences*, New York: Holt Rinehart and Winston.

Chivers, J. 1995. *Team building with teachers*. London: Kogan Page.

Costa, A. L., and Garmston, R. 1994. *Cognitive coaching a foundation for renaissance schools*. Norwood, MA: Christopher-Gordon Pub. Inc.

Costa, A. L., and Kallick, B. 1995. *Assessment in the learning organization: Shifting the paradigm*. Alexandria, VA: Association for Supervision and Curriculum Development.

Danielson, C. 1996. *Enhancing professional practice: A framework for teaching*. Alexandria, VA: Association for Supervision and Curriculum Development.

Darling-Hammong, L. 1997. *The right to learn: A blueprint for creating schools that work*. San Francisco: Jossey-Bass Publishers.

de Charms, R. 1976. *Enhancing motivation: Change in the classroom*. New York: Irvington.

DeGaetano, Y., Williams, L., Volk, D. 1998. *Kaleidoscope: A multicultural approach for the primary school classroom*. New Jersey: Merrill.

Doll, R. C. 1989. *Curriculum improvement: Decision making and process* (6th ed.), Boston: Allyn and Bacon.

Educational Leadership. 1987a. Theme issue: Staff Development through Coaching 44(4).

Educational Leadership. 1987b. Theme issue: Collegial Learning 45(3).

Educational Leadership. 1987c. Theme issue: Progress in Evaluating Teaching 44(7).

Eisner, E. W., and Peshkin, A. 1990. *Qualitative inquiry in education*. New York: Teachers College.

Elmore, R. F. and Rothman, R. (Eds.). 1999. *Testing, teaching, and learning: A guide for states and school districts*. Washington, D.C.: National Academy Press.

Etzioni, A. 1993. *The spirit of community: Rights, responsibility and the communitarian agenda.* New York: Crown Publishers.

Glickman, C. D. 1981. *Developmental supervision: Alternative practices for helping teachers improve instruction.* Alexandria, VA: Association for Supervision and Curriculum Development.

Guskey, T. R. 1986. Staff development and the process of teacher change. *Educational Research* 15 (5): 5–12.

Houser, N. O. 1990. Teacher-researcher: The synthesis of roles for teacher empowerment. *Action in Teacher Education* 12 (2): 55–60.

Journal of Staff Development. 1987. *Theme issue: Peer Coaching,* 8 (1).

Joyce, B., Calhoun, E., and Hopkins, D. 1999. *The new structure of school improvement: inquiring schools and achieving students.* Philadelphia: Open University Press.

Joyce, B., and Showers, B. 1988. *Student achievement through staff development.* New York: Longman.

Kaufman, R. 1991. *Strategic planning plus.* Glenview, IL: Scott Foresman.

Kohn, A. 1999. *The schools our children deserve.* Boston: Houghton Mifflin Co.

Lantieri, L. and Patti, J. 1996. *Waging peace in our schools.* Boston: Beacon Press.

Lieberman, A. 1992. The meaning of scholarly activity and the building of community. *The Education Researcher* 21 (6): 5–12.

Little, J. W. 1982. Norms of collegiality and experimentation: Workplace conditions of school success. *American Educational Research Journal* 19(3): 325–340.

Maeroff, G. I. 1993. *Teambuilding for school change.* New York: Teachers College Press.

McCloskey, W., and Egelson, P. 1993. *Designing teacher evaluation systems that support professional growth.* Greensboro, NC: Southeastern Regional Vision for Education, School of Education, University of North Carolina at Greensboro. (ERIC ED 367 772)

McGreal, T. L. 1989. Necessary ingredients for successful instructional improvement incentives. *Journal of Staff Development* 10(1): 35–41.

Mohlman-Sparks, G. 1986. The effectiveness of alternative training activities in changing teaching practices. *American Educational Research Journal* 23 (2): 217–225.

Morgan, M. 1984. Reward-induced decrements and increments in intrinsic motivation. *Review of Educational Research* 54(1): 5–30.

Naller, E., and Kleine, P. 2001. *Using educational research: A school administrator's guide.* New York: Addison Wesley Longman, Inc.

Oja, S. N., and Reiman, A. J. 1997. Describing and promoting supervision for teacher development across the career span. In J. Firth and E. Pajak (Eds.), *Handbook of research on school supervision.* New York: Macmillan.

Olivia, P. F. 1992. *Developing the curriculum* (3rd ed.). New York: HarperCollins.

Pajak, E. 1993. *Approaches to Clinical Supervision.* Norwood MA: Christopher-Gordon Pub. Inc.

Paulson, F. L., Paulson, P. R., and Meyer, C. A. 1991. What makes a portfolio a portfolio? *Educational Leadership* 48 (5): 60–63.

Phillips, M. D., and Glickman, C. D. 1991. Peer coaching: Developmental approach to enhancing teacher thinking. *Journal of Staff Development* 12(2):20–25

Pophan, J. 1988. The dysfunctional marriage of formative and summative evaluation. *Journal of Personnel Evaluation in Education* 1: 269–273.

Postman, N. (1992). *Technology.* New York: Knopf.

Reiman, A. J., and Thies-Sprinthall, L. (1993). Promoting the development of mentor teachers: Theory and research programs using guided reflection. *Journal of Research and Development* 26 (2), 179–185.

Rosenshine, B. V. 1986. Synthesis of research on explicit teaching. *Educational Leadership* 43(7):60–69).

Russell, T., and Munby, H. (Eds.). 1992. *Teachers and teaching: From classrooms to reflection.* London: Falmer.

Sparka, G. M., and Bruder, S. 1987. How school-based peer coaching improves collegiality and experimentation. Paper presented at the annual meeting of the American *Educational Research Association,* Washington, D.C. April.

Wasley, P. 1994. *Stirring the chalkdust.* New York: Teachers College Press.

Zina, J. E., Weissberg, R. P., Wang, M. C., and Walberg, H. J. (in press). *Promoting school success on social emotional learning.* New York: Teachers College Press.

Index

Printed in the United States
77032LV00001B/12